THE EUROPEAN UNION SERIE

General Editors: Neill Nugent, William E. Paters(

The European Union series provides an authoritative library on the ranging from general introductory texts to definitive assessments of key institutions a... actors, issues, policies and policy processes, and the role of member states.

Books in the series are written by leading scholars in their fields and reflect the most up-to-date research and debate. Particular attention is paid to accessibility and clear presentation for a wide audience of students, practitioners and interested general readers.

The series editors are **Neill Nugent**, Professor of Politics and Jean Monnet Professor of European Integration, Manchester Metropolitan University, and **William E. Paterson**, Honourary Professor in German and European Studies, University of Aston. Their co-editor until his death in July 1999, **Vincent Wright**, was a Fellow of Nuffield College, Oxford University.

Feedback on the series and book proposals are always welcome and should be sent to Steven Kennedy, Palgrave Macmillan, Houndmills, Basingstoke, Hampshire RG21 6XS, UK, or by e-mail to s.kennedy@palgrave.com

General textbooks

Published

Desmond Dinan **Encyclopedia of the European Union**
[Rights: Europe only]
Desmond Dinan **Europe Recast: A History of European Union**
[Rights: Europe only]
Desmond Dinan **Ever Closer Union: An Introduction to European Integration** (4th edn)
[Rights: Europe only]
Mette Eilstrup Sangiovanni (ed.) **Debates on European Integration: A Reader**
Simon Hix and Bjørn Høyland **The Political System of the European Union** (3rd edn)
Paul Magnette **What is the European Union? Nature and Prospects**
John McCormick **Understanding the European Union: A Concise Introduction** (5th edn)
Brent F. Nelsen and Alexander Stubb **The European Union: Readings on the Theory and Practice of European Integration** (3rd edn)
[Rights: Europe only]
Neill Nugent (ed.) **European Union Enlargement**

Neill Nugent **The Government and Politics of the European Union** (7th edn)
John Peterson and Elizabeth Bomberg **Decision-Making in the European Union**
Ben Rosamond **Theories of European Integration**
Esther Versluis, Mendeltje van Keulen and Paul Stephenson **Analyzing the European Union Policy Process**

Forthcoming

Laurie Buonanno and Neill Nugent **Policies and Policy Processes of the European Union**
Dirk Leuffen, Berthold Rittberger and Frank Schimmelfennig **Differentiated Integration**
Sabine Saurugger **Theoretical Approaches to European Integration**

Also planned

The Political Economy of European Integration

Series Standing Order (outside North America only)
ISBN 0–333–71695–7 hardback
ISBN 0–333–69352–3 paperback
Full details from www.palgrave.com

Visit Palgrave Macmillan's
EU Resource area at
www.palgrave.com/politics/eu/

Development Policy of the European Union

Martin Holland
and
Mathew Doidge

First published 2012 by
PALGRAVE MACMILLAN

Palgrave Macmillan in the UK is an imprint of Macmillan Publishers
Limited, registered in England, company number 785998, of Houndmills,
Basingstoke, Hampshire RG21 6XS.

Palgrave Macmillan in the US is a division of St Martin's Press LLC,
175 Fifth Avenue, New York, NY 10010.

Palgrave Macmillan is the global academic imprint of the above companies
and has companies and representatives throughout the world.

Palgrave® and Macmillan® are registered trademarks in the United States,
the United Kingdom, Europe and other countries

ISBN 978–0–230–01989–8 hardback
ISBN 978–0–230–01990–4 paperback

This book is printed on paper suitable for recycling and made from
fully managed and sustained forest sources. Logging, pulping and
manufacturing processes are expected to conform to the environmental
regulations of the country of origin.

A catalogue record for this book is available from the British Library.

A catalog record for this book is available from the Library of Congress.

10   9   8   7   6   5   4   3   2   1
21   20   19   18   17   16   15   14   13   12

Printed in China

This volume was completed in the aftermath of the earthquakes that struck Christchurch, New Zealand, on Saturday 4 September 2010, Tuesday 22 February and Monday 13 June 2011. It is dedicated to the city, the victims of the earthquakes and their families.

Also by Martin Holland

An Introduction to the European Community in the 1980s (1983)
Candidates for Europe: The British Experience (1986)
*The European Community and South Africa: European Political
Cooperation under Strain* (1988)
European Community Integration (1993)
European Integration: from Community to Union (1994)
*European Union Common Foreign Policy: CFSP Joint Action in
South Africa* (1995)
The European Union and the Third World (2002)

Also by Mathew Doidge

*The European Union and Interregionalism: Patterns of
Engagement* (2011)

Contents

List of Illustrative Material

Boxes

Figures

Tables

Map

Preface

This has been without any doubt a difficult book to write. Not only is the topic vast and complex, but the parameters within which the EU has operated its policy with the developing world have undergone radical and seemingly continual reform over the last decade. This book addresses all these significant changes, including the progressive implementation of the Cotonou Economic Partnership Agreements since 2000, the Everything But Arms initiative of 2001, the 2005 'European Consensus on Development' as well as the most recent EU perspectives on achieving the Millennium Development Goals. We hope the analysis will remain both provocative and relevant for years to come, even if the policy details continue to change in the future. The analysis poses a number of simple but related questions. First, can the EU demonstrate a distinct development policy separate and superior to that of the member states? Second, how far have traditional development policy assumptions been replaced by a global liberalized agenda based on free trade? Third, how successfully has the EU linked development policy with its foreign policy activities under the 2009 Lisbon Treaty? And lastly, what is the impact of external relations – particularly development policy – on the integration process per se?

This book was conceived as a replacement volume for my 2002 book *The European Union and the Third World*, but it has taken much longer to conceptualize and execute than I ever anticipated and would most likely never have been completed without the contribution of my co-author, Mathew Doidge. Institutionally, the support provided by the National Centre for Research on Europe at the University of Canterbury, New Zealand, has been greatly appreciated. The insights and questions raised by graduate students across Asia, America and the Pacific have added to the richness and contemporary relevance of this book and I am eternally indebted to all of you who have studied with me in New Zealand, Thailand, Malaysia and the USA.

Dudley House, Christchurch   MARTIN HOLLAND

Authors' Notes

Throughout this book, it can safely be assumed that one euro equals one ECU and/or EUA.

For simplicity's sake the term 'European Union' (EU) rather than 'European Community' (EC) is often used to describe actions that pre-dated the 1993 Maastricht Treaty.

List of Abbreviations

ACP	African, Caribbean and Pacific countries
AEMM	ASEAN–EC Ministerial Meeting
ALA	Asia–Latin America Regulation
APEC	Asia–Pacific Economic Cooperation
APRIS	ASEAN Programme for Regional Integration Support
ASEAN	Association of Southeast Asian Nations
ASEM	Asia–Europe Meeting
BRICS	Brazil, Russia, India, China and South Africa
CAN	Andean Community
CAP	Common Agricultural Policy
CEEC	Central and Eastern European Countries
CFSP	Common Foreign and Security Policy
CI	(ECHO) Crisis Index
CIDA	Canadian International Development Agency
COREPER	Committee of Permanent Representatives
CSDP	Common Security and Defence Policy
DAC	Development Assistance Committee (of the OECD)
DCI	Financing Instrument for Development Cooperation
DEVE	Development Committee of the European Parliament
DFID	(UK) Department for International Development
DG	(Commission) Directorate-General
DG-DEV	Directorate-General for Development
DG-DEVCO	Directorate-General for Development and Cooperation – EuropeAid
EAMA	Associated African States and Madagascar
EBA	Everything But Arms
EC	European Community
ECHO	DG Humanitarian Aid and Civil Protection (after the Lisbon Treaty; formerly the European Community Humanitarian Aid Office)

ECU	European Currency Unit
EDF	European Development Fund
EEAS	European External Action Service
EEC	European Economic Community
EIB	European Investment Bank
EMU	Economic and Monetary Union
ENPI	European Neighbourhood and Partnership Instrument
EP	European Parliament
EPA	Economic Partnership Agreement
ESAF	Enhanced Structural Adjustment Facility
EU	European Union
EU12	The 12 EU member states that joined in the 2004 and 2007 enlargements
EU15	The 15 EU member states that joined prior to the 2004 enlargement
EUA	European Units of Account
EU–LAC	EU–Latin American and Caribbean
FAC	Foreign Affairs Council
FCA	(ECHO) Forgotten Crisis Assessment
FDI	foreign direct investment
FTA	Free Trade Agreement
FTAA	Free Trade Area of the Americas
GATT	General Agreement on Tariffs and Trade
GDP	gross domestic product
GNA	(ECHO) Global Needs Assessment
GNI	gross national income
GSP	Generalized System of Preferences
HAC	Humanitarian Aid Committee
HDI	Human Development Index
HIPC	Heavily Indebted Poor Countries
IMF	International Monetary Fund
LAC	Latin America and Caribbean
LDC	Least Developed Country
MDGs	Millennium Development Goals
MERCOSUR	Common Market of the South (Mercado Común del Sur)
MFN	Most Favoured Nation
NGO	Non-Governmental Organization
NIC	newly industrialized country
NIEO	New International Economic Order

OCT	(French) Overseas Collectivities/Countries and Territories
ODA	Official Development Assistance
OECD	Organisation for Economic Co-operation and Development
PAIRCA	Programme of Support to Central American Integration
PPP	purchasing power parity
RELEX	Directorate-General for External Relations
SAARC	South Asian Association for Regional Cooperation
SADC	Southern African Development Community
SAP	Structural Adjustment Programme
SCR	Common Service for External Relations (Service Commun Relex)
SEM	Single European Market
SOM	Senior Officials Meeting
STABEX	Stabilization of Export Earnings Scheme
SYSMIN	Stabilization Scheme for Mineral Products
TAO	Technical Assistance Office
TEC	Treaty Establishing the European Community
TEU	Treaty on European Union
TFEU	Treaty on the Functioning of the European Union
UK	United Kingdom
UN	United Nations
UNAIDS	Joint United Nations Programme on HIV and AIDS
UNDP	United Nations Development Programme
UNHCR	United Nations High Commissioner for Refugees
USA	United States of America
USAID	United States Agency for International Development
VI	(ECHO) Vulnerability Index
WHO	World Health Organization
WTO	World Trade Organization

Introduction

The study of European Union (EU) development policy presents something of a paradox. Development policy constitutes an area where the EU can rightly claim to be an international leader with significant influence shaping global agendas: and yet academic studies devoted to development policy are few, especially in comparison with the ever-expanding literature on Europe's Common Foreign and Security Policy (CFSP). This book begins to redress this imbalance by providing both a comprehensive and a contemporary analysis of EU development policy. Whilst Europe's formal relations with the developing world are as old as the integration process itself, the shape and the content of those relations have altered significantly since the signing of the Treaty of Rome in 1957. Successive enlargements, differential rates of global development, the collapse of communist ideology in Central and Eastern Europe, the reorganization of international trade under the auspices of the World Trade Organization (WTO) have all contributed to reshaping the EU's external relations with the developing world. Most recently, the Millennium Development Goals (MDGs) and the introduction of the Lisbon Treaty have begun to redefine fundamentally both Europe's development objectives and its implementation mechanisms. This book examines these changes from both an empirical and a conceptual perspective: significantly, EU development policy is categorized as an aspect of Europe's broader role as an emerging international actor and is addressed within the wider context of Europe's integration process. It is argued that contemporary theories of integration provide the appropriate tools for understanding not just the EU's internal dynamics, but its external relations as well.

Overview

While the EU developmental framework is considered in greater detail in subsequent chapters, what follows is a brief introductory overview of the evolution of the Union's external relations with the developing world. As already noted, a European development policy dates back to the Treaty of Rome of 1957, though no such element was initially conceived by the six founding member states, despite ongoing ties of four of the six to their colonial and ex-colonial possessions. As Hewitt and Whiteman (2004: 134) acknowledge, 'that the new democratic Europe should have colonial entanglements associated with the past era of aggressive nationalism, least of all by the Dutch (who had already lost Indonesia) and by the newly democratic Germans who saw empire as one more trapping of the Wilhelmine and Prussian past', had not been envisaged until, at the eleventh hour, French negotiators put the issue on the table. Confronted, in the wake of the Second World War, with its increasing inability to fund the heavy costs of its colonial possessions, France saw the new European architecture as a solution to its problems. Thus, in a somewhat cynical ploy to disburse the costs (particularly to Bonn) of maintaining its political influence in its colonial territories, the French government made its signing of the Treaty and thus continuing participation in the integration process conditional upon the establishment of an institutionalized and treaty-based relationship between the Community and the developing world (essentially francophone Africa). This relationship was to involve reciprocal trade access to the European Community (EC) and the establishment of a European Development Fund (EDF) to which Germany and France were each to provide one-third. As a consequence, Article 3(k) was inserted into the Treaty of Rome, stipulating 'the association of the overseas countries and territories in order to increase trade and to promote jointly economic and social development'.

While the EDF budget line has remained the foundation for cooperation with the former colonies, the framework within which it is couched has undergone considerable evolution over time (see Chapter 2). Following the conclusion of the Treaty of Rome, relations with the developing world as outlined in Article 3(k) were formally realized with the conclusion of the 1963 Yaoundé Agreement between the EC and the 18 Associated African States and Madagascar (known under the French acronym EAMA). Clearly, the EAMA represented a very narrow definition of the developing world, the first iteration of a European approach that has placed a premium on historical ties. In 1971, with the introduction of the Generalized System of Preferences (GSP) offering non-reciprocal market access to a range of developing countries, the

European development approach began to shift from this narrow francophone African focus of the EAMA to one somewhat more global in nature. This was reinforced when in 1973 the United Kingdom joined the Community, bringing its own set of ties with the developing world and requiring an expansion in the architecture of EC development policy. The product was the 1975 Lomé Convention to replace Yaoundé, and a new grouping – the African, Caribbean and Pacific (ACP) states – to replace the EAMA. The Lomé Convention remained the framework of cooperation with the ACP until the Cotonou Agreement entered into force in 2003, a replacement necessitated by the apparent failure of Lomé to alter fundamentally the circumstances of the states of Africa, the Caribbean and the Pacific, and by the renewed emphasis of the WTO on the principle of reciprocity in international trade, a principle of which Lomé was in clear violation.

While the development relationship with what are now the 79 states of the ACP can be traced as far back as the Treaty of Rome, developing countries outside of this framework found it much more difficult to access European aid (with South Africa joining the ACP in 1998, and being covered only in a qualified fashion by the Cotonou Agreement, we will for simplicity's sake hereafter restrict the definition of the ACP to 78 states).

The states of Latin America and Asia in particular have historically been a low priority for EU development assistance (see Chapters 5 and 6), and it was not until 1974 that a specific financing instrument – the Asia–Latin America (ALA) Regulation – was put in place to assist them. The ALA was essentially an ad hoc innovation, resembling a collection of leftovers not included within the ACP. In 2006 the regulation was bundled with a range of other geographic and thematic instruments into the new Financing Instrument for Development Cooperation (DCI) covering 47 states in Asia, Latin America, the Middle East and South Africa. At a very basic level, relations with these non-ACP states have always followed a markedly different path. An emphasis on liberalization and reciprocity in market access, for example, has been a clear characteristic since the outset, though it was not until the Cotonou Agreement that this was to surface in relations with the ACP.

The ad hoc nature of early development policy evolution, most clearly embodied through the method of its inclusion in the Treaty of Rome, was reflected in the institutional structures for its administration (see Chapter 4). Aside from the problems of policy fragmentation – which up until the second Barroso Commission saw the Directorate-General (DG) for Trade responsible for trade and commercial policy, DG External Relations responsible for relations (including development) with Asia and Latin America, and DG Development responsible for the ACP – specific structures for the implementation of the development programme were also somewhat lacking. The administration of EDF and ALA assistance remained the responsibility of DG staff, who increasingly contracted it out via a series of Technical Assistance Offices (TAOs). It was not until 1992 that the first dedicated structures for the administration of assistance began to emerge, with the establishment of ECHO – the European Community Humanitarian Aid Office (now DG Humanitarian Aid and Civil Protection) – a response to increased demand for humanitarian assistance and the global ambitions of Europe. Notwithstanding the emergence of ECHO, these structures remained particularly weak and became the target of increased criticism throughout the 1990s, culminating in a series of critical reports from a Committee of Independent Experts and the Organisation for Economic Co-operation and Development's (OECD) Development Assistance Committee (DAC). The initial response was to establish a new grouping to coordinate assistance – the Common Service for External Relations (again usually known by its French acronym, SCR: Service Commun Relex) – which became operational in 1998. Nevertheless ongoing problems necessitated another rethink only a few years later, and the EuropeAid Cooperation Office was established in 2001, which for the next decade remained the primary structure responsible for the administration of development assistance.

What can be seen from the above, therefore, is a process of evolution (often ad hoc) in the development architecture of the EU. In order to contextualize development policy, the EU's global engagement with the developing world is best described as a policy patchwork (albeit one with trade liberalization an increasingly common thread). Separate regimes exist for relations with the ACP states, Latin America, Central America, China, India and the Association of Southeast Asian Nations (ASEAN) – a dialogue which is itself further refined through the partially overlapping Asia–Europe Meeting (ASEM) process (see Chapter 6). Additionally, the EU also has special relationships with a multitude of member state overseas departments and territories. However, the most structured and historically important relationship has always been with the ACP states through the Lomé Convention and subsequently the Cotonou Agreement. A consequence of seeing past EU development policy primarily through the Lomé prism has seen the EU interact in a geographically specific way, rather than globally. For decades, the developing world was defined as principally those former member state colonies in Africa, the Caribbean and the Pacific and dealt with under the Lomé framework; only this relationship was historical, institutionalized, comprehensive and based on the principle of non-reciprocity. In contrast, relations with the Indian subcontinent, Asia and Latin America have been comparatively new incremental initiatives, fragmented and generally more limited in scope.

Such a dichotomy (based on past practice rather than development criteria) was always difficult to sustain, and became increasingly indefensible. The collapse of communism in Central and Eastern Europe further complicated this untenable position: throughout the 1990s development aid was increasingly shifted in favour of these emerging democratic European states. Europe's traditional definition of development needs were proving inadequate, raising the need for a radical reconceptualization and a more coordinated, consistent and complementary approach. Consequently, a more inclusive definition of the developing world was needed that recognized regional disparities while seeking common approaches to common problems. Geography and history were no longer sufficient, and in the last decade the EU has fundamentally reviewed its network of relations with regions of its traditional partners in the developing world in an attempt to produce a new policy paradigm that was consistent, comprehensive and common in origin, approach and criteria. Formally, if somewhat belatedly, this motivation reflected the treaty obligations of the 1993 Treaty on European Union (TEU) and which have been reasserted again under the 2009 Lisbon Treaty. Specifically:

> Community policy in the sphere of development cooperation, which shall be complementary to the policies pursued by the Member States, shall foster:
> - the sustainable economic and social development of the developing countries, and more particularly the most disadvantaged among them;
> - the smooth and gradual integration of the developing countries into the world economy;
> - the campaign against poverty in the developing countries.

The principles of coordination, coherence and complementarity that guided the EU's external and foreign policies were also to be reflected in development policy. The first decade of the twenty-first century witnessed Europe's relations with the developing world coming under greater scrutiny with past practices being challenged both externally and internally. Simultaneously, it became increasingly unfashionable for states and international organizations to follow traditional development strategies because of their modest successes over the second half of the twentieth century (see Chapter 1). With more immediate priority given to the transitional economies of the Central and Eastern European Countries (CEECs) at the expense of the non-European developing world, a reconceptualization of development strategy was needed. These historical trends were given additional institutional authority with the implementation of the Lisbon Treaty on 1 December 2009 whereby development policy has become increasingly incorporated within the EU's emerging global foreign policy agenda.

Institutional and external contexts

It became commonplace to underline the complications introduced by the pillared approach to EU policy-making under the 1993 Maastricht Treaty. The TEU's intergovernmental compromise, which introduced the idea of policy pillars that distinguished between competences and decision-making methods according to policy sector, undoubtedly reduced the ability and perception of the EU to act as a single actor. The cordoning and sanitization of 'foreign policy' as a pillar II intergovernmental competence under CFSP excessively narrowed the domain of EU foreign policy action. In almost every instance, pillar I Community competences were required to implement CFSP in practice. This consequence was nowhere more clearly evident than in relations with the developing world, which illustrated both the impracticality of this segmentation, as well as the policy contradictions that could result. Of course, at the time this policy apartheid was necessary for reasons related to intra-European debates on integration, and the price in terms of a diluted EU external presence was one that a majority of member states were willing to pay. For third countries the notion that Europe's relations with the South (particular through Lomé) constituted something other than foreign policy was absurd. But it was an absurdity that the EU insisted on preserving for some 16 years until the eventual introduction of the Lisbon Treaty in 2009 saw a ubiquitous rather than divided policy-making framework re-emerge.

The CFSP's joint actions and common positions – and since 2003 the more than two dozen Common Security and Defence Policy (CSDP) missions that have been undertaken – inevitably compromised the TEU's policy pillars, especially where pillar I trade relations between the EU and the developing world became CFSP tools. The range of CFSP joint actions, common positions and decisions associated with developing countries has been consistently high, constituting the major EU foreign policy focus after the Balkans and Eastern Europe. For example, in 1998 Africa accounted for six of the 22 common positions taken by the EU, and Asia a further five: three of the EU's 20 joint actions related to Africa (Allen and Smith 1999: 89). More recently, half of all CSDP missions undertaken up until 2010 (both military and civilian in nature) had been carried out in either Africa (covering Guinea-Bissau, Somalia, Darfur, Chad and the Democratic Republic of Congo) or Asia (Afghanistan and Aceh) – a clear recognition that the securitization of development had become a well-established phenomenon prior to the Lisbon Treaty initiatives. Fortunately – for both EU policy-makers as well as third countries – EU foreign affairs appear finally to be organized in a streamlined and coherent manner and the traditional problems of coordination between CFSP objectives and those conducted by the EU under pillar I are no longer evident. While historically there is no doubt that the existence of the CFSP both complemented and complicated EU development policy, it is still too early to judge conclusively whether the Lisbon Treaty has provided the effective panacea that was so widely sought.

The collapse of the Berlin Wall did more to redefine the context of the EU's development policy than any other contemporary event. The East, not the South, became the principal focus of EU development assistance throughout the 1990s. This new geopolitical context also cast a shadow in the form of enlargement. Between 2004 and 2007 the EU expanded to include 12 new members – the vast majority of which were comparatively poor by EU standards (despite the development assistance they received during the 1990s) and none had any tradition of being aid donors. Rather than increasing the EU's capacity to meet its stated 0.7 per cent ODA (Official Development Assistance) target as well as the MDGs by 2015, enlargement has caused some to question the

continued willingness or ability of the EU to even maintain its traditional development support, let alone increase it to these new levels.
Consequently, whilst at one level the negotiations for enlarging the
EU were a strictly intra-EU issue, their implications continue to
affect existing and future relations with the developing world. Any
further enlargement to embrace the Balkans, Iceland or Turkey can
only exacerbate the tension between global development as a priority and the counter-view that charity is first needed closer to home.

It will be interesting to see how the new institutional architecture
of the Lisbon Treaty impacts upon the EU's development policy –
both in direct and indirect ways (see Chapter 4 for institutional
details). The early indications suggest that the new High
Representative for Foreign Affairs has a clear ambition to draw
development policy increasingly into her sphere in order to align
better the various parts of EU foreign policy-making: how this
evolves over the first five years of the Treaty's implementation will
provide an important guideline, as will her role in balancing the
Commission's and Council's overlapping involvement in development policy. More speculatively, an increased emphasis on
enhanced cooperation as a decision-making style could see the EU
adopting differentiated layers of relationships with the developing
world. No longer may it be necessary for the EU27 to find a consensus to formulate policy: an inner core group of states may prefer to
extend their joint activity to introduce a more extensive collective
European policy. Of course, no such policy can contradict the existing *acquis* but undoubtedly this flexibility can be regarded as a
potential policy vanguard and as such it can implicitly set the future
policy direction of the EU as a whole. Potentially, enhanced cooperation can create path-dependency by creating a new level of collective policy for the core group of states that can ultimately lead to a
new collective future policy status quo for all member states. This
tendency can be applied – at least in theory – to initiatives in development policy. As past and more recent enlargements have shown,
eastern, northern and southern EU states have quite substantially
different development policy perspectives: it is not beyond the
realms of possibility that the four member states who by 2010 had
achieved the 0.7 per cent aid commitment could use enhanced cooperation to advance collective development policy, for example. Such
possibilities do influence the context of EU decision-making: the use
of consensus as a policy brake, if not redundant as a threat, is no
longer an absolute veto.

Turning from the internal European contexts that help to shape development perspectives, there are three important external arenas that have constrained EU policy: the WTO; global debt-reduction initiatives; and the 2008 global financial crisis. The continuing Doha Development Round as well as the failed 1999 Seattle WTO meeting illustrate both the interrelated nature of the EU and WTO agendas and the importance (and difficulty) of incorporating development concerns as a central feature of global liberalization. Simply, whatever independent initiatives the EU may wish to make in development policy, these need to be both compatible with WTO rules and consistent with developing country aspirations. As the seemingly unending banana saga of the late 1990s illustrated, the global context of WTO institutions is a clear and legitimate constraint on EU policy formation. Similarly, the G7 initiative of 1998–99 on global debt reduction for developing countries helped to shape the emergence of a common EU stance and eventual action on the issue. Conversely, however, the global financial crisis put into stark relief the EU's priority of self-interest when balanced against assisting developing countries to cope with the crisis. With commendable frankness, the EU response was clear – no additional financial resources would be made available within the development policy framework. Rather, the more effective use of existing commitments was the new ambition. Thus institutional frameworks and unanticipated events outside the EU have had – and will continue to have – an impact on the direction and application of EU development policy.

Other examples could be added to this list of external and internal agents – the global consensus on poverty, environmental sustainability and climate change, and women's development in particular. However, the important point, at least from the perspective of this text, is that clearly context does matter. Despite being the world's largest trader and having experienced some 60 years of collective action the EU cannot act in a fully autonomous manner but is, like all international actors, constrained by a multiple series of contexts, both intra-European and global. Europe's development policy does not operate in a vacuum. Policy choices are constrained by these varied contexts within which the EU operates. This general conclusion has significant policy implications and in this section we have sought to outline a number of particular contexts that have influenced the EU's relationship with the developing world.

The focus of this book

The purpose of this text is to explore the mosaic of relations that characterize EU–developing world relations (historically, institutionally and in terms of contemporary policies) and to provide a comprehensive overview that respects the uniqueness of each policy sector yet demonstrates, where appropriate, the commonalities within the EU's global relations. This tension has been the hallmark of EU–developing world relations to date, notwithstanding the post-2000 reforms and the 2009 Lisbon Treaty which were in part designed to address the issue of differentiation.

An aspect of integration?

The EU policy-making process is the organizational principle around which this book is constructed. In particular, the link between internal EU integration and external relations is emphasized. The debates pertaining to a deeper Union and the integration process are not confined purely to Europe's own Single Market and Economic and Monetary Union (EMU) programmes; they influence and help direct the policies adopted towards the external world. At a theoretical level, this analysis suggests that there is an implied 'spillover' from the level of political and economic integration within the EU into the area of development policy. Collective external action is dependent on the political will of the EU's decision-making elite without whose agreement policy reformulation is impossible given its still pervasive intergovernmental character. We do not attempt to provide a detailed description of each EU–developing country bilateral relationship, or even an exhaustive account of the various treaties and agreements. Rather, we offer a thematic analysis and overview that locates development policy within the wider integration debate (as discussed in Chapter 1). Where specific examples and cases are discussed in various chapters, these are by way of illustration of more general issues.

A case for subsidiarity?

A fundamental question posed in this analysis is to what extent there should be an EU development policy. What can the EU do better – in terms of global development – than the member states individually? Can a more effective development policy be conducted bilaterally between member states and third countries directly than can be achieved 'collectively' at the EU level? Given the miniscule development aid contributions made by all of the post-2004 new member states, increased veracity has been given to those who argue that development may be better delivered bilaterally than through the imperfect mechanism of the EU. Simply, if provocatively, is development policy a case for subsidiarity?

The concept of subsidiarity introduced in the Maastricht Treaty has traditionally (and legally) been confined to discussions of intra-EU policy competences. Subsidiarity is interpreted legally as a requirement that EU policy only be implemented where there is a clear advantage over the bilateral implementation of that policy by individual member states. Brussels has to demonstrate that things can be done better collectively than by the individual governments acting separately. Within the EU's internal policies this concept has been problematic enough: in external relations, both intergovernmental and Community, the difficulties are magnified.

However, the principle (in a general if not precise legal sense) is relevant to the current external relations debate. The onus is on the EU to demonstrate that the EU is better at conducting and delivering development policy to the developing world than are the member states. If this cannot be demonstrated a renationalization of development policy could emerge, a tendency consistent with the general intergovernmental interpretation of subsidiarity. The challenge, then, is to what extent can the EU demonstrate both a *distinct* development role for itself as well as a *superior* one to that of the member states?

Whilst development policy may well continue to be an area of mixed competences and commitments between the member states and the EU, the clear trend has been towards enhancing the role of the Union. And yet to avoid duplication the EU needs to establish a distinct role in development policy separate from that already conducted by the member states. There seems little point in Europe running an additional programme that duplicates the existing activities of the EU27 merely for the sake of it. Member states can choose whether to commit their resources bilaterally or through the EU system: what clear advantages can the EU route offer? Historically, what has been lacking is a coherent and accepted yardstick to determine those aspects of development cooperation that are best done bilaterally by member states, and those that are better done collectively at the EU level.

In many respects the EU makes a unique contribution to global development. First, under the Lomé Convention the EU sought to introduce a greater degree of equality and partnership into the development relationship in contrast to typical traditional bilateral arrangements. Second, thanks to pressure from the European Parliament, Europe initiated policy and led the debate on a number of new development issues, such as women and development, reproductive healthcare, AIDS, environmental sustainability and refugees. Third, a bottom-up philosophy tended to emphasize cooperation with Non-Governmental Organizations (NGOs) as the appropriate deliverer of development assistance. Overall, it can be argued that collective EU development policy adds value if only by virtue of its coordination role and the scale of assistance, particularly in areas such as emergency food aid and through Lomé and Cotonou financing. Historically, however, ambiguity rather than clarity has surrounded the nature of Europe's distinctive development role and what policy elements were best coordinated at an EU level. Only after 2000 did the Commission finally begin to address this fundamental concern.

Whilst, since Maastricht, the EU's treaties have listed distinctive features of EU development policy, these were not exclusive domains: however, they do provide a guide to the future EU–member state division of development policy sectors. Various proposals to define and specify a distinct EU role have been tabled. For example, the EU could focus primarily on poverty alleviation (as now required by the Lisbon Treaty and the MDGs). This radical approach would see EU assistance focus on the least developed countries (utilizing the Everything But Arms – EBA – initiative), leaving bilateral member-state relations to cover the other developing countries. Such a division runs counter to 25 years of Lomé relations that grouped all types of developing countries together under a single framework. As the Cotonou Partnership Agreement has illustrated, any dismantling of the ACP framework should anticipate resistance and require significant member-state cooperation and goodwill in order to placate anxieties and cover any potential omissions. Obviously this touches on the sensitive issue of balance in Commission–Council relations.

Intergovernmental agendas suggest that neither the extension of EU policy competences nor a redistribution of competences between the Union and its member states will be easily achieved. Other suggestions have called for the EU to act as the 'wholesaler' of development assistance (providing the structure for development) with member states acting as 'retailers' in the local markets (actually implementing specific programmes on the ground). Another proposal – and one where the EU's claim to a distinctive role may be the strongest – emphasizes political conditionality ('democracy and the rule of law ... human rights and fundamental freedoms') as an appropriate EU-level policy competence. Thus whatever bilateral relations might exist, these would be governed by common EU-level definitions of human rights and democratic conditionality. In practice, such an overarching EU role has begun to emerge especially in the context of the adoption of the MDGs. Of course, an unintended consequence of the national financial constraints that have confronted member states since 2008 may be enhanced EU-level activity and rationalization to the benefit of developing countries in the second decade of the twenty-first century. Cynics have already noted, however, that it may be easier for the EU to achieve finally its 0.7 per cent ODA target by simply maintaining existing aid levels in a sinking GDP (gross domestic product) environment. These and related themes are explored in greater detail in the following chapters.

Related to the question of subsidiarity is an additional and fundamental question – does the EU need a development policy? Is any such policy merely an optional policy choice within the process of integration, or does it represent a core function? We cannot take as given the necessity of a development policy beyond the technical framework established by the Common Commercial Policy. However, there are a number of altruistic as well as self-interested reasons that suggest that a development policy is not optional but fundamental to the process of European integration and the EU's global role as defined by the Lisbon Treaty.

Among the motivations based on self-interest is the one to avoid intra-European social destabilization resulting from increased illegal immigration and refugee crises. Whilst a Europe just for Europeans is not the policy of the EU, improving the living standards in the developing world serves to reduce the economic attraction of migration to Europe. The maintenance of resource supplies remains vital to Europe's economic growth, and China's expansion into Africa in the last five years has again underlined the EU's resource dependency. Similarly, while the collapse of the Soviet Union initially presented an opening up of markets and resources in the former Soviet sphere, the EU's continued reliance on Russian energy has underlined the necessity for the EU to continue to look to developing countries for resources and raw materials. A further motivation can be found in the EU's support for the exploitation of export markets and the general promotion of global free trade. As is discussed elsewhere throughout this book, the EU is committed to integrating the developing world into the global trading system, though on the basis of free trade, despite the scepticism held by many in the developing world. Lastly, the EU has long held a desire to emerge as a global actor – both economic as well as political – with some believing that the new provisions for foreign affairs in the Lisbon Treaty finally provide the structural capacity to realize this ambition. The development agenda creates the potential for Europe to play such a political foreign affairs role through its economic power as the world's largest trader and ODA provider.

More altruistically, the EU's development policy expresses its belief in democracy. The pervasive application of conditionality concerning human rights, good governance and democracy should not be simply dismissed as the imposition of European values on reluctant developing states. Often, developing countries welcome this conditionality as it can help them safeguard and extend democratic practices domestically. Similarly, EU policy encourages and supports regional integration for the developing world. Under the past Lomé umbrella, as well as the current Cotonou framework, provisions and funding for the promotion of regional integration projects have been designated. Obviously, as the world's most advanced form of law-based regional cooperation, the EU has a philosophical commitment to integration; however, it would be somewhat churlish to regard this as a selfish motivation. The rationale is primarily altruistic: regionalization is seen as a core element of development. Finally, there is the assumption (already touched on) that Europe's own internal integration should not be considered in isolation and the necessary link with external relations acknowledged. What happens within the EU integration process has fundamental repercussions for the developing world – economically, socially and environmentally. The consequences of a failed Single Market or Monetary Union would not be confined to Europe: they would impact directly on the fragile economies of the developing world, evidence of which has already been apparent in the wake of the 2008 financial crisis. Global development, whether in Africa, Asia or Latin America, is therefore inextricably linked to the internal success of European integration.

By necessity this book provides an empirical account of the historical evolution of the EU's development policy; however, it offers more than a descriptive and statistical recital of information easily found elsewhere (see Grilli 1993; Lister 1997a; Carbone 2009). Rather, it presents thematic and theoretical arguments that provide the context for analysing EU policy. Obviously, the reform of the Lomé Convention and the introduction of Economic Partnership Agreements (EPAs) under Cotonou is a significant theme, but, as already argued above, the EU's policy towards developing countries reaches far beyond these treaty-based agreements with the ACP states, best illustrated by the shift in emphasis towards the MDGs during the last decade. Both the strengths and the weaknesses of EU policy (in content and scope) are the focus of this analysis.

Change, reform and differentiation

There is no ideal time to write about the EU: it is constantly evolving and susceptible to the vagaries of electoral change in the member states. The same is true for Europe's policy with the developing world. The last decade of the twentieth century witnessed monumental global change – ideological, economic and strategic – and these changes directly impacted on the perceptions and expectations surrounding development policy. Since the mid-1990s Europe's development policy has been in a state of flux, a situation that was compounded by the enlargements of 2004 and 2007. Despite the seemingly unifying theme of the MDGs, as the EU enters the second decade of the new millennium, development policy remains a work-in-progress. Consequently, this book presents the debates that have shaped the policy options and offers broad parameters within which future changes can be located and interpreted. Why did the EU undertake such a complete re-evaluation of its development framework at the end of the twentieth century? The rationale for reform was initiated by a growing dissatisfaction with the Lomé structures, the motivations for which were diverse, but cumulatively compelling, at least from a European perspective. And yet, why, after ten years of implementation, is the new development paradigm still largely unproven and, for many, unloved?

First, there was the record of European assistance. Too few ACP countries had seen a radical transformation in their economic well-being: dependency continued to define their relationship with Europe. Second, as noted already, the preferences and resources given to Central and Eastern Europe had largely been at the expense of the ACP: the cake had not sufficiently increased to cope with both these development appetites. Third, the WTO began to cast a critical eye in general over preferential agreements and, specifically, with respect to the Lomé preferences (an interim WTO waiver notwithstanding), arguing that these were inconsistent with the trend towards open markets. In response, the European Commission actively promoted a global free-trade philosophy. Fourth, if paradoxically, trade figures suggested that the 'privileged' position of ACP countries and the value of their preferential treatment had become significantly eroded after 1989. The Lomé states were no longer at the apex of the 'pyramid of privilege'. Further, almost every state in Asia had substantially out-performed those of the ACP, despite not receiving any such concessionary privileges.

Last, the calls for reform reflected a growing recognition of the diversity within the developing world and the obvious inconsistencies in the EU's geographical ambit. It became increasingly difficult to explain what common interests bound the Lomé states together or distinguished them from the majority of non-Lomé developing countries. The ACP was an acronym, but it had also become increasingly anachronistic. Nonetheless, the ACP argued that the rationale for the grouping was more than post-colonial history and clearly the large size of the ACP group has provided certain negotiating advantages (for both the ACP and the EU). However, the existence of regional provisions within Lomé, and even more explicitly under the Cotonou framework, endeavoured to emphasize the diversity of needs rather than enhance the 'coherence' of the ACP community. Increasingly 'differentiation' has become the clarion call for the development policy agenda of the twenty-first century. The protracted negotiations towards EPAs that are now falling into place across the ACP reflect this new approach, although their success so far remains as much a matter of belief as of evidence.

This book outlines many of the future challenges that the EU's policy towards the developing world faces up until 2020. First is the question of development funding. Between 2004 and 2009 the EU experienced the effects of both the global financial crisis and of enlargement from 15 to 27 member states. As a consequence it is far from guaranteed that previous levels of financial assistance available for global development will continue, especially given the extremely low levels of development aid given by member states from Central and Eastern Europe. As noted already, the

Commission's initial response to the 2008 global financial crisis perhaps gives the clearest indication: no increase in aid levels was offered; the more effective use of existing aid was the preference. Second, the lessons from past enlargements suggest that the next wave of membership will impact on the EU's development policy: unless more affluent candidates can be attracted (Norway or Switzerland), the accession of comparatively poor new member states can only increase intra-EU pressures on development funding. Third, within the changing context some member states may strive to maintain and protect their special historical ties with particular developing countries or regions. Fourth, global trends will influence the EU's policy options. The WTO provides a constraint upon EU policy as the new EPA trade relationships have to be consistent with WTO regulations including the post-Doha perspective. Fifth, and related, is the move towards global regionalism that provoked the restructuring of the EU's development relations in 2000. Since then, the EU has reoriented its approach to differentiate between levels, or types, of developing country, discriminating between countries that previously had largely been treated on an equal footing. Quite whether the implicit contradictions and overlaps between EU policies such as EPAs and EBA can be reconciled remains to be seen. Sixth, the framework for relations will remain contentious. The principle of non-reciprocity at present has been retained for the world's 48 Least Developed Countries (LDCs), but pressures to extend the philosophy of Free Trade Agreements (FTAs) uniformly – irrespective of the level of development – are unlikely to disappear entirely. Seventh, as set out in the Maastricht Treaty and reaffirmed under Lisbon, as well as enshrined in the EU's embrace of the MDGs, the reduction of poverty is the principal development policy goal. However, has the EU provided itself with adequate and appropriate instruments and policies for such an ambitious task? Indeed, is such a humanitarian policy goal achievable? And lastly, has the EU's development approach been out-flanked by China's more pragmatic and non-conditional engagement with developing countries, particularly those in Africa? The EU remains bound by its own norms and values as expressed through the treaties and may find its traditional development recipients less willing to accommodate these demands now that China represents an alternative development partner.

As is typically the case in most EU policy areas, relations with developing countries combine a number of otherwise discrete policy sectors and institutional actors. For example, development policy involves external trade relations in general as well as EPA relations specifically: the role of ECHO has increased significantly whereas the CFSP and even CSDP have been used periodically to support development policy goals. Consequently, prior to the Lisbon reforms simplifying decision-making, pillar I Community competences had been utilized in conjunction with pillar II intergovernmental procedures. The actors include the member states in the Council, the European Parliament and the Commission (which itself still divides competence for development policy across several Directorates-General and the post of the High Representative for Foreign Affairs and Security Policy). As is explored in the following chapters, whilst such policy diversification has both strengths and weaknesses, the problems of coordination and complementarity are undoubtedly exacerbated by such diffusion.

The current relationship between the CFSP and development policy is a clear illustration of this problem. The Maastricht Treaty (Article C) demanded a linkage, despite the pillared structure that separates development policy from intergovernmental CFSP:

> The Union shall in particular ensure the consistency of its external activities as a whole in the context of its external relations, security, economic and development policies. The Council and Commission shall be responsible for ensuring such consistency. They shall ensure the implementation of these policies, each in accordance with its respective powers.

Article 21 of the Lisbon Treaty (now Article 21 TEU) has included development goals under its general principles guiding foreign affairs as follows:

> 1. The Union's action on the international scene shall be guided by the principles which have inspired its own creation, development and enlargement, and which it seeks to advance in the wider world: democracy, the rule of law, the universality and indivisibility of human rights and fundamental freedoms, respect for human dignity, the principles of equality and solidarity, and respect for the principles of the United Nations Charter and international law ...
> 2. (d) foster the sustainable economic, social and environmental development of developing countries, with the primary aim of eradicating poverty;

(e) encourage the integration of all countries into the world economy, including through the progressive abolition of restrictions on international trade.

The challenge is to balance Europe's array of external objectives and responsibilities. Development policy, in its broadest sense, is part of the EU's CFSP personality and one of its instruments. Joint actions, for example, can have development implications. As a global actor the EU requires a comprehensive network of external policies that combine trade, environment, development as well as the more traditionally recognizable foreign policy issues together. Achieving coordination, coherence and complementarity between and across these sectors within the Union is a mammoth task; but it is also an essential one and, as already suggested, unavoidably linked to the integration debate per se. In such a scenario development policy cannot be an optional extra, but constitutes a core component of Europe's external relations and CFSP.

The chapters

The remainder of this introduction provides a synopsis of the individual chapters and some concluding remarks about the purpose of the book. Whilst each chapter focuses on a specific area of European development policy, the themes and ideas raised in this introduction permeate the discussion throughout.

Since 2000, the EU has undertaken a fundamental revision of its relations with the developing world. As such it is legitimate and necessary to question whether these changes are based on a coherent philosophy or reflect a series of disjointed political compromises that have done little fundamentally to reconceptualize development policy. Why should there be an EU policy? What should be its content? How is it to be executed? Who are the actors? What is the relationship to United Nations and bilateral policies? And, crucially, how is development policy to be funded? These are all central issues that require analysis.

Chapter 1 addresses the issue of defining development. Here we consider changes within the EU's vision of development, linking this to the evolution of development thinking more broadly. This theoretical consideration is taken further by exploring the extent to which integration theory helps to explain the priorities within the EU development agenda. Finally, we confront the issue of defining the developing world itself, a necessary first step in any developmental initiative.

Chapters 2 and 3 provide an historical overview of EU–developing world relations through the prism of the ACP. In Chapter 2 we consider the origins, motivations and content of Europe's development policy towards the ACP and contrast the earliest period of relations (the Yaoundé Convention) with the successive Lomé Conventions and the negotiations that led to the Cotonou Agreement. In Chapter 3 we continue this theme with a closer examination of the nature of Cotonou and the protracted introduction of EPAs, and we consider the parallel evolution of the 2001 EBA initiatives aimed at the LDCs globally.

Chapter 4 addresses the institutional settings of development policies, policy-making process and implementation. We begin by placing an emphasis on the consequences of administrative reforms – under Jacques Santer (1995–99), Romano Prodi (1999–2004) and José Manuel Barroso (2004–) – and on the emergence of the 2005 'European Consensus on Development', designed to establish clear guidelines structuring the Union's role towards the developing world. We also address policy implementation, focusing principally on ECHO and EuropeAid, as well as considering the post-Lisbon round of reforms, including the emergence of the European External Action Service (EEAS) and its impact on the administration and implementation of development.

In Chapters 5 and 6 we explore the comparatively rudimentary relations with Latin America and with Asia. First, the recent history of the EU's relationship with Latin America is traced, exposing the significant change in relations. Originally very much an afterthought, relations with Latin America have evolved into a dialogue where the EU has clear foreign and economic policy goals, the pursuit of which has been increasingly facilitated through the provision of aid. As with Latin America, development has typically been a low priority in the EU–Asia relationship, and as discussed in Chapter 6 the Union's interests in the region have been primarily economic. Focusing on trade and competition, the relationship has been channelled through interregional structures: the EU–ASEAN relationship and the ASEM process. In this chapter we consider these interregional economic ties alongside the more limited aid and development relationship.

In Chapter 7 we debate the merits, effects and consequences of two specific EU concerns: complementarity and conditionality.

Complementarity has become a guiding principle for the organization of all EU policy sectors. The realization of this goal in development policy has been, however, complex and problematic. Political conditionality (in the form of good governance, democracy, the rule of law and human rights) is a pervasive element of EU external relations, and yet its application remains disputed. Economic conditionality (structural adjustment, liberalization and debt) is similarly contentious, though it remains a core element of European policy.

In Chapter 8 we explore the place of the EU in the broader global development architecture. The EU has been a leading voice alongside key multilateral institutions in establishing the new development agenda over the last two decades. Particular consideration is given to the relation of the EU to debates on ODA commitments, untying aid, the reprioritization of Africa and, most importantly, the UN's MDGs. In exploring links between EU development policy and that of the broader global community, we question whether development policy is enhanced by complementarity or reduced through duplication and competition.

To conclude: in the focus of this analysis of EU development policy we have consciously chosen to adopt a region-to-region approach. Thus the chapters are concerned with EU relations with the four principal blocs that describe the developing world – the ACP, MERCOSUR (Common Market of the South), ASEAN and ASEM. This approach is obviously open to the criticism that bilateral relations between the EU and individual developing countries are not given sufficient recognition. For example, relations with India or Pakistan are not included here, nor are the separate countries of Central America. However, this individual level of analysis is the necessary and unavoidable price to be paid for providing a broader perspective of EU development policy. The text – mirroring the EU itself – utilizes economies of scale by looking at region-to-region relations. Indeed, the very fact that the EU seeks such regional dialogues and agreements underlines that this approach is the appropriate perspective.

Writing about development policy as the process evolves is as precarious as it is ambitious. In this book we seek to identify the content of the policy debate and to theorize about the relationship between EU development policy and the integration process. As such, the ideas adopted are innovative and hypothetical. However, a core theoretical lacuna has been suggested that necessitates an answer: *does the EU play a distinct role in development policy?*

Subsidiarity might provide the answer, albeit one critical of the EU's claim to distinctiveness. Conversely, perhaps development policy is no longer a core policy within the Union, but one where a variable geometry approach is more appropriate. However, any such reformulation of the EU's role has to recognize and accommodate the objective of consistency in external relations and development policy as expressly articulated in the treaties from Maastricht to Lisbon.

For much of the developing world the reality of the new millennium started on 29 February 2000, the date the Lomé IV Convention expired. For 25 years under Lomé, the EU was the developing world's most significant democratic partner. However, the changes under Cotonou, particularly the introduction of EPAs, have launched a new and different era which many believe may fundamentally alter this relationship. The emergence of China, and latterly India, as alternative development partners has only served to exacerbate this tension. Development policy continues to face a crossroads and many of the assumptions and certainties of the past are now under constant and unprecedented scrutiny.

Development policy reform is a continual process, the outcome of which remains undecided and susceptible to sudden change. Forging a consensus within the EU member states is always hard and the European Parliament will certainly be active – and its approval is required for any new treaty-based agreements. Despite the clear free-trade policy tendencies of Europe, the history of the EU suggests that ambitious proposals that challenge the status quo more often lead to incremental and pragmatic change than to wholesale reform. However, the response of the developing world is crucial. Collectively they may be able to influence the debate to their mutual advantage; however, where no consensus emerges on their shared interests the EU will again be able to dictate the terms of the dialogue from now until at least 2020. Whether the late-1990s reform process was just another manifestation of *fin de siècle* euphoria, or a more sober re-evaluation of the EU's global role and limitations, the new millennium is witnessing a watershed in development policy.

Chapter 1

Theories and Concepts

This chapter explores a range of conceptual issues that impact upon the assessment of the EU's relationship with the developing world. The first is a recognition that the Union's conception of development has transformed over time, reflecting the continuing evolution of, and tension between, theoretical models of development. EU development policy is in many ways a reflection of this evolution. But these external models must also be supplemented by an understanding of European integration theory, which can be used to elucidate changing priorities in the Union's development agenda. Internal debates on the nature and functioning of the EU, coupled with the supranational–intergovernmental dynamics of integration, have played an important role in structuring external engagement, not least that with the developing world. Finally, at a more empirical level, we consider the definition of the 'developing world' itself. Myriad competing conceptions of what constitutes the developing world exist, creating a source of tension with the Union's own development policy, structured as it has been by historical realities more than objective considerations.

The changing vision of development

The historical evolution of EU–ACP relations also reflected a more general reconsideration of the concept of development itself. The changes in the EU approach were influenced by the wider developmental debates that had surfaced since the launch of the EU's development project, which saw, over time, a fundamental transformation in the European conception of development. Before examining these changes in detail later on in this text, these general tendencies are briefly outlined in this section.

The 1960s Yaoundé Convention conformed to many of the expectations of Modernization Theory of the early development period, informed largely by the goal of allowing the developing

23

world to catch up with the developed world -- a Eurocentric and unilinear formulation involving the emulation of the development trajectories of Northern states (as typified by Rostow's (1960) well-known five stages of economic growth). Yaoundé thus focused on trade – a source of much-needed foreign exchange – as a mechanism for development, together with technical assistance, training, investment and capital movements, as a means of fostering the progression of francophone African states along the path to development. Accordingly, development was defined in terms of 'the industrialization of the Associated States and the diversification of their economies, with a view to enabling them to strengthen their economic independence and stability' (Preamble to the Yaoundé Convention).

This market-centric notion of development, however, came under sustained attack during the late 1960s, as Dependency theorists linked 'underdevelopment' with the incorporation of developing countries into the capitalist economy, and questioned whether a focus on external trade and integration into international markets (which characterized European development policy) would in fact narrow the development gap as supporters of the Modernization approach asserted. The experience of the Yaoundé Conventions seems to have vindicated this pessimism. The free trade relationship encapsulated within Yaoundé, rather than altering the historical metropolis–satellite relationship, was regarded by many as further entrenching dependency, leading some to view the convention as merely an extension of French colonial policy.

At the extreme, Dependency Theory advocated a radical break with the capitalist international economy; milder forms, however, led to a push for a renegotiation of the North–South economic relationship with calls for a New International Economic Order (NIEO), a concept that was to become the cause célèbre of developing countries during the 1970s. Intrinsic to this Third Worldist perspective was a demand that international trade be reoriented to: ensure better and more stable prices for commodity exports upon which developing country economies were dependent; provide preferential access to markets in the developed world for emerging industries; and provide greater volumes of economic and technical assistance free of conditions.

It is in the context of Dependency Theory and the NIEO that the Lomé Convention emerged. In its 1971 'Memorandum on a Community Policy for Development Co-operation', an important precursor to Lomé, the European Commission argued for a future development policy that was 'the joint responsibility of the developing countries and the industrialized countries' with relationships based on 'close co-operation and organized solidarity', with Europe making 'its own contribution to the establishment of a more just international order' (Commission 1971: 8). The first Lomé Convention articulated these ideals and reflected many of the demands of the Third World, with the Commission appearing uniquely willing to 'buck the trend in international development' (Arts and Dickson 2004: 1) and respond to the criticisms levelled by Dependency Theory and the NIEO approach. As a reflection of the emphasis on a 'fairer' model of cooperation between Europe and the ACP states, the principles of partnership and a contractual approach were stressed, non-reciprocity of preferential market access commitments introduced, and STABEX (Stabilization of Export Earnings Scheme) and subsequently SYSMIN (Stabilization Scheme for Mineral Products) used to address directly the demand for stability in commodity prices. As a result, the Lomé Convention was at that time lauded as a model for development cooperation and North–South relations in general.

By the 1980s, however, the concept of development experienced another transformation. The structural crisis of the 1970s, followed by the Latin American Debt Crisis of the 1980s, underlay the emergence of the neoliberal counter-revolution in development economics, the rise of the Washington Consensus, and their application to the developing world in the form of International Monetary Fund (IMF) and World Bank-led structural adjustment. This new orthodoxy saw the free market once again as the surest path to global development. With the rise of adjustment conditionalities in the development strategies of the dominant international financial institutions, the European Commission was forced to come to terms with the new realities of global development and, prior to Lomé IV, accept that the implementation of neoliberal reforms through the medium of structural adjustment programmes had for developing countries become 'the *sine qua non* of their dialogue with the outside world', and that the only substantive choice now available to them was between an 'ordered, properly managed adjustment or forced adjustment' (Frisch and Boidin 1988: 67–8).

Despite initial efforts to develop a uniquely European adjustment support package consistent with Lomé's 'partnership' principle (rather than just paralleling the 'often dogmatic and too exclusively economic and financial' approach of the Bretton Woods institutions (*The Courier* 1988: 73)), the Commission's efforts were undermined by a lack of financial resources and the preference of the majority of member states who favoured the World Bank and IMF framework. In the event, Lomé IV reflected the interests of the member states: European adjustment support was explicitly linked with World Bank/IMF programmes. Thus, all recipients of European support became subject to Bretton Woods Structural Adjustment Programmes (SAPs), meaning in practice that Commission programmes provided de facto support only to World Bank and IMF activities (Brown 2004: 23).

The 'normalizing' of European development policy was further evident under the final convention which reflected the move within the development community during the 1990s to place greater emphasis on poverty reduction. This had been signposted most prominently in the World Bank's 1990 *Word Development Report*, and found expression in the European context in the Maastricht Treaty (subsequently Article 208 of the Treaty on the Functioning of the European Union – TFEU – formerly the Treaty Establishing the European Community – TEC) and the Lomé IV mid-term review which required that due account be taken of European development cooperation policy (Article 4), in other words the new Maastricht components of the TEC. While continuing to acknowledge 'the right of each state to determine its own political, social, cultural and economic policy options' (Article 2), Lomé IV further brought the European approach closer to the development mainstream by introducing political provisions on the promotion of human rights, good governance and the rule of law.

The Cotonou Agreement reinforced this string of changes, consigning the remaining uniquely European elements of Lomé to history and bringing the EU–ACP relationship closer to the framework of global governance, particularly trade governance under the WTO. Thus the ACP states are now being disaggregated, with the conclusion of WTO-compatible regional EPAs becoming the norm (see Chapter 3). Further, in line with the broader development community, poverty reduction has been highlighted as the 'central objective' of EU–ACP cooperation (Article 19), with conditionalities (on democracy, human rights, the rule of law and good governance) being linked to the receipt of assistance, establishing what is seen as being a more integrated approach to poverty. This holistic development approach has been taken even further by linking development policy with the CFSP goals of peace-building and conflict prevention (Article 11). Cotonou clearly signalled the closer integration of development within the broader external relations of the EU. This politicization of development has continued in the wake of Cotonou, with Europe also responding to the increased security emphasis of the post-9/11 world by introducing the fight against terrorism and weapons of mass-destruction into the existing Article 11 as a result of the 2005 Review of the Cotonou Agreement (see pp. 84–7). The most recent Lisbon Treaty changes have further underlined this trend with the High Representative for Foreign Affairs and Security Policy assuming new and substantive responsibilities for development policy.

In summary, there has been considerable evolution in Europe's approach to development policy since the early days of the Yaoundé Convention. An initial focus on development as economic growth was subsequently transformed into a uniquely European position under Lomé, which sought to address the concerns of the Third World directly. Latterly, however, Europe has returned to the mainstream. While development is now defined in terms of poverty reduction, integration into the global economy has been embraced as the key mechanism in pursuit of this goal. This perspective has also promoted conditionalities specifying inter alia the pursuit of good governance, defined in a manner consistent with the broader development community. These transformations were concretized in the Cotonou Agreement, which also began the process of integrating development policy more closely with EU external relations, arguably leading to a further politicization of development as witnessed under the 2009 Lisbon Treaty.

Development and integration theory

While *development theory* presents a broad conceptual context within which to locate Europe's development initiatives over the past half-century and more, *integration theory* – something specific to the European experience – can also be used to interpret and explicate the changing priorities in the EU's development agenda. Often the EU's external actions are more the consequences of its own internal integration dynamics than of external realities. A number of other texts emphasize the priority that should be given to integration theory. In *Developments in the European Union* the authors remind us it is vital to contextualize empirical information (whether policies or decisions) within theoretical and conceptual approaches, so as to understand the 'facts' better as well as to assess and develop the nature of integration theory (Cram et al. 1999: 17). In a similar vein, in *Decision-Making in the European Union* the authors distinguish between three levels of theorizing (super-systemic, systemic and sub-systemic) and argue – rightly – that it is important to differentiate between these levels when considering the appropriate choice of theoretical framework (Peterson and Blomberg 1999). Simply, the level of analysis required will determine the usefulness as well as the applicability of each theoretical approach. As the authors argue, 'a theory which seeks to explain or predict "big decisions", such as the launch of EMU, should not be judged by how well it explains or predicts a decision to change the way pig carcasses are measured' (ibid.: 9). Applying this logic here, the usefulness of grand integration theories (such as neo-functionalism, constructivism or intergovernmentalism) in explaining the changing outlines of EU development policy should not be confused with different lower-level approaches that might better explain a specific humanitarian action, ODA or trade concessions.

The general EU literature since the 1990s has been characterized by a renewed interest in these broader integration issues: in this discussion the theories associated primarily with the work of Moravcsik, Marks, Bulmer, Peterson and Wendt are applied to development policy. How far can these general integration theories be used to interpret the EU's specific policy towards the developing world? Such an approach runs the danger of creating the appearance of coherence; however, the application of a general approach can, through its very generality, create a false impression of cohesion and coherence, where in fact the policy is fragmented and a response to different catalysts.

Liberal intergovernmentalism, at its most basic level, places the state as the key actor in determining EU outcomes. Although its most influential proponent, Moravcsik (1991, 1993, 1995; Moravcsik and Nicolaïdis 1999), specifically circumscribes the applicability of liberal intergovernmentalism to what he calls history or polity-making events, its logic and explanation has been extended by others in an attempt to form a more general grand theory of integration. However, as Sartori (1976) long ago warned, concepts do not automatically 'travel' well and the cost of increased stretching is often an unsatisfactory fit between theory and practice. While acknowledging this potential constraint, many of the general assumptions of intergovernmentalism have direct applicability to theorizing the EU's development policy. Thus for intergovernmentalists, integration is fundamentally realized through interstate bargaining by rational economically self-interested governments influenced by their domestic settings and is not the outcome of any independent dynamic process or non-state actors. Crudely put, what you see is what you get: states exercise power and therefore all decisions made by the EU must reflect, to some degree, a realpolitik perspective. Typically, outcomes are based on the lowest common denominator. In Europe's international relations not all states are deemed equal, with France, the United Kingdom (UK) and Germany often the dominant actors; however, the importance of all member states is argued to exceed that of any supranational institution which, for intergovernmentalists, are peripheral and provide an inadequate account of the EU's grand decisions.

A key question implicit in this examination of the EU's policy towards the developing world is: who is driving the policy agenda? Liberal intergovernmentalism provides one set of conceptual lenses for intellectualizing this question. The answers it provides are distinct, provocative and possibly mutually exclusive with other integration theories. Whether intuitively appealing, or fundamentally flawed, the importance of intergovernmentalism is that it clearly establishes an extreme explanatory pole against which other theories can be located, compared and contrasted. Thus, an intergovernmentalist perspective towards EU development policy argues that the policy-making process is determined by the member states. In this book we cite many examples that correspond to such an approach. As will be discussed in Chapter 2, historically the introduction of a development focus (through Yaoundé and Lomé) was largely driven by national government concerns (primarily French and British respectively). This was complemented by the emergence of a Latin American policy after the accession of Spain and Portugal (see Chapter 5). Member states were also the primary source for the increased concern for good governance and other aspects of conditionality (Chapter 7). And although Romano Prodi instigated the reform of the Commission, his selection as President of the Commission was a direct response to member state pressures demanding restructuring and more effective policy implementation.

As outlined in Chapter 3, the negotiation of Cotonou provides some of the richest evidence of intergovernmentalism in EU policy-making. Importantly, for any agreement to proceed there had to be consensus on all points on the EU side. While trade-offs and concessions are the typical mechanism for determining EU policy, this does not undermine the fundamental point that any single state can veto a consensus and prevent it from emerging. Chapter 3 provides a series of examples where the negative role of member states was evident in the constraints imposed upon the negotiating mandate given to the Commission. Agricultural concessions were largely prohibited due to expected member state opposition. The issue of immigration and repatriation was again the result of explicit member state involvement. More positively, the involvement of the UK and Germany was the determining factor in changing the EU position on both debt relief and on the treatment of LDCs. The change in government in the UK was instrumental in finally bringing debt relief within the ACP framework – a policy that previous EU governments had avoided. Similarly, the decision not to extend reciprocal free trade principles to the LDCs was strongly advocated by the UK, Germany and the Netherlands, underlining both the legal and moral authority of member states in determining EU development policy.

The application of liberal intergovernmentalism to development policy reminds us of the primacy of the member states. The 27 determine the broad parameters for the large decisions – such as the 'Consensus on Development' or adoption of the MDGs – that set the context for micropolicy choices. Their political will – or at least their collective acquiescence – is required. However, there are also clearly disadvantages in only using such an elite-focused approach to policy-making. The EU institutions are marginalized in such an analysis: in the context of development policy, the omission of the Commission as a significant policy initiator is conceptually unrealistic and misleading, and the European Parliament's new authority as a full co-legislative power under the Lisbon Treaty means that this supranational institution is set to play a greater development policy role than in the past and that concepts, if they are to remain useful, need to accommodate this changing context.

An alternative theoretical approach– neo-functionalism – has been applied to the integration process since the 1950s and its classical application is best represented by the work of Ernst B. Haas. Generally, neo-functionalism is identified as the opposite theoretical pole to intergovernmentalism; however, the contrast should not be seen as fundamentally antagonistic, but rather that different aspects and actors involved in the integration process are given different emphases and explanatory power. Peterson and Bomberg (1999: 15) go as far as to state that the two approaches 'are complementary more than they are competitive'. As theory, intergovernmentalism focuses on process whereas neo-functionalism highlights context. Neo-functionalism does not deny that states are important actors; but it does argue that other supranational actors (such as the Commission, Parliament and the Court) may often be of greater importance in explaining outcomes. In essence, neo-functionalism tends to identify a wider range of actors and a greater complexity of relationships when characterizing integration. What it shares with intergovernmentalism is an aspiration to offer a comprehensive super-systemic-level explanation of the process.

The idea of 'spillover' is neo-functionalism's most celebrated – and controversial – theoretical contribution. For Haas, spillover manifests at least three elements: the functional, the political and the geographical. The logic is straightforward. Neo-functionalism argues that policy sectors and decisions are not isolated or autonomous. Rather they are located within a network, or policy community, and that decisions have repercussions beyond their immediate policy area. Actions that promote deeper integration in one policy area will have implications, consequences and effects upon a number of related policy areas. For example, a decision to create a European single market has influenced more than internal trade barriers. Neo-functionalists would argue that it has necessitated a common response to issues as diverse as citizenship, immigration, trade sanctions and tax harmonization.

Within the development policy context, a neo-functional based analysis would see connections between the EU's reform of the Lomé Convention and its approach to a CFSP, enlargement as well as trade relations in general. Most obviously, Maastricht provided the possibility – and Lisbon now the reality – for spillover to occur from CFSP to development policy (see p.135). The EBA debates on free market access for all LDCs arguably also display neo-functional characteristics. Having conceded that LDCs should receive special treatment under Cotonou, this policy concession crucially informed the EBA debate. Without any concessions for the ACP LDCs, support for the EBA may not have emerged. In the past, considerable debate has focused on whether this spillover effect is inevitable or 'automatic'. While most now agree with Keohane and Hoffmann (1990) that any such spillover is usually preceded by an 'intergovernmental bargain', only crude intergovernmentalists deny that this dynamic is evident in the integration process. The idea of spillover merely acknowledges the interrelated nature of policy development within the EU – which can have both positive and negative outcomes.

Some of the most interesting conceptual developments over recent decades are consistent with and build upon a basic neo-functional foundation. Perhaps the most influential is the 'multi-level governance' perspective first elaborated by Marks, Hooghe and Blank. They reject a uni-dimensional theoretical framework in favour of a more complex model that identifies a range of actors across different policy levels, characterized by 'mutual dependence, complementary functions and overlapping competences' (Marks et al. 1996: 378). Significantly, this approach both incorporates and moderates the intergovernmentalist preoccupation with the central role of the state. The crucial modification is that multi-level governance considers that states (represented through the Council) share decision-making authority with the supranational institutions; consequently, states – while they remain important actors – cannot guarantee desired outcomes and are themselves constrained by domestic interests and influences. In the context of Europe's external development relations, the recognition of other actors (such as the ACP states and the EU–ACP institutions as well as the Commission and the Parliament) suggests that this policy sector may possibly exhibit an even more extreme form of multi-level governance than that found for internal EU policies (Holland 2000).

Numerous examples of multi-level governance can be found in this book. The most obvious relate to the reform of the Commission and to the Cotonou negotiations covered in Chapters 3 and 4. As noted above, the member states were important in promoting the reform of Commission procedures – but they were not the only actors. The critical report that led to the resignation of the Santer Commission in 1999, pressure from the European Parliament as well as the agenda of the subsequent Prodi Commission were at least of equal importance. A combination of national and supranational factors was at work. The Cotonou negotiations provide an even broader example. Clearly, the Commission was instrumental in setting the parameters for the debate. Although none of the Green Paper options was endorsed without qualification, the focus of the reform debate was in practice set by the Commission and by its resultant guidelines. Had the Commission not signalled a preference for regional FTAs, it is hard to see how this concept would have emerged at the Council level. Of course, as discussed above, the Council can and did modify the Commission proposals – most notably with respect to separate treatment of LDCs – but overall as demonstrated in Chapter 3 the framework of the Cotonou Agreement and the current EPAs can be traced back to the Commission's earliest 1996 proposals. The advantage of multi-level governance is that it allows the analysis to accommodate the roles of non-state actors and institutions and as such adds a much-needed layer of conceptual sophistication to a basic intergovernmental theory.

The conceptual roots of multi-level governance can be traced to the earlier work of Bulmer (1983) that was influential in repositioning 'domestic politics' as a key variable in explanations of European decision-making. Clearly, too, the approach is sympathetic to the neo-functionalists' emphasis on supranational institutions, particularly the role of the Commission. At its most incisive, multi-level governance theorizes the enhanced authority of the supranational institutions at the expense of the state and national sovereignty. However, it goes beyond these earlier frameworks to stress the complexity and interacting nature of different policy levels – local, regional, national, transnational and international – that collectively shape integration. This complexity, of course, presents its own methodological challenges, but it is nonetheless a welcome correction to the over-simplification presented in many intergovernmentalist analyses.

Another approach that is compatible with multi-level governance considers the influence of public policy literature on integration theory, particularly the idea of policy networks (Peterson 1995; Richardson 1996). Simply, this approach argues that general public policy theories derived from national studies can be applied equally successfully to the EU policy process: in that respect they suggest that *sui generis* theories of integration are unnecessary. For example, agenda management and implementation processes have been used to enrich analyses of EU behaviour. The major contribution of the public policy literature has been at the micro-decision-making level and these approaches are less well able to operate at the level of grand theory. However, the recognition of interlocking policy networks at EU, state and substate levels is consistent with a multi-level governance perspective and helps to challenge further an exclusive reliance of intergovernmental explanations. In relation to development policy, the problems associated with policy implementation or with assessing good governance (as examined in Chapter 7) may best be dealt with through such network policy theories. As such they may present a useful framework for evaluating the EU's adoption and implementation of the MDGs, which is the focus of Chapter 8.

Another contemporary development that is consistent with neo-functionalism is 'new institutionalism' (see Bulmer 1994; Pierson 1996). Here, the emphasis is on the role of the supranational institutions in shaping the EU agenda, policies and decisions. This approach confronts the intergovernmentalist view that institutions are merely objective agents and not actors with their own motivations and interests. The European Parliament, the Commission and the Court of Justice both effect and are affected by the integration process. Values, norms, the very 'politics' of interaction, are used to explain outcomes. A dynamic rather than static view of institutions is assumed which clearly requires an institutional learning capacity. Not only do institutions matter, they evolve, adapt and respond within their contemporary and historical contexts. Of course, this dynamic characteristic reflects the reality of changing political elites (at least within the Commission and Parliament) that can alter the definition of institutional self-interest at any given moment. Consequently, new institutionalism argues that outcomes are rarely optimal: policy gaps and unintended consequences are evident especially where decisions are made within the context of short-term institutional horizons. The potential conflict between the EBA and Cotonou free trade areas to be discussed in Chapter 3 seems a clear example of this dynamic that may be explained by new institutionalism. Historical precedent and timing are identified as crucial limitations: future options are constrained by past decisions and the logic of 'path dependency' is influential. Applying these insights to the EU's development policies again enriches our understanding. For example, it reminds us of the power of the status quo. Innovations must operate within the context of existing policy parameters, and these will inevitably preclude some outcomes and favour others. Similarly, the European Parliament's desire to participate in the reform debates on Lomé may reflect both a concern with development policy per se, but it may also reflect the wider issues of defining policy competences between competing institutional actors in general. A legal or purely formal understanding of the policy process ignores these vital contexts; but, inevitably, accommodating new institutionalism further adds to the complexity and messy nature of theory building.

The most recent conceptual school that demands consideration as a potential framework that may help explain EU development policy is constructivism. Constructivism is not itself a 'grand theory' of European integration (Christiansen et al. 1999: 530), though attempts have, for example, been made to elucidate a constructivist approach to processes of socialization in Europe (e.g. Checkel 2003). Rather, constructivism offers an ontological perspective that can be applied to the integration process: the world is viewed as social rather than material, and identities and interests are seen as being endogenously constructed through inter-subjective interaction, rather than exogenously given (i.e. the product of domestic pressures alone) (Wendt 1992: 394). Structure and agent, in this view, are mutually constitutive (Giddens 1984).

Constructivism therefore sets out clear challenges to integration theory, most notably concerning the rationalist focus on agents – be they states alone, in the case of liberal intergovernmentalism, or a broader understanding incorporating also supranational institutions, as is the case with neo-functionalism and multi-level governance – recognizing the importance of structure and social learning. Agents, in this view, act according to their own interests, but also according to the rules of the institutions in which they are embedded. And yet constructivism also offers certain overlaps with integration theory, most notably with neo-functionalist assertions concerning, for example, the shift of loyalties to supranational institutions or redefinitions of interest of social and political actors (Ruggie 1998: 862).

A key element of the constructivist approach to European integration, then, is a recognition that integration has had a transformative impact on the state system (Christiansen et al. 1999: 529), which in turn has an impact on integration itself. Constructivist research on European integration therefore focuses on the ways in which norms and expectations are transformed over time, and the way state identities are transformed as a product of interaction within the European space. To go back to the question, raised above in relation to liberal intergovernmentalism, of who sets the policy agenda, constructivism suggests that even if member states are the most important actors, their own interests are constructed and transformed though interaction within this European policy space, implying a gradual Europeanizing of member state interests and policy formation.

In the context of development policy, constructivist approaches might point to the progression of EU policy-making from the narrowly defined largely instrumental set of policies of its early years – on the provision of food aid or market access – to a more proactive approach pursuing a broader Union interest in its development policy, one centred on the values seen to lie at the heart of the EU itself, such as good governance and improving the quality of life, as discussed in Chapters 7 and 8. In this respect, development policy may increasingly represent a socially constructed set of interests about the correct role of the Union in the world – a Europeanization of development policy. Within such a constructivist approach, of interest is the extent to which processes of social learning will bring member state interests closer, and the extent to which European norms and values penetrate into national polities, thus influencing policy formation at both domestic and European levels, and impacting on the success with which these policies are formed and implemented – the issues of coordination and complementarity.

In summary, the theoretical point being made here is a simple one: theories that are typically used to explain the internal processes of European integration – and even polity-making decisions – may be used with equal validity and relevance for understanding Europe's external relations. Thus integration theory can offer an appropriate conceptual framework for thinking about the EU's relations with the developing world. The decisions, non-decisions, policies and programmes both reflect and are informed by this wider integration context. However, as this discussion has outlined, the purpose of theorizing about European integration is not to find a single macro-theory. Rather it is to discriminate between alternative theories depending upon the level of analysis chosen and the nature of the actual empirical case. At different times within this book alternative theories are engaged – intergovernmentalism, neo-functionalism, multi-level governance and so on – in order to shed the greatest light upon specific aspects of EU development policy. Such an inclusive theoretical position – if somewhat frustrating for those seeking simple answers – is the only valid approach.

Where is the developing world?

From the EU's perspective, determining what constitutes the developing world has been complicated rather than simplified by its past reliance on the Lomé Convention as the principal line of demarcation. But the Lomé framework, whilst extensive, never provided a comprehensive approach towards the developing world, and one of its greatest weaknesses was its somewhat idiosyncratic and incremental nature. For example, consider the following comparison of two countries at the end of the 1990s. Both shared a European colonial legacy; they had comparably poor per capita GDPs; displayed similar low literacy and life expectancy levels; and the external trade patterns for both were based on a limited range of primary products. Both, clearly, were developing countries, arguably amongst the least developed. In this example, however, only one, Angola, was a member of the Lomé Convention, the EU's then preferred framework for relations with the developing world. The other, Cambodia, remained outside. Similar parallels can be made between Nigeria (a comparatively affluent Lomé state) and India (a developing country outside the Convention), or between Dominica and Vietnam. Out of the 48 LDCs in the world as defined by the United Nations (UN) before 2000, nine were excluded from the fourth Lomé Convention.

These illustrations symbolize a central historical problem – the patchwork nature of the EU's development policy. A consistent and comprehensive approach had been absent: incrementalism and adhocery spiced with pragmatism and post-colonial angst resulted in Europe's fragmented and increasingly complex relations with the countries of Africa, Asia, the Caribbean, Latin America and the Pacific Island states. Vociferous critics argued that such a status quo was indefensible and questioned whether this geographical diversity required policy pluralism, or if a simple coherent global approach was more appropriate and ultimately more effective in realizing development goals.

Defining the developing world has always been problematic. Which criteria should be applied: ideology, poverty, geography, economic performance, aid or exclusion from the global economy? Obviously, reliance on just a single criterion is inadequate. However, each, at some time, has been utilized as the demarcation between the 'First' and 'Third' World. Analysis as recent as 1990 defined the Third World as 'non-European, non-communist and poor' (O'Neill and Vincent 1990: ix). The tumultuous international events of the 1990s overturned not just communism, but also the simplicity of ideology as a definitional development criterion. The former stability of global political geography dissipated to such an extent that the traditional usage of the term 'developing country' is no longer a clearly delineated concept. The variety of nomenclature is revealing: the 'Third World', 'Developing World', 'the South', 'under-developed', 'non-industrialized' or even 'Other World' have all been applied to the same general category of countries, albeit each with specific inclusions and exclusions. To further complicate matters, just after the birth of the European Community in the late 1950s there were just 83 member countries in the UN. By 1989 this had risen to 156 members and by 2006 to 192, with further expansion likely as, for example, the status of Kosovo, Palestine and South Sudan are settled. Faced with more than one hundred 'new' nations, old designations have seemed increasingly redundant.

Until recently, the developing world was defined most simply by identifying geographically what constitutes the First and Second/transitional Worlds – definition by exclusion of the 'other'. If we accept this proposition the developing world is composed of all states other than those of Western, Central and Eastern Europe, Russia and the Commonwealth of Independent States, Japan, Australasia and North America, mirroring a broad North–South divide (the Antipodes excepted). Such simplicity sits uneasily with and of course ignores the new global BRICS framework of Brazil, Russia, India, China and South Africa which collectively covers more than 40 per cent of the world's population.

An alternative strategy is to work from the bottom up. The 48 LDCs obviously fit the rubric; so too do all the 78 ACP full member states of the 2000 Cotonou Partnership Agreement, the successor to the previous Lomé Conventions. Once the arithmetic encroaches on three figures, choices become open to interpretation. What of the states on Europe's southern border? Do, perhaps, the economies still in transition of Eastern Europe, or those developing countries on the Mediterranean rim, qualify, particularly after the economic, political and social upheavals of the Arab Spring of 2011? Further afield, is it valid to classify Latin America, China, India and the vast majority of Asia as an undifferentiated developing world category?

What criteria, then, can Europe use to distinguish between the complex and differentiated categories of the developed and developing world? Certainly any crude dichotomy is unsatisfactory. Can statistics provide a reliable guide to this definitional problem? If so, whose statistics should be used: the OECD, the World Bank, the European Union or the third countries themselves?

The World Bank's *World Development Report 2010* uses 2008 gross national income (GNI) per capita statistics as the main criterion for establishing four basic categories of development (covering 211 'countries'). These are (World Bank 2010b: 375–6):

TABLE 1.1   *ACP LDCs' Human Development Index, 2010*

Country	Population (millions)	HDI	HDI ranking
Democratic Republic of Congo	67.8	0.239	168
Niger	15.9	0.261	167
Burundi	8.5	0.282	166
Mozambique	23.4	0.284	165
Guinea-Bissau	1.6	0.289	164
Chad	11.5	0.295	163
Liberia	4.1	0.300	162
Burkina Faso	16.3	0.305	161
Mali	13.3	0.309	160
Central African Republic	4.5	0.315	159
Sierra Leone	5.8	0.317	158
Ethiopia	85.0	0.328	157
Guinea	10.3	0.340	156
Sudan	43.2	0.379	154
Malawi	15.7	0.385	153
Rwanda	10.3	0.385	152
Gambia	1.8	0.390	151
Zambia	13.3	0.395	150
Tanzania	45.0	0.398	148
Djibouti	0.9	0.402	147
Angola	19.0	0.403	146
Haiti ~	10.2	0.404	145
Senegal	12.9	0.411	144
Uganda	33.8	0.422	143
Lesotho	2.1	0.427	141
Comoros	0.7	0.428	140
Togo	6.8	0.428	139
Mauritania	3.4	0.433	136
Madagascar	20.1	0.435	135
Benin	9.2	0.435	134
São Tomé and Príncipe	0.2	0.488	127
Solomon Islands ~	0.5	0.494	123
Timor Leste	1.2	0.502	120
Equatorial Guinea	0.7	0.538	117
Eritrea	5.2	n.a.	n.a.
Kiribati ~	0.1	n.a.	n.a.
Samoa ~	0.2	n.a.	n.a.
Somalia	9.4	n.a.	n.a.
Tuvalu ~	+	n.a.	n.a.
Vanuatu ~	0.2	n.a.	n.a.

n.a. HDI data not available for these countries.

~ Non-African LDC.

+ Population is less than 0.1 million.

Source: UNDP (2010: 143–6, 184–7).

TABLE 1.2 *Other ACP states' Human Development Index, 2010*

(i) Other non-LDC ACP African countries (15)			
Country	*Population (millions)*	*HDI*	*HDI ranking*
Zimbabwe	12.6	0.140	169
Côte d'Ivoire	21.6	0.397	149
Nigeria	158.3	0.423	142
Cameroon	20.0	0.460	131
Ghana	24.3	0.467	130
Kenya	40.9	0.470	128
Congo	3.8	0.489	126
Swaziland	1.2	0.498	121
Cape Verde	0.5	0.534	118
South Africa	50.5	0.597	110
Namibia	2.2	0.606	105
Botswana	2.0	0.633	98
Gabon	1.5	0.648	93
Mauritius	1.3	0.701	72
Seychelles	0.1	n.a.	n.a.

(ii) ACP Caribbean countries (15)*			
Country	*Population (millions)*	*HDI*	*HDI ranking*
Haiti*	10.2	0.404	145
Guyana	0.8	0.611	104
Suriname	0.5	0.646	94
Dominican Republic	10.2	0.663	88
Jamaica	2.7	0.688	80
Belize	0.3	0.694	78
Trinidad and Tobago	1.3	0.736	59

→

(ii) ACP Caribbean countries (15)*

Country	Population (millions)	HDI	HDI ranking
Bahamas	0.3	0.784	43
Barbados	0.3	0.788	42
Antigua and Barbuda	0.1	n.a.	n.a.
Dominica	0.1	n.a.	n.a.
Grenada	0.1	n.a.	n.a.
St Kitts and Nevis	0.1	n.a.	n.a.
St Lucia	0.2	n.a.	n.a.
St Vincent and the Grenadines	0.1	n.a.	n.a.

(iii) ACP Pacific Island countries (14)*

Country	Population (millions)	HDI	HDI ranking
Papua New Guinea	6.9	0.431	137
Solomon Islands	0.5	0.494	123
Micronesia	0.1	0.614	103
Fiji	0.9	0.669	86
Tonga	0.1	0.677	85
Cook Islands	+	n.a.	n.a.
Kiribati*	0.1	n.a.	n.a.
Marshall Islands	0.1	n.a.	n.a.
Nauru	+	n.a.	n.a.
Niue	+	n.a.	n.a.
Palau	+	n.a.	n.a.
Samoa*	0.2	n.a.	n.a.
Tuvalu*	+	n.a.	n.a.
Vanuatu*	0.2	n.a.	n.a.

n.a. HDI data not available for these countries.
* Includes LDC countries given in Table 1.1.
+ Population is less than 0.1 million.
Source: UNDP (2010: 143–6, 184–7).

- Low income (US$975 or less in 2008);
- Lower-middle income (US$976–3,855);
- Upper-middle income (US$3,856–11,906);
- High income (US$11,907 and above).

The analysis identified 43 low-income, 55 lower-middle-income, 46 upper-middle-income and the remaining 67 as high-income economies. The World Bank asserts elsewhere that low- and middle-income economies 'are sometimes referred to as developing economies'; but whilst the 'use of the term is convenient ... Classification by income does not necessarily reflect development status'(!) (World Bank 2011).

In the OECD Development Assistance Committee's 2010 *Development Co-operation Report* a different but related methodology is adopted. Focusing on just those developing countries that were ODA recipients, four categories were identified, again using the criterion of per capita GNI, though based on 2007 data (OECD-DAC 2010: 271–2):

- Least Developed Countries (LDCs);
- Low-Income Countries (LICs) (per capita GNI less than US$935);
- Lower Middle-Income Countries (LMICs) (US$936–3,705);
- Upper Middle-Income Countries (UMICs) (US$3,706–11,455).

Forty-nine LDCs, 12 LICs, 47 LMICs and 43 UMICs were identified (ibid.: 270).

The Human Development Index (HDI) offers yet another perspective. This United Nations Development Programme (UNDP) approach supplements indices that focus crudely on GNI bases. It employs indicators based on the criteria of longevity (life expectancy), educational level and income per head; whilst still imperfect, many argue that it gives a better assessment of 'development' as opposed to poverty. The 2010 HDI Report (UNDP 2010) rank-ordered 169 countries (with 25 further countries unable to be assessed due to insufficient data) and produced some surprising results. For example, the ACP countries of Barbados (42) and Bahamas (43) ranked above EU member states such as Lithuania (44), Latvia (48), Romania (50) and Bulgaria (58), and only just below Portugal (40) and Poland (41). Less surprisingly, all but one country (Afghanistan) ranked below 140 was an ACP member

TABLE 1.3 *Non-ACP LDCs' Human Development Index,*
2010

Country	Population (millions)	HDI	HDI ranking
Afghanistan	29.1	0.349	155
Nepal	29.9	0.428	138
Yemen	24.3	0.439	133
Myanmar	50.5	0.451	132
Bangladesh	164.4	0.469	129
Cambodia	15.1	0.494	124
Laos	6.4	0.497	122
Bhutan	0.7	n.a.	n.a.

n.a. HDI data not available for these countries.
Source: UNDP (2010: 143–6, 184–7).

(144–7). Of further interest from this HDI perspective is the fact that nine LDCs, five of which fall into the UNDP's 'Low Human Development' category, are not members of the ACP grouping of states. A summary of the HDI for ACP countries and other non-ACP LDC states may be found in Tables 1.1, 1.2 and 1.3.

Faced with this ambiguity, in this book a precise GNP per capita definition of the developing world is avoided in favour of an essentially geographically based interpretation that reflects the reality and actual practice of the EU's development relations. The developing world is defined as those states covered by the European Union's key development funding instruments – the EDF and the DCI. In contrast to other EU external-relations budget lines that have been formally merged under the umbrella of the new post-Lisbon Treaty European External Action Service, these are the primary responsibility of DG Development and Cooperation – EuropeAid (DG-DEVCO, formerly DG Development) (see Chapter 4). As such, the developing word is defined in EU terms as the 78 ACP states covered by the EDF, alongside those primarily Asian and Latin American states covered by the DCI. This clearly excludes the states of Central and Eastern Europe and the Mediterranean. While there are clearly developmental aspects to the EU's relationship with these states,

MAP 1.1 *ECHO Field Offices and Key External Relations Funding Instruments (EDF, DCI, ENPI), 2010*

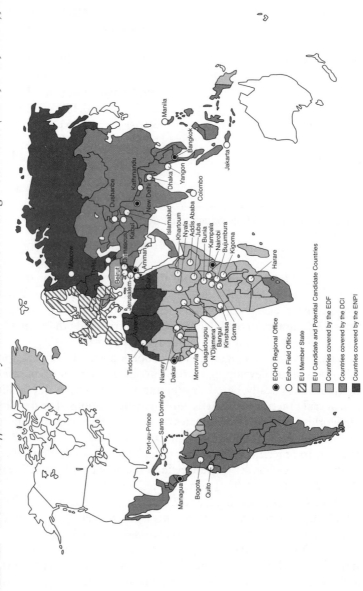

they are accorded a 'privileged relationship' with the Union stemming from their geographic location. In what is effectively a concentric circles approach to its neighbourhood, these states have either become members of the EU themselves, have been designated as candidates for membership or viewed as potential future candidates, or are seen as part of a broadly conceived European political and economic space. This differs markedly from the more at-arms' length conception of the states covered by the EDF and DCI. The primary funding instrument for the Eastern European and Mediterranean states is the European Neighbourhood and Partnership Instrument (ENPI) (see Map 1.1).

To conclude, this chapter has provided the necessary theoretical frameworks within which the following empirical chapters can be located. While each chapter can stand individually as a contemporary description of the nature of EU development policy towards specific regions or as thematic examinations of development objectives, the conceptual approaches identified offer an additional explanatory perspective to the analysis. The difficulty in identifying those countries that legitimately consitute the developing world has also been examined, with the EDF and DCI mechanisms used (for the EU at least) to operationalize this definition. With these ideas in hand, we now turn to the substance of contemporary EU development policy.

Chapter 2

The ACP: From Yaoundé to Cotonou

We begin this chapter by addressing two basic questions. What were the origins of the EU's development policy? What were the motivations? These simple questions need to be examined in some detail in order to convey the context within which development policy has evolved since 1957. Many of the current debates concerning the restructuring of development policy can only be understood through such a historical perspective.

The 1957 Treaty of Rome establishing the European Economic Community (EEC) was a document that challenged pre-existing assumptions about state sovereignty. These assumptions were not exclusively internal in their implications but extended to a state's external affairs as well. The internal integration of the European market had direct and serious consequences for third countries, and the position of the developing world was addressed, albeit imperfectly, in the founding Treaty. Of course, bilateral relations have persisted and act to complement the European relationship with the developing world; significantly, however, the scope and scale of these bilateral ties have been progressively modified. Whilst the Treaty was myopic in its largely francophone definition of the then Third World, this framework represents the origin of Europe's fragmented and differentiated approach.

The original signatories to the Treaty of Rome all sought special arrangements for those matters that were of particular importance to them: agricultural, political and colonial. For France, the protection of the relationship with its colonial dependencies was one such priority. Significantly, throughout the discussions that led to the Spaak Report, which set the framework for the original Community, no mention was made of colonial relations, and only as late as May 1956 did France table the issue. The other member states were reluctant to involve the EC in what was to most a French external affair, with the Dutch and the Germans the most critical. However, as one commentator noted, 'France's move was shrewdly timed: by making a satisfactory agreement on provisions for its dependencies a *sine qua non* for its signature of the Treaty, French bargaining power was maximized' (Ravenhill 1985: 48). Consequently, on French insistence, provisions for 'association' for all dependencies were included in Part IV of the Treaty: a contractual treaty-based relationship was created that established both the basis and the rationale for subsequent arrangements such as the Yaoundé and Lomé Conventions and the current Cotonou Partnership Agreement.

Associated status was given to specific Overseas Collectivities and Territories (OCTs) that had 'special relations' with a member state. Initially this only involved relations between 31 OCTs and four member states (France, Belgium, Italy and the Netherlands) but was expanded with the first enlargement in 1973. French colonial ties predominated and incorporated the states of French West Africa, French Equatorial Africa as well as island dependencies in the Pacific and elsewhere. Article 182 of the Treaty of Rome set out the parameters of these original provisions:

> The purpose of association shall be to promote the economic and social development of the countries and territories and to establish close economic relations between them and the Community as a whole.
>
> ... association shall serve primarily to further the interests and prosperity of the inhabitants ... in order to lead them to the economic, social and cultural development to which they aspire.

In essence, both member states and colonial dependencies were to be treated similarly with respect to trade access, investment and the reduction and eventual abolition of customs duties (with the exception of certain 'sensitive' products). A consequence of this was that other third country developing states were discriminated against. The contractual nature of the relationship was important as a legal obligation was established on member states to 'contribute to the investments required for the progressive development of these countries and territories' (Article 183.3). The exclusive mechanism chosen for the task of providing aid was the EDF. The role of the EDF has grown significantly (both in the scale and scope of funding

TABLE 2.1　　*Financing of development cooperation, 1958–2013*

Convention	Fund	Date	No. of states	EDF* (ECU millions)
Treaty of Rome	EDF 1	1/1/1958	31	581
Yaoundé I	EDF 2	1/7/1964	18	666
Yaoundé II	EDF 3	1/1/1971	19	843
Lomé I	EDF 4	1/4/1976	46	3,124
Lomé II	EDF 5	1/1/1981	57	4,754
Lomé III	EDF 6	1/5/1986	66	7,754
Lomé IV	EDF 7	1/3/1990	69	10,800
Lomé IV (review)	EDF 8	4/11/1995	70	12,967
Cotonou	EDF 9	1/1/2002	76	13,500
Cotonou (review)	EDF 10	1/1/2008	78	22,682

* Includes grants, special loans, STABEX and SYSMIN.
Sources: Glaser (1990: 26), Vernier (1996: 12), Commission (2002b) and Council of the EU (2006).

– see Table 2.1) and it continues to remain one of the key instruments of Europe's policy towards the developing world. Despite this assistance and the market preferences given to their exports, the associated states generally failed to improve their economic prospects.

Not surprisingly, Articles 182–7 were criticized for perpetuating existing colonial dependency. Whilst with hindsight this certainly seems the case, two ancillary factors are pertinent. First, in the context of the time, these Articles were more significant for underlining at the very beginning of European integration that an external developmental relationship could not be ignored. Clearly, Europe's global role and responsibility were to be valued and part of the wider notion of integration: the then Community was much more ambitious than is perhaps commonly acknowledged. As Monnet (1978: 392) argued, the Community was 'not a coal and steel producers' association: it is the beginning of Europe' – with all that phrase implies internally and externally. But second, the selectivity of the countries included foreshadowed what was to become the central problem in Europe's relationship with the developing world

– historical ties rather than need had been the driving rationale behind preferential treatment. It has taken half a century to unravel this selectivity in Europe's definition of the developing world.

The Yaoundé Conventions

The association provisions still apply to a small number of what are now referred to as Overseas Countries and Territories linked to Denmark, France, the Netherlands and the UK (seven in the Caribbean, four in the Pacific, one in the Indian Ocean, and seven in the Atlantic), though the issuing in 2008 of a Green Paper on *Future Relations between the EU and OCTs* (Commission 2008) suggests that the era of association may be coming to an end, probably when the current Overseas Association Decision (comprising a funding envelope of €286 million) expires in 2013.

Despite this ongoing hangover from the original association provision, by the early 1960s the majority of OCTs gained their independence and new arrangements were appropriate and necessary. Consequently, by the mid-1960s the vast majority of African states found their relations with Europe structured through a completely new and separate treaty: the first Yaoundé Convention. The foundation of the Convention was the recognition of the national sovereignty of the participating countries. It established preferential trading arrangements between the Six and 18, principally francophone, countries known as the EAMA: Burundi, Cameroon, the Central African Republic, Chad, Congo, Dahomey, Gabon, Ivory Coast, Madagascar, Mali, Mauritania, Niger, Rwanda, Senegal, Somalia, Togo, Upper Volta and Zaire.

There were three distinctive and original features to the Convention: its comprehensive character; the multilateral framework; and the joint institutions. First, uniquely for the time, the Convention linked a range of separate development policies under a single integrated approach. Financial aid, technical assistance and training, trade preferences, and investment and capital movements were all covered. Second, the Convention was the first example of a common contractual basis for relations between the industrialized and the developing world. This multilateral framework made it easier to adopt a regional approach to issues and promoted regional cooperation amongst the EAMA group. Third, three joint institutions were created (the Council, the Parliamentary Conference and the Court of Arbitration). The Council contained one representative from each of the EAMA and European member states, met annually and could issue binding decisions based on joint agreement. The Parliamentary Conference had only advisory status, whereas the Court was the final arbiter where informal procedures in the Council were unable to resolve disputes arising under the Convention (it was never called upon to do so, however).

The first Yaoundé Convention expired in 1969 – although its provisions were renewed for a further five-year period ending in 1975. During the lifetime of this second Convention the first enlargement of the European Community took place. UK membership and the question of Commonwealth relations necessitated a major review of external relations: however, this first decade of treaty-based relations between Europe and the developing world provided the context within which the subsequent Lomé Conventions were debated and designed. Financial support for the EAMA was directed principally through the EDF and the European Investment Bank (EIB). Under Yaoundé I a total of 666 million EUA (European Units of Account) was provided in EDF aid and a further 64 million in the form of EIB loans (see Table 2.1). Under Yaoundé II, EDF aid rose to 843 million with a further 90 million provided by EIB loans (Commission 1986: 15). During this period the Community provided approximately 20 per cent of the total official aid received by the 18 signatory states. Three times this amount, however, was provided by continued bilateral assistance from individual member states (mainly France, Belgium and increasingly Germany). This combination of Community/EU-level aid and bilateral aid continues to be the hallmark of Europe's past and present relationship with the developing world. Whilst the balance may have changed from convention to convention, this shared arrangement has never been challenged. Community/EU-level aid supplements and supports bilateral action: it has never been proposed that it should replace it entirely.

Two serious problems underlay the seeming largesse of the EDF: disbursement of funds and narrow sectoral support. First, typically, from 1957 to 1975 only a third of EDF funds were successfully disbursed during the lifetime of the respective agreements. Second, the greatest proportion of EDF aid was given to infrastructural projects virtually excluding development of the industrial sector. As such, the EDF mirrored the bilateral practices of former colonial donor states.

The basic principles of the Convention followed those found in the Treaty of Rome and partly foreshadowed the core elements of the Cotonou Agreement that was signed in the year 2000. Over time it was hoped that there would be established: the abolition of customs barriers; reciprocal duty-free access; abolition on quantitative quotas on exports; and the extension of Most Favoured Nation (MFN) status to EU member states. The trade content of the Conventions provided for EAMA imports into Europe free from customs duties and quotas for all agricultural and industrial products – except those that were in direct competition with European producers. Whilst the exceptions were criticized, under Yaoundé II EAMA producers in these categories were given limited but preferential access over other third countries. More importantly, the trade preferences enjoyed by the EAMA were progressively eroded due to the lowering or abolition of duties on a range of tropical products – such as coffee, cocoa, tea, pineapples and nutmeg. In addition, products such as copper, iron ore, cotton, rubber and oil seed, the main EAMA exports, were never subject to European tariffs in general. Consequently, the Convention could not provide them with any preferential access to the European market. Overall, the economic benefits provided by the Convention appeared marginal and were openly criticized by the 18 signatories and two member states, Germany and the Netherlands. The impression was given that the Yaoundé states were just 'suppliers of the residual market that the Community producers could not fill and at best provided them with a slight advantage over third countries' (Ravenhill 1985: 56). To compound the trading problem, Yaoundé was based upon the principle of reciprocity.

The Yaoundé Convention only linked Europe to a small segment of the developing world, and in it the seeds of Europe's future piecemeal approach can be traced. Obviously, the 18 Yaoundé countries' share in total external trade was relatively small. Importantly, however, the pattern of trade over the 1958–67 period declined. In 1958, 5.6 per cent of Community imports came from the Yaoundé States, this figure falling to 4.2 per cent by 1967. Community exports to the EAMA stood at 4.4 per cent in 1958, but only represented 2.9 per cent a decade later (Holland 2002: 30) and the resultant trade deficit with the Yaoundé States rose from US$22 million to US$378 million over the period. There was a typical asymmetry in the goods traded: 72 per cent of Yaoundé exports to Europe were primary products whereas 85 per cent of their imports from Europe were industrial in origin (Commission 1969: 10).

Whilst the first ten years of the Treaty of Rome saw a general increase in the member states' share of world trade (which by 1967 saw the Community as the leading global importer (18 per cent) and exporter (20 per cent)), as noted above the developing world's share of this trade declined. Overall, trade with the developing world – like that with the Yaoundé States – declined during this first decade. In 1958 the developing countries supplied 42 per cent of the EC's imports and took 39 per cent of Europe's exports. By 1967 these figures had fallen to 38 and 27 per cent respectively. During the same period Europe reduced its import of raw materials from 30 to 22 per cent. Consequently the trade deficit with the developing world rose from US$700 million in 1958 to $3,225 million by 1967. What is perhaps most surprising is that if these figures are broken down by region, Latin America, non-EAMA Africa and the Middle East were all more important markets for the EC. Only trade with South East Asia approximated to the modest levels of the Yaoundé States (Holland 2002: 30). And yet at this stage Europe's relationship with the wider developing world lacked the formalized relationship of the Yaoundé Convention. No special privileges existed that gave concessions to these nations. This broader trend continued to be reflected for the duration of Yaoundé II.

What, then, was so special about the Yaoundé States and what were Europe's motivations? Were they purely economic and arguably neo-colonial, or more developmental in origin? Certainly, Europe's global competitors, especially the United States of America (USA), may have viewed the association as prejudicial and incompatible with the framework of the General Agreement on Tariffs and Trade (GATT). The difficulties that were to become endemic within the economies of the developing world were already apparent by the time the Yaoundé Convention was signed. Its provisions lacked the necessary drive to alter the historical relationship. Whilst the free trade principle was seen as assisting development, in practice the limited concessions tended to maintain, even strengthen, the dependency relationship. Without the principle of non-reciprocity, the charge of economic neo-colonialism was hard to refute – a perspective that has returned to colour EPA discussions some 35 years later.

More critically, many interpreted the Yaoundé Convention as a poorly disguised extension of French foreign and colonial policy. As one analysis pointed out, the undeniable dependency of francophone Africa on France for aid and trade 'existed independently of the

EEC and was in no way consequential to it' with the majority of original member states 'extremely loath to become involved with former African colonies' (Cosgrove-Twitchett 1978: 122). There was no political dimension to the Convention whatsoever: the notion of good governance conditionality had yet to be conceived. The relationship was essentially one that was a consequence of historical ties that were increasingly difficult to organize as the EC began to expand from its clear francophone base to incorporate the English-speaking developing world.

In summary, many of the issues pertinent to European development policy under subsequent Lomé Conventions and the Cotonou Agreement can be traced to these earlier Yaoundé arrangements. As discussed here, they include ineffectual trading concessions; the disbursement of EDF funds; the colonial basis for preferences and country selectivity; an emphasis on infrastructure aid; the question of reciprocity; and last, but far from least, the influence of French interest in Europe's development agenda.

The Lomé Conventions: I and II (1976–85)

More than any other factor, the enlargement of the EC from the original Six to the Nine in 1973 foreshadowed a restructuring of external relations. Whilst Denmark and Ireland did not have any colonial legacies, one of the key areas of concern raised by British membership was protecting and maintaining relations with Commonwealth developing countries. Geographically this demanded extending the African focus of Yaoundé to include both Caribbean and Pacific states – although the Indian subcontinent was to remain excluded. There was a profound distinction between the Commonwealth ethos based upon an open trading relationship and respect for sovereignty, and the paternalism of France and latterly the EC that 'suggested the Community had little respect for the newly won sovereignty of the Associates' (Ravenhill 1985: 72). Conceptually, it became necessary to mesh the narrowly defined EAMA interests with the more diverse needs of Commonwealth countries. A simple extension of the Yaoundé provisions was contemplated and explored, but ultimately a specifically tailored and integrated Convention was produced that sought to protect French sensitivities yet meet British demands. The views of the developing countries, whilst sought, were of secondary importance to the process.

A further motivation behind this new definition of European development policy was the widely felt disappointment about the impact of Yaoundé. As already noted, the trading preferences were progressively eroded and the introduction of the GSP scheme in 1971 was indicative of a broadening of Europe's external relations. The development objectives of the Convention remained unfulfilled and the largely francophone membership exclusivity encouraged charges of neo-colonialism. Some member states viewed the prospect of future British membership as an opportunity to open a wider development debate, an idea that was vigorously supported by the Commission who wished to see its bureaucratic authority strengthened in this policy area.

Formal negotiations between Europe and the respective developing countries began in mid-July 1973, some 18 months prior to the expiry of Yaoundé II (Holland 2002: 34). It was not until July 1974, however, that the Nine forged a consensus on the outline for the new agreement. Eventually, French opposition to a non-reciprocal arrangement was dropped, an agricultural compromise was fashioned, and on German insistence an aid ceiling was established. Only the question of how to balance Britain's Commonwealth sugar preferences within the CAP remained, though this was eventually resolved (ibid.).

The resulting Lomé Convention replaced one acronym and political and economic entity (EAMA) on the world stage with a new configuration: the African, Caribbean and Pacific states – the ACP. Lomé I was signed on 28 February 1975 and came into force on 1 April 1976 linking the then nine EC states with 46 developing countries. This new ACP grouping comprised the original 18 Yaoundé states and Mauritius; six other African states; and 21 less-developed Commonwealth countries. Of these Commonwealth states 12 were African, six from the Caribbean and three the Pacific. However, during the five-year duration of Lomé I the number of signatories rose to 53 – signalling a consistent future growth in Lomé membership that continued until the end of the twentieth century.

The most distinctive feature of the Lomé Convention was a commitment to equal partnership between Europe and the ACP. The preamble committed the signatory states 'to establish, on the basis of complete equality between partners, close and continuing cooperation in a spirit of international solidarity' and to 'seek a more just and more balanced economic order'. In part, this change in approach was a response to the perception that the Yaoundé arrangements had perpetuated dependency rather than promoted development. In part, too, it was a reflection of the Commonwealth philosophy in contrast to the francophone style of colonial relations. At one level the idea of partnership was formally reflected in the trade relationship, its legal base and in the structure of the institutional framework. At another level, a simple commitment to the principle of partnership can be criticized as ineffectual because such a dialogue could never be between equal partners: the European agenda has clearly prevailed. This mismatch between ambition and actual practice notwithstanding, the goals of the Convention were innovative and established a First–Third World relationship that was progressive and unparalleled for its time.

The major policy objectives of the Convention were as commendable as they were ambitious: the promotion of European–ACP trade; agricultural and industrial development; special aid for the LDCs; and support for regional cooperation. At the policy level, Lomé I was much more than just an extension of the preceding Convention. The shortcomings of Yaoundé had been rightly criticized and Lomé sought to address these in two specific ways: first, by dropping reciprocity; and second, by the introduction of an export stabilization scheme. The decision to relinquish reverse preferences and embrace non-reciprocity was of greater psychological than economic importance. The ACP states were now required simply to treat European exports at least as favourably as exports from other developed nations. The effect on the EC's pattern of external trade was, however, marginal.

STABEX – the system for the stabilization of export earnings from agricultural commodities – was the major innovation of Lomé I. Its objective was to provide funds to ACP countries to cover production shortfalls or price fluctuations for specific agricultural products exported to Europe. Because many ACP states were dependent on a limited number of products, making them especially susceptible to variations in world market prices, STABEX was particularly important. It can be equated with an insurance policy for the ACP: the EC guaranteed a minimum earnings threshold for these specified exports and compensated for any loss of revenue caused by lower prices or loss of production. Twenty-nine products were covered under the first Convention, rising to 44 in Lomé II.

Obviously, the benefits were not equally distributed among the ACP. Under Lomé I more than one-third of available support went to groundnut production (ECU 139.4 million), and just three states

(Senegal, Sudan and Mauritania) accounted for 38.1 per cent of the available funds. This uneven spread continued under Lomé II, albeit with some product and country variation. Three products (coffee, cocoa and groundnuts) took four-fifths of the budget (Holland 2002: 37) with three states (Senegal, Ghana and Côte d'Ivoire) accounting for 38.5 per cent between them (Commission 1986: 25). The underlying philosophy of STABEX proved to be its Achilles heel during these initial years. Global recession and a fall in commodity prices saw requests for STABEX compensation exceed the allocated budget. By 1980, the start of the second Convention, the budget could only match roughly half of all funding requests, and a year later there was a deficit of ECU 341 million. Whilst the budget was in balance by the end of Lomé II, the scheme was clearly a victim of its own success and inevitably an inadequate response to fluctuations in the global economy.

Despite these initial problems Lomé's popularity increased; seven newly independent former British dependencies joined the Convention, making a total of 60 signatories, with a further three joining during the five years of the agreement. Only one of these (Zimbabwe) was from Africa, the remainder being Pacific or Caribbean island states, signalling a changing geopolitical balance within the ACP grouping. Although Lomé II varied little from Lomé I, two developments were introduced – a greater emphasis on the LDCs and the introduction of SYSMIN. At the beginning of Lomé I, 24 of the 46 states were classified as LDCs. Over the next decade this rose to 35 and resulted in Lomé II placing a renewed emphasis on LDCs as well as on landlocked states. SYSMIN was arguably a more immediately significant extension. This 'special financing facility' for mineral exports was based on principles similar to those of STABEX and provided those ACP states that were heavily dependent on mining exports to Europe a degree of protection from loss of production or price collapses.

Any assessment of the impact of the first decade of the Lomé Convention has to begin by acknowledging its foresight in its commitment to partnership and a desire to help integrate the economies of the developing countries into the global market. Second, Lomé eschewed any form of neo-colonial ties: the ACP states were not required to offer Europe any special preferences, nor were they prohibited from trading with other developed countries. Third, no political conditionality was imposed: the domestic politics of signatory states were largely ignored. And, as indicated in the above analysis, a range of development assistance programmes as well as trade preferences was introduced. However, any evaluation also has to acknowledge the gap between the Convention's intentions and its actual effect. Perhaps most critically, the impact on the balance of trade was marginal. Whilst the ACP enjoyed a trade surplus with Europe, this was also the position prior to Lomé. In terms of product, the Convention had the perverse effect of promoting ACP dependency on raw materials as an export base in exchange for importing primarily industrial goods from Europe. During the negotiations for Lomé II the European Parliament issued a particularly critical Report:

> The structure of ACP–EEC trade reveals an acute imbalance, both among products exported and among the ACP exporting countries ... this structure has changed very little and largely retains the features of the colonial period ... The rule of free trade is meaningless for countries which, at the present stage, because of their production structures, have practically nothing to export to the Community. (Focke Report 1980: 14)

The often-quoted figure of 99.5 per cent customs-free access for ACP exports was misleading. Not only were specific agricultural exports excluded, the figure referred to only existing products, not to potential future exports. Finished products in the industrial, agricultural and commercial sectors were excluded and something like 70 per cent of ACP exports could enter Europe duty-free under GSP arrangements anyhow. Even the well-intentioned STABEX and SYSMIN schemes were criticized for rewarding failure rather than success. They could act as a disincentive as neither encouraged better production or efficiency. Those countries that actually increased their production capacity and exports gained nothing under the schemes. Lastly, even the more inclusive scope of Lomé covered only a small percentage of Europe's trade with the developing world and, consequently, was only a modest contribution to the North–South dialogue.

On balance, Lomé was superior to its predecessor, the Yaoundé Convention, and it did symbolize a watershed in post-colonial relations with the developing world. Lomé not only removed reciprocity, it expanded the scope of relations beyond the historical aspects of trade. Equality and stability replaced dependency as the defining characteristics. Obviously, not every ACP or European demand could be met – indeed, both sides were guilty of creating future problems by seeing only their interpretation of the agreement. The first Lomé decade has been characterized as one of decreasing hopes, even if the culprit was the successive oil crises and global recession rather than the Convention. But Lomé was historically important for creating a new actor in international affairs – the ACP – and it was this framework that dominated Europe's perspective on development policy for the remainder of the twentieth century. Whether the motivations were selfish or altruistic remains largely a matter of interpretation.

The Lomé Conventions: III and IV (1985–2000)

The external global context has always been influential in determining the parameters for Europe's development policy. The oil shocks and resultant recession of the 1970s fundamentally changed the context within which Europe conducted its relations with the developing world. It became increasingly apparent that the economic decline in Africa (and to a lesser extent the Pacific and Caribbean states) was not a temporary phenomenon; if development were to be achieved, Lomé III would have to do more than continue the existing framework. For example, between 1980 and 1987 African per capita GDP declined by an annual average of 2.6 per cent, and investment fell whilst simultaneously the debt burden rose inexorably. In contrast, the 1980s witnessed a period of phenomenal economic growth in the emerging economies of South East Asia. Increasingly, international financial institutions such as the World Bank and the IMF became instrumental to the management of development and brought with them the new disciplines and doctrines of SAPs, introduced as a consequence of the debt crisis of the 1980s. By 1989, 30 such programmes were in place in Africa alone (Glaser 1990: 27). Consequently, the focus of Europe's policy began to change to address these broader adjustment issues and to look for an international consensus on macroeconomic assistance.

It was in this context that Lomé III was negotiated. Greece had joined the Community in 1981 and Spain and Portugal were set to do so in 1986. It was the then Twelve and the 66 ACP states that were party to Lomé III. Whilst still imperfect in its geographical spread, these 66 states represented roughly half of the total global number of developing states and contained 15 per cent of the developing world's population. Africa continued to dominate (45 states); 29 ACP states were also Commonwealth members with a further 21 being members of the Franco–African summit. Despite ten years of interaction the ACP only clearly expressed its identity in relation to Europe: individual ACP states took on a variety of group identities depending on the chosen fora. Consequently, Europe's relations with the developing world remained at best idiosyncratic and incomplete. But Lomé continued to symbolize Europe's imperfect definition of development cooperation.

The third Convention sought to 'promote and expedite the economic, cultural and social development of the ACP states and consolidate and diversify relations in a spirit of solidarity and mutual trust' (Article 1). In concrete terms, however, there were comparatively few innovations to the Lomé framework, and as such it failed to address adequately the development crisis that emerged during the 1980s. The euphoria and hyperbole that greeted the signing of the first Convention in 1975 was markedly absent. Lomé no longer appeared to be the best model for development, given the deterioration of most developing country economies. Indeed, there is a strong case that rather than heralding a new interdependence, Lomé had merely re-established North–South dependency (Grilli 1993: 36). The new emphasis on thematic issues (climate, environment, health) as well as commitments to social and cultural cooperation lacked substance. The more significant change was the application of conditionality, something that the ACP had previously resisted. Agreements on private-investment safeguards and conditional funding for adjustment programmes heralded a watershed in the relationship and provided a glimpse of a new agenda that was to dominate the 1990s. Any economic bargaining power the ACP had previously enjoyed began to dissipate and any leverage provided by moral arguments appeared increasingly ineffective.

Unlike previous Conventions, Lomé IV was a ten-year agreement (with a mid-term financial review) scheduled to expire in the year 2000. Once again, changes in the international environment were to dictate the content and direction of policy. Compounding the plight of the Lomé countries, the collapse of communism heralded a new and more immediate development priority for Europe – that of Eastern and Central Europe. Throughout the 1990s Europe's funding priorities clearly shifted from the traditional Lomé states to those closer to home (see p.8). In addition, the '1992' Single European

Market (SEM) project, the GATT Uruguay Round and the establishment of the WTO all posed potentially new trade challenges to an already embattled developing world. If not forgotten, the Lomé states faced increasing marginalization.

After 14 months of negotiations the new Convention between the Twelve and the 68 ACP states was signed on 15 December 1989, once more in the Togolese capital of Lomé. Initially Lomé IV covered more than 450 million people, rising to 570 million in some 70 states by the time of the mid-term review in 1995. However, it was only in the last months of 1989 that the agreement was cobbled together under the then French EU presidency. In general, Europe dictated the agenda, and ACP demands at that time – such as debt relief – went unheeded. The EDF budget was increased to ECU 10.8 billion (a nominal increase of around 40 per cent from the Lomé III figure of ECU 7.7 billion). In real terms, however, the increase was marginal and significantly below that called for by the ACP; the amount was raised to ECU 13 billion at the 1995 mid-term review (see Table 2.1). Such outcomes reflected both the hardening attitude of member states as well as the limited bureaucratic resources of the ACP Secretariat, which constrained its ability to negotiate more effectively. The much-prized principle of partnership at the core of the Lomé model appeared distinctly compromised.

A key element in Lomé IV was the renewed emphasis on conditionality – economic and political. For the first time, aid was explicitly earmarked for Structural Adjustment Support with financial resources coming from the existing EDF budget. Approximately 10 per cent of funds were designated for this purpose – ECU 1,150 million in EDF7, rising to 1,400 million in EDF8. Flexibility rather than a standard approach was emphasized in the new Convention. Article 244 guaranteed that

(a) the ACP States shall bear primary responsibility for the analysis of the problems to be solved and the preparation of reform programmes;
(b) support programmes shall be adapted to the different situation in each ACP State and be sensitive to the social conditions, culture and environment of these States; ...
(e) the right of the ACP States to determine the direction of their development strategies and priorities shall be recognized and respected; ...

(i) support shall be given in the context of a joint assessment between the Community and the ACP State concerned on the reform measures being undertaken or contemplated either at a macro-economic or sectoral level.

Whilst ACP states were included in the policy debate on economic reform, clearly European approval was a funding prerequisite. Article 243 defined as appropriate the type of initiatives that promoted GDP and employment, increased productivity and fostered economic diversification, whilst simultaneously improving 'the social and economic well-being' of the population and ensuring 'that adjustment is economically viable and socially and politically bearable'. These structural reform conditions were only modestly amended in 1995 by extending the process to the regional level. Broadly speaking, the EU mirrored the World Bank view on SAPs – despite the lack of any strong empirical evidence that such an approach was generally beneficial for development (see pp. 28–9; Lister 1997b: 116). The Convention's assertion that the ACP 'shall determine the development principles, strategies and models for their economies and societies in all sovereignty' (Article 3) sat uncomfortably with this recognition of realpolitik. It was only during the 1997–98 Green Paper debate on Europe's post-Lomé relations with the developing world that this established orthodoxy began to be challenged.

Only minor modifications were made to the trade preferences of Lomé IV – despite the erosion of the so-called pyramid of privilege for ACP states – although some relaxation in the 'rules of origin' for manufactured products were gained. The only significant EU concession was to extend the funding basis of STABEX and SYSMIN, although this fell far short of ACP expectations. Debt, rather than trade preferences, had become the more important problem by the end of the 1980s. Whilst Articles 239–42 introduced the issue of debt repayment on to the European agenda, this 'major development issue' remained largely the primary domain of member states and international organizations. At this stage, Europe did not want to establish a new precedent in this area. Once again, the importance of consistency and complementarity between EU and member state policy was highlighted. The recognition of this issue was welcome, yet Europe's collective response remained cautious and respected the role of the member states. Given the EU's limited financial involvement (just 1.2 per cent of the ACP debt-servicing costs were with the EU) it was argued that it was inappropriate and ineffective for the EU to become the dominant forum for addressing debt relief (a position that the EU maintained until at least 2005). Whether this view was justified or not, ignoring the EU-level dimension on debt conflicted with the wider Lomé philosophy of partnership.

Conversely, the new Convention included a number of policy innovations: the environment; human rights; women; and cultural cooperation. The emphasis on human rights was arguably the most ambitious of these. The general principles and objectives of the Convention directly linked development with 'respect for and promotion of all human rights' and economic well-being. Here, for example, the EU supported ACP efforts aimed at 'enhancing the status of women, improving their living conditions, expanding their economic and social role and promoting their full participation in the production and development process on equal terms with men' (Article 153). Other social policies included health, education and training, population issues and the environment. Cumulatively these further extended the Convention's scope beyond its purely trade-related origins and confirmed that political and social conditionality was to constitute a new direction in European development policy. The differences, rather than the similarities, between the original Convention and Lomé IV were becoming increasingly pronounced. Whilst the status quo was retained in the overall trade relationship, new motivations heralded a psychological shift in EU–developing world relations.

By the time of the scheduled 1995 mid-term review, the global development context had once again significantly shifted from the parameters that had shaped the 1989 agreement – and the shift further disadvantaged the developing countries. A number of states faced increasing economic crises and donor fatigue was becoming endemic. The traditional ideological and geostrategic balance had collapsed as former communist societies increasingly embraced democratization. Internally, the Maastricht Treaty established new development-cooperation objectives and obligations and the 1995 enlargement saw different development perspectives introduced by the new member states of Austria, Finland and Sweden (Vernier 1996: 8). Only the mid-term renewal of the financial protocol of Lomé IV was mandatory; in all other respects it was anticipated that the Convention would run unaltered for a decade. However, largely on EU insistence, the review process was extended beyond funding issues in response to the changing global context, the effect of liberalization on the erosion of preferences, and problems associated with the actual implementation of the Lomé system.

By employing the provisions under Article 366, both the ACP and the member states were entitled to modify aspects of the agreement. Although all decisions were consensual, the modifications adopted principally reflected the EU's new agenda rather than ACP concerns. The review lasted 13 months with the revised agreement being signed by 70 ACP states in November 1995. Three broad areas were reviewed: institutional and political issues; trade and sectoral issues; and development financing. Consensus existed on amending a wide range of issues, notably reference to democratic principles, the fundamental importance of trade in the development process and the introduction of two-tranche programming. Conversely, differences existed over EDF funding, access to the SEM and the relaxation of the rules of origin for ACP products.

The main focus of the trade debates departed from the traditional Lomé preoccupation with preferential access to a more inclusive approach for creating a better trading environment. The arguments were as much political as they were economic and reflected the agenda of the then GATT negotiations. Two new Articles introduced the idea of trade development and were aimed at 'developing, diversifying and increasing ACP States' trade and improving their competitiveness' domestically and internationally (Article 15a). Mirroring the commitment of the Maastricht Treaty, Article 6a called for the gradual integration of the ACP economies into the world economy and described the function of trade as 'energizing the development process'. Preferential access was not totally absent from the mid-term review and the debate proved contentious. A compromise position saw a modest expansion in product access and a relaxation in quantitative restrictions. The most acrimonious area, however, concerned rules of origin. Finally only modest changes were accepted that encouraged regional cooperation between member and non-member states. In contrast, the reform of STABEX was not controversial and funds for the system were raised by some 20 per cent to ECU 1.8 billion.

The final issue to be renegotiated was the new financial protocol – EDF8. This increased overall funding for Lomé by 22 per cent to ECU 14.6 billion, although in real terms the value remained static: one member state, the UK, even reduced its contribution! The difficulties in obtaining a financial agreement were further underlined by the ratification process. It was June 1998 before the EDF8 began distributing these new funds. Given that enlargement meant that there were now 15 rather than 12 donors, the overall funding level disappointed the ACP recipients. Again, this reflected the EU's new development priorities in Central and Eastern Europe and a general worldwide downward trend affecting bilateral and multilateral aid. Programme aid remained at the heart of the EU's approach. Minor changes were made to the structural adjustment provisions and the application of EIB resources. The EU successfully resisted a request for the unilateral cancellation of ACP debts but did offer some financial relief (worth ECU 135 million in loans) and drafted a new declaration annexed to the Convention in which:

> The Community reaffirms its willingness to contribute constructively and actively to the alleviation of the debt burden of the ACP States.
> In this context, it agrees to transform into grants all the special loans of the previous Conventions, which have not yet been committed.
> The Community also confirms its determination to pursue the discussion of these questions in the appropriate fora, taking into account the specific difficulties of the ACP States.
>
> (Annex LXXXIV)

This latter commitment was in fact honoured and contributed to the start of the international debt relief programme in 2005.

One innovation, however, introduced broad conditionality to the objectives of EU aid policy. The Convention was amended to read: 'In support of the development strategies of the ACP States, due account shall be taken of the objectives and priorities of the Community's cooperation policy, and the ACP States' development policies and priorities' (Article 4). The EU objectives and priorities were derived from the Maastricht Treaty (now Article 208 TFEU) and mirrored commitments given elsewhere, namely: sustainable economic and social development; the reintegration of ACP economies into the world economy; alleviation of poverty; support for democratic and legitimate government; and the protection of human rights and liberties. Although a policy 'dialogue' was established, clearly ACP states were expected to embrace these principles within their own respective development approaches if Lomé assistance was to be granted. The most direct expression of this new expectation was in the move to a two-tranche system for indicative programmes. By withholding 30 per cent of funds until effective implementation of a programme was established, the EU could sanction those states that failed to meet the agreed 'dialogue' objectives.

The 1996–2000 Reform Process

While the Lomé Convention was traditionally the major development framework, the rationale was largely historical than rational. However, what became increasingly clear during the last five years of Lomé IV was that the ACP countries could no longer rely upon either privileged access or continued financial aid from this special relationship. Lomé IV provoked concern about the longer-term viability of its preferential philosophy. The Uruguay Round of GATT drew attention to Lomé's inconsistencies with the broad principles of trade liberalization. Whilst a waiver was eventually granted under the GATT and the subsequent WTO regime, existing practice was becoming increasingly indefensible.

Consequently, by the mid-1990s the need for fundamental reform of the EU's relations with the ACP was becoming increasingly evident, with challenges to the existing structure emerging on several fronts. First, there was the record of European assistance. Few Lomé countries had seen a radical transformation in their economies: dependency continued to define the relationship with Europe. Not only had the Lomé framework failed fundamentally to improve the economic positions of the vast majority of ACP states, some critics suggested that the historic pattern of First–Third World dependency had become even more deeply embedded. This disillusionment, coupled with the domestic financial constraint on the EU budget and pressures from key member states, combined to make policy reform a priority.

The enormous changes witnessed in the international environment during the 1990s provided a second motivation for change. As noted already, prior to 1989 Europe's development policy had been exclusively focused on the 'traditional' developing world. With the collapse of communism development priorities were increasingly switched to the newly democratic transitional economies of Eastern and Central Europe. For the EU, charity, or at least aid, increasingly began closer to home. In many ways, the integration process and the necessity of Eastern enlargement presented detrimental (if unintended) consequences for the developing world beyond Europe's borders.

Third, the parameters of the global environment changed. This presented new opportunities – and dangers – based around technology and the globalization of trading and financial systems. Crucially, the pervasive trend towards trade liberalization and the WTO orthodoxy were at odds with the traditional preferential aspects of Lomé. The WTO had begun to examine preferential agreements generally, and with respect to Lomé specifically. Although Lomé IV had been granted a WTO waiver, clearly this anomaly could not be maintained in the medium term. Whether the WTO position on Lomé simply reflected the EU's own free trade prejudices or acted as a catalyst for them is a matter of dispute. However, a free trade agenda became part of the EU's new ideology and played a central role in defining the shape of the future EU–ACP dialogue.

Fourth and somewhat paradoxically, both in terms of trade and aid, the once privileged status of the Lomé states was effectively downgraded and other group-to-group dialogues provided equivalent access to the European market. From a position at the apex of the so-called 'pyramid of privilege' in the 1970s, the ACP states saw their position progressively eroded: the CEECs, the Mediterranean associates as well as a number of bilateral agreements all provided better preferential access which further marginalized the ACP's competitive position.

Lastly, the diversity within the developing world and the obvious inconsistencies in the EU's geographical organization became unsustainable. The dissimilar treatment of similar developing countries was increasingly difficult to explain. Post-colonial ties and historical links were the obvious explanations for this tradition of differentiation. But the patchwork and incremental nature of Lomé has undoubtedly been regarded as its greatest weakness. Both the subsequent Cotonou Partnership Agreement and the EBA initiative reflected this new reality.

The Green Paper, Commission guidelines and the Council negotiating mandate

In response to these and other demands, in November 1996 the European Commission issued its discussion Green Paper on the future of Lomé. The Green Paper was designed to initiate a broad participatory and transparent policy debate on these proposals involving the ACP, member states as well as institutions such as the

European Parliament (Holland 2002: 178). Based on the results of this extensive if compressed consultation (lasting nine months), in October 1997 the Commission issued its guidelines for negotiating the future of the ACP–EU dialogue (which in turn formed the basis for the negotiation mandate agreed to by the Council in June 1998). The guidelines sought to reconcile 'flexibility and efficiency with a multi-pronged, integrated approach to cooperation' thereby placing the EU–ACP partnership on a new footing (Commission 1997a: 3). In essence this meant constructing a new overall agreement with the ACP that permitted differentiation and was open and flexible enough to accommodate changing circumstances. The five principal components were: political dialogue; alleviation of poverty; economic partnership; effectiveness; and geographical differentiation (see Chapter 3 for further details).

On the basis of Commission recommendations, the Council's negotiating mandate for reforming Lomé was finally agreed in June 1998, with formal negotiations commencing three months later. The timing was important: the UK held the EU presidency for the first half of 1998 and the recently elected British Labour Government had strong views on development priorities and sought actively to shape the mandate at this late stage. As is discussed further below, irrespective of the institutional openness of the process and the novelty of the consultative Green Paper, the negotiations between the EU and the ACP were vastly unequal. Those changes that did appear in the negotiating mandate were more likely to come from the member states and even the European Parliament than from the ACP. For reasons of domestic politics there were simply concessions that the EU was unable to make.

As early as March 1998 the areas of conflict became evident, with two primary axes of disagreement. First, whilst the Council supported the Commission's general trade liberalization thrust, a number of member states (the UK and the Scandinavian countries in particular) were critical of this being imposed on all ACP states and promoted alternative mechanisms for those ACP states unable or unwilling to move towards reciprocity and liberalization. In the event, the British presidency managed to forge an agreement that permitted the LDCs to retain their existing Lomé preferences rather than having to adopt automatically the new free trade regime. This meant that for these 39 ACP LDCs zero duty access to the European market was maintained for all current Lomé products on the existing non-reciprocal basis. This constituted a significant policy change from the Green Paper proposals, and, whilst there was general consensus on this principle, the time frame was more problematic; the final decision set 2005 as the cut-off date for these non-reciprocal arrangements.

Second, policy towards those remaining ACP countries that were not LDCs highlighted the tensions within the European 'consensus' and emphasized the key role that can be played by the presidency. The Dutch, thinking beyond the ACP mandate, wanted the GSP approach extended to all developing countries; conversely Spain objected to any discussion of GSP, arguing that this was outside the remit of the Lomé talks. France, Italy and Germany were concerned that the GSP option would negate the incentives for the ACP to move towards reciprocal free trade and actually undermine this core objective of the negotiations. It was finally accepted that any ACP country that was either unwilling, or unable, to join a free trade regime would retain at least the current preferences offered through the GSP system. This signalled a substantive change of position within the member states and was indicative of the persuasive power of the UK presidency. Consequently, with respect to trading relations at least, the 1998 negotiating mandate was more sympathetic to the ACP's development agenda than most readings of the earlier Green Paper had suggested.

Conclusion

To summarize, this historical overview of EU–ACP relations forms the starting point for any current analysis of the EU's relations with the developing world. The rationale for the original Yaoundé Convention and its successor Lomé Convention was historical rather than rational. What became increasingly clear, however, particularly towards the end of the lifetime of Lomé, was that the ACP could not continue to rely upon either privileged access or financial aid as part of this special relationship. Lomé IV was increasingly viewed through the prism of its inconsistencies with the increasingly institutionalized architecture of global governance, and particularly the GATT/WTO and the Bretton Woods institutions.

The 'solution' was the Cotonou Agreement, an attempt to reconcile the demands of the ACP with those of the global community (see Chapter 3). However, Cotonou's emphasis of geographic and economic differentiation seemed to some to be essentially incompatible with the notion of an overall framework that respected and defended the ACP as a singular group. The rationale was political. It was a necessary compromise to placate the ACP vested interests and offered at least the appearance of an agreement that recognized the integrity of the ACP grouping. However, economically, that integrity has rapidly diminished. Not only was the ACP subsequently divided by free trade reciprocity, for the LDC the exclusiveness of Lomé was also threatened. Foreshadowing what was to become a future policy change (under EBA), a consensus has emerged around treating all LDCs, both ACP and non-ACP, in an identical fashion (see Chapter 3). Whilst such uniformity is laudable, it does undermine the necessity of maintaining the ACP grouping. What function can the ACP really serve? Persisting with this recognition of colonial ties hardly seemed an appropriate principle for reform or for guiding international relations in the twenty-first century. To have abandoned the overall Lomé framework would have caused serious political and institutional protest – from the ACP, some member states and European institutions. To persist with the facade of a collective agreement was perhaps the only possible option in the transition from uniform non-reciprocity to the new regionalized free trade regimes favoured by Brussels and implemented through Cotonou.

Conversely, the Commission and others continue to argue that there is nothing inherently contradictory between having an overall framework and specialized regional or country-specific provisions. That the ACP itself values the coherence of the grouping is perhaps proof enough for its longevity. The institutions, procedures, as well as Lomé's own *acquis* are important foundations: to have discarded them outright would have suggested that 25 years of past development experience had been worthless. Although imperfect, the Lomé experience did and can continue to contribute to a better development-policy paradigm and remains the starting point for an understanding of the objectives and motivations underpinning Cotonou.

Chapter 3

Parallel Paradigms: Cotonou, Economic Partnership Agreements and Everything But Arms

The focus of this chapter is on the post-2000 changes and challenges that EU development policy has addressed. First, the negotiation process leading to the Cotonou Agreement is outlined; second, the issues raised by the introduction of Cotonou are discussed, including the amendments made in the 2005 and 2010 review processes; third, the actual EPA implementation process up until 2010 is analysed; and fourth, the parallel policy initiative – the 2001 Everything But Arms regulation – is outlined and examined as an element of Europe's more coherent global development approach. Given the ongoing nature of both the EPA and EBA initiatives, we seek to contextualize these policy innovations and point to any policy consequences (intended or otherwise) that may emerge during the life of Cotonou to 2020.

Negotiating Cotonou

The leitmotif of Lomé was always its claim of partnership. The 1999 Cotonou negotiating process, however, was marked more by inequality and one-way conditionality than parity, leading one commentator to describe the negotiations 'as a situation of total power asymmetry, where the normative consensus of the EU leaves little room for concessions' (Elgström 2000: 195). Not that such an outcome was particularly surprising or unique: each of the successive Lomé revisions had seen essentially the European perspective predominate.

For the EU, five principal objectives drove the negotiations. First, Cotonou presented an opportunity for Europe to enhance both its capacity and credibility as an effective international actor through the construction of a renewed political dialogue with the developing world. As such, the incorporation of development into a broader European foreign policy was part of a wider EU agenda, ensuring its consistency with the objectives of the CFSP, a familiar refrain still heard today despite the expectations of the Lisbon Treaty.

Second, reflecting changing European development priorities, the goal of alleviating poverty was emphasized. Mirroring policy debates in the UN forum, this new development priority combined economic, social and environmental dimensions. Thus, for example, combating gender discrimination and environmental degradation was linked to the question of poverty as well as the more traditional concerns of healthcare and educational opportunities. This new approach also stressed the developmental importance of creating a climate conducive to fostering the private sector, growth, competitiveness and employment, areas where EU support was offered.

Third, and the most radical innovation, the existing basis of EU–ACP economic relations was to be replaced by country-specific partnerships. Whilst an overall EU–ACP agreement was to be maintained, strengthening regional integration by signing individual EU agreements with Africa (subdivided regionally), the Caribbean and the Pacific was seen as the non-negotiable long-term objective.

The effectiveness of aid was the fourth objective. Despite Lomé's contractual basis, the actual application of aid had failed to match expectations (largely due to the variety and complexity of aid instruments that impeded consistency). The simplification and rationalization of instruments became a priority. Conditionality was to remain, however, to encourage policy reform – although the EU was increasingly sensitive to the negative perceptions this entailed.

The final objective was to complement an overall Cotonou Agreement with geographical differentiation – even if critics argued that these two objectives were inherently contradictory. The overall framework was to cover the general objectives, principles and institutional aspects of the EU–ACP relationship, whilst geographic differentiation reflected the regional dimension of political dialogue, economic and trade cooperation and integration. A key ambition was to construct an economic framework that could encourage greater regional integration. In addition, whilst respecting the integrity of the ACP grouping, the extension of non-reciprocity to non-ACP countries of comparable levels of development (the LDCs) was envisaged – and eventually enacted through the 2001 EBA initiative.

Underlining the increased importance of the EU–ACP political dialogue in the negotiations, there was a broad European consensus on the main elements of democratization, human rights and good governance. Unsurprisingly, political conditionality was contentious. For the ACP the concept of partnership and new forms of conditionality were viewed as antagonistic; conversely, a political 'dialogue' focused on good governance was central to the EU's notion of partnership and development. The ACP did not question the elements of conditionality that had previously been introduced in Lomé IV. What was resisted was the EU's agenda to extend the scope of good governance as a development prerequisite, particularly given the varied interpretations of what constituted good governance. Whilst the ACP subscribed to the principle of good governance, they rejected the European position that it should be the principle on which trade was made conditional. They argued that good governance was in part a result of institutional development and sustained efforts to build national capabilities (especially legislative, judicial and executive): these levels of institutional development varied widely across the ACP and could only improve through continued and guaranteed support. Indeed, they contended that to make trade or aid conditional could perversely undermine such institution building.

However, the asymmetry that had typified successive Lomé agreements was extended to good governance. The concept was largely defined in European terms and by European standards that risked being incompatible with individual ACP cultures and institutional capacities. Common assumptions and motivations guiding the good governance agenda could not be presumed. Although there were shared concerns (conflict prevention, post-conflict reconstruction and sustainable development), the EU's priorities were given precedence (such as human rights, democracy, drugs and crime, gender equality), while the ACP agenda (focused on the impact of EU arms sales, activities of European transnationals and nuclear testing) was marginalized. Not only were the standards of good governance viewed as Eurocentric, the EU insisted on the unilateral right to suspend any form of development assistance if it concluded that good governance had been breached. Not surprisingly, the exclusion of any joint mechanism for measuring good governance or any joint procedures for suspension produced vociferous, albeit ineffective, ACP opposition.

Debt relief was another political issue that divided the two sides. For the ACP, debt relief was a development priority. The cancellation of all debts accrued under the four Lomé Conventions was called for, together with an assurance that the EU would promote the issue of debt relief at the international level. In response, during the negotiations, the German EU presidency proposed abolishing debt for the most heavily indebted ACP states (a process which was finally commenced in 2005).

Finally, concerning the management of the relationship, differentiation between ACP states (rewarding successful and appropriate cooperation practices) was a key European political objective. Equal treatment irrespective of past performance was no longer acceptable from the EU perspective. Whilst need was to remain a core determinant for resource allocations (assessed according to population size, income levels, LDC status and specific vulnerabilities), this was to be supplemented by estimates of performance. Conversely, the ACP opposed the limitation of aid based on any performance criteria and called for the EU to meet the international standard of 0.7 per cent of GDP devoted to ODA (as well as honouring its own Treaty-based objective of reducing poverty). According to 1997 DAC figures, only three EU member states met this target – Denmark (0.97 per cent), the Netherlands (0.81 per cent) and Sweden (0.76 per cent) (a situation that had not significantly improved by 2010 when only four states met the target – Sweden (1.12 per cent), Luxembourg (1.01 per cent), Denmark (0.88 per cent) and the Netherlands (0.82 per cent)). Whilst France and Germany contributed the highest European ODA totals (US$6.3 and US$5.9 billion) this only represented 0.45 and 0.28 per cent respectively in 1997.

These significant differences in the EU and ACP perspectives and objectives described above were the subject of intense negotiations through 1999; however, it would be misleading to characterize the process as excessively conflictual: the final outcome produced a broad agreement on the general aspects of the accord. This consensus included the eradication of poverty and the gradual integration of the ACP into the world economy; the incorporation of the private sector within development strategies; the promotion of regional integration; linkages between sustainable development and the environment; and the role of civil society in promoting peace and stability.

Implementing Cotonou

At the risk of repetition, the core elements of Cotonou can be summarized as the reduction (and eventually eradication) of poverty while assisting the sustainable development and the gradual integration of ACP into the world economy. The eventual Agreement was based upon a set of binding fundamental principles that have already been discussed in greater detail, but can be listed here as:

- The equality of partners and the local ownership and choice of development strategies. Notwithstanding the Agreement, the ACP states remain 'in all sovereignty' to determine how their societies and economies develop.
- Broad-based participation involving not just ACP governments but – an innovation in its time – extended to include civil society, private sector and local government.
- Political dialogue with obligations and conditionalities, particularly the 'essential elements' of human rights, good governance and the rule of law.
- The introduction of differentiation in treatment between the LDCs and other ACP states, and regionalization of the ACP group into seven EPAs.

Within these broad principles Cotonou used both trade arrangements as well as substantial aid provisions to achieve the objectives of poverty reduction and economic development. But the shadow of political dialogue dominated the original Agreement and also took centre stage in the 2005 and 2010 review processes (discussed later in this chapter).

At the time of its launch, supporters of the Partnership Agreement argued strongly that within the context of increasing and irreversible globalization, only Cotonou was able to provide an effective framework for development. Globalization had already demonstrated a capacity to marginalize permanently certain ACP regions: the intention and spirit of Cotonou was to ensure that the ACP were included rather than excluded from globalization and to influence the direction of this process to secure more equitable development. The EU was explicit in expressing its political commitment to defending the principles of the Cotonou Agreement in all international fora, particular at the WTO. Yet despite this highest level of political will, the Partnership Agreement has faced a number of important challenges, some of which remained unresolved by 2011.

Perhaps the most fundamental challenge to be faced during the existence of the EPAs is a psychological one. Cotonou undoubtedly presented an opportunity for EU–ACP relations to prosper and does offer innovative – if contentious – solutions to historic dilemmas. But the extent to which the new philosophy and ambitions have been embraced has varied across the three regions, and a Lomé mentality has shown great persistence, especially in the Pacific and much of Africa. It was one thing to agree to the principle of trade liberalization, but quite another to implement the necessary domestic reforms to create that reality in the ACP states. As has proved the case, it was wishful thinking in the extreme to presume that all of the 38 non-LDC signatory states would be in a position to sign regional free trade agreements by Cotonou's original 2008 deadline.

The negotiations that led to the 1999 South African FTA were instructive in shaping the trade aspects of the Cotonou Agreement. The successful 'first wave' of the regional EPAs has also been instructive and influential, as well as helping to make more transparent the merits and pitfalls of experimenting with free trade for those less enthusiastic or economically less-well-suited ACP states. Thus the detailed provisions, timing and selection of appropriate states, as the test case, were crucial. The EPA between the EU and the Caribbean provided such an example: however, the lessons learnt persuaded some ACP regions as to the suitability of free trade, but for others underlined its inapplicability for African and Pacific economies. Of course, external factors have also played a part, not least the emergence of China as a development option since 2005, with its preference for trade, aid and investment without political conditionalities. Were the financial crisis of 2008 to continue to undermine the international consensus to meet the MDGs, as well as finally to achieve the long-promised 0.7 per cent ODA target, the ACP may begin to shy away from the EU's more intrusive, rule-based and liberalized trading regime. There is no alternative framework on offer.

A further challenge has been the LDCs. Insisting on the LDCs adopting the same timetable towards economic partnership as the other better-developed ACP states (as proposed in the original Commission Green Paper) would have been catastrophic – and was successfully resisted. However, by providing essentially the Lomé status quo for these 39 LDCs, the EU has created an unintended paradox. If, as is widely accepted, Lomé's non-reciprocal arrangements helped to exacerbate the economic decline of the ACP, how can their continuation be advantageous? How, if at all, can the LDCs reach an economic position whereby economic liberalization becomes a possibility? Is the new Cotonou reality, however unintentionally, condemning them to third-class status in perpetuity? Clearly, the nature and global scale of these problems go far beyond the scope of the Partnership Agreement. Nonetheless, to be effective the Cotonou Agreement has to recognize and operate within the global economy if the mistakes of Lomé are not to be repeated.

In addition to the economic challenges, the Cotonou Partnership Agreement set an ambitious agenda relating to civil society. Lomé adopted an essentially government-to-government approach: to transform and decentralize this to involve non-state actors – some of whom may be in conflict with their government – is something the Commission recognized might be difficult to implement (Petit 2000: 18). Not all ACP countries have a well-defined civil society that is capable of participating in development initiatives; in others the government may be reluctant to empower potential opposition groups. However, the development of legitimate and representative groups within civil society and their effective participation in the formulation of development policies remains a core element in the Cotonou approach. Indeed, Cotonou defines the involvement of non-state actors as a 'fundamental principle' and their involvement is required across a wide range of policy sectors covered in the Agreement (Desesquelles 2000: 8). For the EU, successful development is now predicated on having effective democratic processes and pluralistic participation in order to provide the necessary institutional foundations for economic policy. Civil society is therefore an explicit and essential element of development and one where continued EU support (financial, political and even moral) is required. While this is non-controversial, it still remains to be seen whether the Partnership Agreements can institutionalize effective and enduring mechanisms adequate for achieving these objectives.

A somewhat more pragmatic challenge that the EPAs have faced is effective implementation. The record shows that both Lomé and the EU's other aid programmes have often been characterized by tardy implementation, inefficiency and weak accountability. As discussed in Chapter 4, to address these deficiencies the Prodi Commission introduced institutional-level reform, Cotonou simplified the use of financial instruments and most recently the Lisbon Treaty brought development policy directly into mainstream EU foreign policy-making. Cumulatively, these reforms ought to increase the efficiency of the EU's development programmes, but they seem unlikely to be sufficient. The EU's institutional capacity is already saturated, and, despite the ambition to be a significant international actor, it is far from certain whether the EU can overcome the increased intergovernmental impetus embodied in the Lisbon Treaty. A stronger and larger Commission with expanding policy competences – the EEAS notwithstanding – now appears incompatible with the direction of the integration process of the early twenty-first century. Without such additional institutional capacity, the procedures envisaged in Cotonou and Lisbon may become impossible to implement effectively. Similarly, better implementation demands increased capacity on the part of the ACP recipients, particularly in relation to decentralized cooperation involving a partnership between state and non-state actors (Desesquelles 2000: 9). Without adequate institution-building (for government and for civil society), the implementation capacity for many ACP countries will be largely unchanged, in effect neutralizing any new policy opportunities presented by an EPA.

It is now widely accepted – at least by the EU – that development requires strong democratic institutional support. A majority of ACP states can demonstrate robust and deep-rooted democratic systems; but for some this process remains fragile and in its infancy. And for a number of states internal or external conflicts during the decade have effectively undermined democratic culture and processes – in Ethiopia, Eritrea, the Democratic Republic of Congo, Rwanda, Sierra Leone, Sudan or Fiji for example. In such circumstances the role of political dialogue, particularly conflict prevention strategies, becomes fundamental to the success of any Partnership Agreement.

A more general challenge is whether the unique EU–ACP relationship can be maintained: the introduction of Cotonou led many to question whether this signalled the break-up of this 'imagined' group. The coherence of the group was first challenged in the 1996 Green Paper, yet despite dire predictions of an imminent death, the ACP has managed to maintain solidarity throughout the post-Lomé reform process and rebuffed criticisms of the contradictions and incompatibility within the ACP concept. Until the ACP wishes to disestablish the group there is little that the EU can effectively do. The political symbolism of the ACP label far outweighs any geographic or economic arguments. At least superficially, Cotonou has guaranteed the status quo until 2020. But as suggested already, beneath this formal unity the new EPAs must inevitably create institutionalized tensions that may result in the ACP imploding and fragmenting into discrete – and competing – regional EPA groupings.

Whereas past diversity was not an impediment to cohesion, future economic competition (disguised as 'positive differentiation') may prove a greater challenge. The ACP faces considerable internal strain as it seeks to balance the interests of LDCs with those of comparatively wealthy states such as Nigeria or South Africa within the concept of regional free-trade areas. Again, Cotonou (perhaps unintentionally) has encouraged and formalized such divisions by treating the LDCs quite differently economically from the other ACP states.

Of course, there are countervailing political arguments in support of maintaining the solidarity of the ACP. As a group of 78 states it presents a more credible presence as a negotiating partner that would be absent were the individual states to interact bilaterally or regionally with the EU. And yet the ACP has sat uncomfortably with the EU's preference for regional dialogues internationally – hence the emphasis on EPAs. The longevity of the ACP may depend on the promotion of the group's identity beyond the EU into other international arenas: acting collectively at the WTO or the UN would enhance its utility and answer critics who see the ACP's sole *raison d'être* as its special relationship with Europe. Successive ACP Heads of Government summits recognized this necessity, but have failed to find a more effective expression in practice (Karl 2000: 22). Although as yet untested, Cotonou does offer an incentive, however, as the EU under the Agreement is committed to promoting the ACP's representation in international organizations.

Lastly, the final challenge still to be overcome is familiar and conceptual in content. Despite 35 years of collective action, the delineation of the EU's development role with respect to that of the member states or other international organizations and donors, remains ambiguous. Cotonou – like its predecessor – constituted a unique agreement unparalleled for its time, linking politics, trade and aid in novel ways. As such Cotonou does contain the essence of a distinct EU development role with its emphasis on regional inte-gration, democratic conditionality and trade facilitation. However, the parallel with the EU's own CFSP is instructive. Just as Europe's foreign policy is diminished (at least in the eyes of third countries) by the continuation of national foreign policies (even where these are 'consistent' with CFSP), so the EU's common development policy, as expressed through the Cotonou Agreement and the 'Consensus on Development', is diminished by the existence of bilateral develop-ment programmes operated by individual member states. Until development policy becomes an exclusive EU competence, questions will always be raised as to the legitimacy of its role and effectiveness of its function. The 20-year duration of Cotonou has precluded the immediate abandonment of an EU development policy: however, the future renationalization of this policy sector cannot be totally discounted. After all, financial support for the Partnership Agreement falls outside the scope of the EU's own budgetary resources and the continuation of the national funding basis of the EDF makes the programme highly dependent on intergovernmental accord. Conversely, an exclusive EU competence for development might be regarded as self-defeating. The complexity and scale of development, particularly in relation to poverty, requires multiple actors and agencies, as witnessed by the emergence of the international approach to the MDGs since 2000. The EU, member states, other OECD countries, the UN, the WTO and others all have roles to play. Where these are overlapping, the institution that can offer 'added value' or comparative advantage should take the lead. Such an approach remains consistent both with a broader understanding of subsidiarity and with a logical approach to development in a globalized context.

Before concluding this assessment of Cotonou, the amendments made to the Agreement in 2005 and in 2010 (under the procedure provided by Article 95(3) for a review) will be briefly outlined. Consistent with the notion of partnership, these amendments were made by consensus between the EU and the ACP.

In the 2005 review, the mutual and growing concern with international crime and the jurisdiction of the International Criminal Court was reaffirmed, whilst the MDGs were described as providing 'a clear vision' that underpinned ACP–EU Cooperation (Cotonou 2005: 32). The most significant addition to the political dialogue concerned the 'Fight against Terrorism' (new Article 11a) where there was agreement to combat terrorism through international cooperation including the exchange of information on terrorist groups, training, technical knowledge and experiences in relation to the prevention of terrorism. Cooperation to counter the proliferation of weapons of mass destruction was also added as an 'essential element' (Article 11b), further deepening the political dialogue content of the Agreement. The non-proliferation mechanisms involved included the agreement to ratify all relevant international instruments and to establish effective national controls for the export and transit of weapons-of-mass-destruction-related goods, including dual use technologies, complemented by effective sanctions. In support, the EU agreed to provide additional new financial and technical resources.

Some minor amendments were also made in relation to trade and ecological change. It was agreed that special consideration would be given to those ACP states with extreme dependence on agricultural and mining exports, particularly those that were 'the least developed, landlocked and island, post-conflict and post natural disaster ACP States' (Article 68). Further support was also flagged for regional cooperation between ACP and non-ACP countries. Lastly, the operation of Article 96 (concerning the 'essential elements' in the political dialogue where a state fails to fulfil an obligation stemming from respect for human rights, democratic principles and the rule of law – see pp. 193–201) was modified in an attempt to rebalance what had been perceived as an unfairly weighted process favouring the EU.

The 2010 review considered amendments in three specific areas: political dialogue; economic cooperation, regional integration and trade; and development, including climate change and the MDGs (Cotonou 2010). The nexus between development and security was an important theme running through the political dialogue review, the logic being that 'without development and poverty reduction there will be no sustainable peace and security and without peace and security there can be no sustainable development' (Article 11.1). The content of the political dialogue was extended and made consistent with the EU's own European Security Strategy concerns: the proliferation of small arms and light weapons, anti-personnel landmines and new security threats, such as organized crime, the trafficking of people, drugs and piracy. The 2010 review identified new collaborative mechanisms to address these challenges including cooperation on border controls and 'enhancing the security of the international supply chain, and improving air, maritime and road transport safeguards' (Article 11.2). Two other familiar themes were also restated – a call for the joint promotion of 'a system of effective multilateralism' (Article 8.2) and for greater policy coherence at the EU level to support better development outcomes. Additional emphasis was placed on conflict prevention initiatives organized at the regional level. The provisions on humanitarian assistance were redrafted in relation to emergency situations and support for ACP efforts in disaster risk reduction and post-conflict reconstruction and rehabilitation. The mixed nature of emergency relief was also reconfirmed by stressing the necessity for comple-mentarity and coordination between EU and member state efforts 'in accordance with best practice in aid-effectiveness' (Article 72.5).

The most significant addition to EU–ACP trade relations concerned the promotion of sustainable fisheries and aquaculture (Article 23a). In particular, the EU agreed to support the necessary infrastructure, provide technical support and build capacity to enable the ACP to take full advantage of their fisheries resources. Importantly, the review guaranteed that any EU–ACP fisheries agreements would be consistent with development needs. Through these mechanisms it is anticipated that significant improvements in employment, food security and poverty levels can be achieved.

Other measures were also modified in line with Cotonou's objec-tive of facilitating the ACP's full participation in international trade – although the wish to see them 'reducing their dependency on commodities ... promoting more diverse economies' (Article 34.4) seems at best remarkably optimistic and at worst to border on naivety. Regional integration was seen to play an essential support-ing role in this endeavour, as well as form the basis for the EPAs. The text related to EPAs specifically was also revised. Article 37.7 opened the door for new states to accede to existing EPAs at a later date and provision was made to allow both the EU and the ACP to engage in other multilateral and bilateral trade liberalization agree-ments, despite the potential negative effects of eroding Cotonou's trade privileges. Where the interests of the ACP may be affected by other EU trade policies a procedure for consultation was established under Article 38.

In terms of development initiatives, the 2010 review called for timely, if optimistic, 'concerted efforts to accelerate progress towards the attainment of the MDGs' (Article 19.2), which had failed to make any significant progress since being first launched in 2000 (see pp. 247–8). A renewed focus on combating HIV/AIDS was highlighted in order to reduce the pandemic's impact on all other areas of development. A link with the EU's broader normative agenda was also made by the requirement to remove 'punitive laws, policies, practices, stigma and discrimination that undermine human rights' (Article 31.e). Once again, regionalism was suggested as a development remedy with the revised Agreement making explicit reference to interregional and intra-ACP cooperation (expressed regionally, at the continental level or between the ACP and other third countries – Article 28.3).

A new Article 32 was introduced that located climate change as a development priority. Specific attention was given to endangered island and low-lying states that faced coastal erosion, cyclones, flooding and environmentally induced migration; and to landlocked states that had to combat, desertification, drought, deforestation and floods. Suggested remedies to mitigate climate-change impact included better use of global carbon markets, environmental technology, emission reductions and better weather early warning systems.

Commenting on the outcome of the 2010 revision of Cotonou, ACP President Bunduku-Latha believed 'that the revised agreement will help to fight against poverty and assist in our efforts to achieve sustainable development and help to mobilize the international community to attain the MDGs' (ACPSec, 2010). This cautious optimism notwithstanding, these comments have to be placed in context and in relation to the one area where the Cotonou Agreement has yet to deliver any significant progress – the establishment of EPAs – and it is to this challenge that we now turn.

Economic Partnership Agreements

What progress has been made in pursuit of Cotonou's economic transformation goals during the first decade since the signing of the Agreement? In particular, just how successful have the regional groupings within the ACP been in negotiating separate EPAs with the EU? Importantly, has this process been based on common understandings or has it been characterized by resistance to and an absence of mutual objectives?

In continuing to grant preferential access to European markets (even as an interim measure), Cotonou, like its Lomé predecessor, was in violation of Article 1 of the General Agreement on Tariffs and Trade which asserted: 'any advantage, favour, privilege or immunity granted by any contracting party to any product originating in or destined for any other country shall be accorded immediately and unconditionally to the like product originating in or destined for the territories of all other contracting parties'. Its ongoing legality was therefore premised upon the existence of a WTO waiver. It was this waiver for the Cotonou Agreement, which was to expire on 31 December 2007 (WTO 2001: §1), that informed the initial time frame for the negotiation of reciprocal EPAs as set out in the Cotonou text.

Formally, EPA negotiations began in September 2002 with an expected completion date of September 2007 for entry into force on 1 January 2008. By 2011, however, only the Caribbean grouping had signed a comprehensive regional EPA, which had been provisionally applied since December 2008 (see Table 3.1). Of the remaining 63 ACP states, 21 have initialled interim EPAs, of which 12 have subsequently been signed. Only ten of the 39 ACP LDCs have chosen to participate: Haiti has signed a full agreement as part of the Caribbean grouping (though it is not currently applied), nine others have initialled interim agreements and two have gone on to sign these agreements. This disappointingly low (from the EU perspective) take-up rate among LDCs is in part explained by the duty- and quota-free access that these countries already possess under the EU's EBA initiative (see below). The majority of ACP LDCs remain unconvinced that the EPAs will provide substantive benefits above what they already receive, and may well present increased economic risks. To compound matters, in all but one of the five designated African groupings the majority of states were classified as LDCs (for Central Africa, Eastern and Southern Africa, the East African Community and West Africa).

Key to the ongoing delays in concluding EPA negotiations have been disagreements on the actual nature and content of regional agreements. While the specific instances of disagreement are myriad, two underlying themes are broadly evident and go to the heart of the new post-Cotonou approach to development. First, questions have been raised as to the exact developmental focus of EPAs, and notably over the impact of reciprocity in the context of relationships between unequal partners. Citing the Commission's own acknowledgement that 'our experience tells us that FTAs between a large market like the EU and small economies are not easily sustainable and often lead to a deficit for the weaker partners' (cited in Coates and Braxton 2006: 2–3), concerns have been expressed as to whether the negotiating process is weighted in favour of the EU rather than the ACP, producing results that are geared more to the market access requirements of the Europeans than the needs of developing countries. Certainly, the experience of the South Africans in their protracted FTA negotiations with the EU during Nelson Mandela's presidency, would tend to confirm this Eurocentric tendency (Holland 2004). In this respect, particular criticism has been levelled at the EU–Pacific EPA process, and the Union's less than enthusiastic response to the Pacific Islands

Table 3.1 *Status of Economic Partnership Agreement Negotiations, 2010*

Grouping	Membership	Negotiations launched	Status of interim EPA	Status of regional EPA
Central Africa	Eight members: Cameroon, *Central African Republic, Chad, Congo, Democratic Republic of Congo,* Equatorial Guinea, Gabon, *São Tomé and Príncipe*	October 2003	Initialled by Cameroon in December 2007 and signed in January 2009.	Negotiations ongoing.
EAC	Five members: Burundi, Kenya *Rwanda, Tanzania, Uganda*	October 2003	Initialled by EAC in November 2007.	Negotiations ongoing.
ESA	Twelve members: *Comoros, Djibouti, Eritrea, Ethiopia, Madagascar, Malawi,* Mauritius, Seychelles, *Somalia, Sudan, Zambia,* Zimbabwe	February 2004	Initialled by Seychelles, *Zambia* and Zimbabwe in November 2007 and *Comoros, Madagascar* and Mauritius in December 2007. Signed by *Madagascar,* Mauritius, Seychelles and Zimbabwe in August 2009.	Negotiations ongoing.
SADC	Seven members: *Angola,* Botswana, *Lesotho, Mozambique,* Namibia, South Africa, Swaziland	February 2004	Initialled by Botswana, *Lesotho, Mozambique,* Namibia and Swaziland in November 2007. Signed by all but Namibia in June 2009.	Negotiations ongoing with target date of end 2010.
West Africa	Sixteen members: *Benin, Burkina Faso,* Cape Verde, Côte d'Ivoire, *Gambia,* Ghana, *Guinea, Guinea-*	October 2003	Initialled by Ghana and Côte d'Ivoire in December 2007. Signed by Côte d'Ivoire in November 2008.	Negotiations ongoing.

	Bissau, Liberia, Mali, Mauritania, Niger, Nigeria, Senegal, Sierra Leone, Togo		
Caribbean	Fifteen members: Antigua and Barbuda, Bahamas, Barbados, Belize, Dominica, Dominican Republic, Grenada, Guyana, *Haiti*, Jamaica, Saint Lucia, Saint Vincent and the Grenadines, Saint Kitts and Nevis, Surinam , Trinidad and Tobago	April 2004	Comprehensive regional agreement initialled in December 2007 and signed in October 2008 (*Haiti* signed December 2009). Provisionally applied since December 2008 (excluding *Haiti*).
Pacific	Fifteen members: Cook Islands, East Timor, Fiji, *Kiribati*, Marshall Islands, Micronesia, Nauru, Niue, Palau, Papua New Guinea, *Samoa, Solomon Islands*, Tonga, *Tuvalu, Vanuatu*	September	Initialled by Fiji and Papua New Guinea in November 2007. Signed by Papua New Guinea in July 2009. Negotiations ongoing.

Notes: Italicized states are LDCs. These states are covered by the EU's EBA initiative. EAC: East African Community; ESA: Eastern and Southern Africa; SADC: Southern African Development Community.
Source: Commission (2010e).

Forum's proposed EPA text. Following the leaking in November 2006 of a letter signed by senior Commission Trade and Development officials (Manservisi and Falkenberg 2006) providing the EU's response to the Pacific proposals, civil society organizations came firmly to the view that elements that could make the EPAs development-friendly were being thwarted (Rampa 2007: 23).

By the end of 2007 discontent with the negotiating process and the perceived outcomes of EPAs was becoming increasingly evident throughout the ACP. The EU, for example, was accused of hijacking the EPAs as a mechanism for getting the so-called Singapore Issues (on competition policy, government procurement, investment and trade facilitation) – which were rejected by developing countries in the Doha Round of WTO negotiations – back onto the agenda. In the run-up to the Lisbon Europe–Africa Summit in December 2007, Senegalese President Abdoulaye Wade warned of the potential negative consequences of the EPAs being negotiated and accused the EU of trying to impose 'a straitjacket that does not work' (*Africa Renewal* 2008: 23). At the Summit itself Alpha Oumar Konaré, Chairman of the Commission of the African Union, echoed this tone, criticizing the Union for forcing agreement on individual countries (ibid.). Similar concerns were also expressed closer to home. In 2006 the European Parliament urged the Commission to ensure that EPAs were above all developmental rather than simply trade agreements, while at the same time in an open letter to their Commission counterparts, the UK Minister for Trade (Ian McCartney) and for Development (Gareth Thomas) called for ACP states to be given as much time as they needed to adjust to market opening, with requisite safeguards against European competition (Kelsey 2007: 84–5).

The second broad area of disagreement has been the coherence of the EU's regional focus. Regional integration is central to the Cotonou Agreement's approach to poverty reduction through integration into the global economy (Article 35[2]), with aggregation into larger groupings seen inter alia as a key mechanism for overcoming many of the problems of small economies in global trade. Two criticisms have been raised. The first is whether the EU approach reinforces regional integrative impulses. The Union's 2006 rejection of the Pacific ACP's preferred regional approach to fisheries negotiations in favour of ongoing bilateral agreements (the EU had pre-existing agreements with the Federated States of Micronesia, Kiribati and the Solomon Islands), for example, has been seen by critics as inconsistent with the espoused regional focus of EPAs as well as being contrary to Pacific development.

A second criticism relates to the selection and definition of ACP regional groupings which have not always corresponded to existing integration arrangements, raising questions about their sustainability and the consequential impact that overlapping memberships might have on other regional structures. Of the 15 members of the SADC, for example, only seven are members of the SADC EPA grouping, while six find themselves in the Eastern and Southern Africa grouping, with one each in the East African Community and Central Africa. While the potential exists for such EPAs to reinforce regional schemes, such overlap could also have a diluting impact or provoke regional realignments, particularly where tensions between regimes of economic liberalization emerge (Stevens 2006: 445–7). This problem was recognized in 2008 by then Commissioner for Development Louis Michel (2008: 43–5), though no solution was posed beyond the assertion that 'the EU is neutral as to the make-up of regional integration areas'.

Disagreement over the path forward for EPAs, particularly on the fundamental issues of their developmental and regional focus, has been a major factor in delaying concluding the agreements, with evident tensions between the EU and its ACP partners. At the Parliamentary High-level Conference on EU–Africa relations convened in Brussels in September 2010, Namibian delegates insisted that the EU was treating its negotiations with the Eastern and Southern African grouping as anything but one between equals. The consequence, they asserted, is that 'what the EU demands at this point will not provide for greater equity' but will instead perpetuate African under-development (Duddy 2010). Further disquiet was expressed immediately prior to the November 2010 EU–Africa Summit over the conduct and content of the EPA negotiations, particularly over a perceived gap between EU rhetoric on development and partnership and its actual practice behind closed doors, which led to an African threat to walk away from the process (Phillips 2010). With such passions running high in the continuing EPA debate, it seems unlikely that substantive process towards the Cotonou goals will be made easily, or in the near future.

Everything But Arms

Both the complexity as well as the dynamic pace of change that came to characterize the EU's development policy at the start of the twenty-first century was reflected in the so-called Everything But Arms (EBA) proposal adopted as a Council Regulation (416/2001) on 28 February 2001. This Commission proposal to the Council was both consistent with the new thrust of the Partnership Agreement and yet simultaneously suggested a fundamental break with the EU's past approach to development policy. As discussed above, Cotonou had introduced the principle of differentiation according to development status and offered special treatment for ACP states classified as LDCs. The Agreement even foreshadowed the general application of this new principle. However, while consistent with the Cotonou philosophy, EBA breached the long-established policy of offering the ACP preferential advantages over all other developing countries. To extend non-reciprocity to non-ACP LDCs suggested – if not endorsed – a view that the ACP as a group was no longer the dominant organizing principle for EU–developing world relations. Within the ACP members, a majority of states were LDCs (40 as of 2011) who now had the option of joining an EPA or being dealt with under a separate new 48-country LDC framework. Those critics who argued that Cotonou was the forerunner to the fragmentation of the ACP group appeared to have been vindicated.

According to a 2000 Commission press release, EBA constituted a 'groundbreaking plan to provide full access for the world's poorest countries into European Union markets' and would grant duty-free access to the world's poorest countries (Commission 2000b). The proposal covered all goods except the arms trade: hence the slogan, 'Everything But Arms'. Thirty-three LDCs are African, eight are located in Asia, six in the Pacific, and just one in the Caribbean region. The European Trade Commissioner who launched the EBA initiative, Pascal Lamy, was forthright in his advocacy for the new proposal.

> There has been plenty of talk about how market access for poor countries is critical if we are to tackle their growing marginalisation in the globalising economy. Everyone seems ready to make the commitment at the political level. But talk is cheap. We now need to move beyond opt-out clauses. It's time to put access to our markets where our mouth is. That means opening up across the board, and for all the poorest countries. So we want to move to liberalise everything but the arms trade. (Ibid.)

The decision to proceed with EBA was in part a response to the failed 1999 Seattle WTO meeting and the perception that developing countries faced potential exclusion from the benefits of global trade liberalization. The EU's initiative was consistent with a wish – still unfulfilled – to see a future WTO round of multilateral trade negotiations successfully launched through which the interests and concerns of the developing countries could be addressed.

Given its implications, the proposal faced opposition from two directions. First, a number of existing ACP beneficiaries feared their interests would be compromised by this more inclusive programme; and second, initially some of the more protectionist-minded EU member states raised critical voices. In order to placate the ACP, concessions were made on transitional arrangements for significant products (rice, sugar and bananas) (see below for details). The potential impact on ACP bananas was, however, still regarded as problematic by several Caribbean states. And of course, these concessions inevitably promoted continued LDC reliance on largely unprocessed raw products with little added-value accruing. Member state concerns over the potential for fraud and the difficulties in monitoring rules-of-origin were addressed in the detail of the eventual regulation and specific measures were established to safeguard the EU from a flood of fraudulent imports under the proposal. A somewhat different criticism was also raised by some LDCs; rather than excluding the duty-free export of Third World arms to Europe, it was argued that greater benefits would result from a cessation of European arms sales to the developing world! This logical, if naive, suggestion of course ran counter to the EU's global export strategy and the stated objectives of the 2004 European Defence Agency which were to make the EU the world's largest arms exporter. Such tensions will clearly prove difficult to resolve for the EU's nascent foreign policy under High Representative Catherine Ashton, even if pragmatism is likely to trump principles on most occasions.

With opposition largely overcome, on 26 February 2001 the Council adopted the EBA Commission proposal as an amendment to the EU's GSP, and just one week later goods from the LDCs began to receive tariff-free access to the EU market for all products other than arms and ammunition. This initiative made the EU the world's first major trading power to commit itself to opening its market fully to the world's most impoverished countries, a significant commitment and step towards matching development aspirations with action.

Duty and quota restrictions were eliminated immediately on all products except for the sensitive ACP issues of sugar, rice and bananas, where full liberalization was phased in over a lengthy transition period. EBA complemented the LDC content of the Cotonou Agreement and triggered a process that saw free access for 'essentially all' LDC products by 2005.

Prior to its launch, there was considerable speculation on the likely effect of the EBA initiative and whether the generous rhetoric would match the economic content. According to Commission figures, the EU had become the major global destination for LDC exports. In 1998, LDCs had global exports for goods worth €15.5 billion: the EU took 56 per cent of this total (worth €8.7 billion), while the USA imported 36 per cent (worth €5.6 billion) and Japan 6 per cent. However, the pre-EBA regime excluded about 10 per cent of the 10,500 tariff lines in the EU's tariff schedule and affected 1 per cent of the total trade flows. The EBA addressed these gaps by granting duty-free and unrestricted quota access to a further 919 lines, covering all products (except arms and ammunition) from all LDCs. The new list left out just 25 tariff lines all of which were related to the arms trade. For the first time all agricultural products were covered, including beef and other meat; dairy products; fresh and processed fruit and vegetables; maize and other cereals; starch; oils; processed sugar products; cocoa products; pasta; and alcoholic beverages. As already noted, only the three most sensitive products – bananas, rice and sugar – were not liberalized immediately. As the Commissioner for Trade commented:

> We have been through this line by line, product by product, and have concluded that we should now take this important further step. Of course, some of the products are relatively sensitive, but there is no point in offering trade concessions on products which LDCs cannot export. We have to make a real difference. We of course recognise that duty free access alone is not enough to enable the poorest countries to benefit from liberalised trade. We need to help them build their capacity to supply goods of export quality, and we reaffirm the Commission's commitment to continued technical and financial assistance to this end. (Commission 2000b)

For three products (bananas, sugar and rice) the implementation of unrestricted access was to take effect in progressive stages. The

ACP banana protocols were also the subject of concerted WTO action and the new provisions had to respect and be consistent with WTO rulings. Consequently, duties on bananas were to be reduced by 20 per cent annually as of 2002 with full elimination of tariffs within five years. Duties on rice and sugar were reduced on a shorter timescale: the first 20-per-cent-level cuts commenced in 2006, with progressive reductions annually until final abolition, which was scheduled for 2009.

To compensate for the delay to fully liberalized market access, the EU agreed to transitional procedures for all LDCs that invoked duty-free quotas for sugar and rice. The quota levels were based on the best figures for LDC exports during the 1990s, plus an additional 15 per cent, and were to increase by 15 per cent each year during the transitional period. For LDC raw sugar, a duty-free quota was set at 74,185 tons for 2001–02, growing to 197,355 tons by 2008–09. Imports of sugar under the ACP–EC Sugar Protocol were additional to this quota (to uphold the integrity of this protocol). Similarly, LDC rice had duty-free status within the limits of a tariff quota of 2,517 tons in 2001–02, increasing to 6,696 tons by 2008–09 (Holland 2002: 230).

The challenges posed by coherence, complementarity and coordination are clearly at play in this new approach. The compromise tried to balance improved trading opportunities for LDCs but gave sufficient time and protection to EU member state producers to adapt to changes required in the Common Agricultural Policy (CAP) (particularly for sensitive products). It also had to take into account the constraints imposed by agreements with other developing countries (the ACP as well as other traditional suppliers of primary products to the EU) and, of course, be consistent with WTO thinking.

This seeming European largesse also had to be balanced against other provisions of the regulation that sought to stabilize the effect of this liberalization and, in extreme circumstances, to protect EU producers and the EU's financial interests. Article 2.7 gave the Commission the authority to 'carefully monitor the imports of rice, bananas and sugar' and, if necessary, move to 'temporary suspension of the preferences'. Typically, the EU designated itself judge and jury in any such cases. More generally, Article 4 provided for measures to combat fraud. Under this heading was included the failure to provide sufficient administrative cooperation to verify the precise country of origin of LDC goods and 'massive increases' in the normal levels of LDC production and export capacity to the EU.

And finally, Article 5 provided for the suspension of preferences by the Commission for a range of particularly sensitive products 'if the import of these products cause serious disturbance to Community markets and their regulatory mechanisms'. A 25 per cent annual increase was deemed sufficient to trigger this procedure. Thus, through these mechanisms the EU is able to monitor carefully imports of rice, sugar and bananas and can apply safeguard measures where necessary: as of 2010 no such action had ever been taken.

There has been criticism of the motivation behind these safeguards, however, with some seeing these omnibus provisions as a self-serving compromise. The defence offered by the Commission that trading benefits should only accrue to the countries for which they are intended (the LDCs) lacks a certain conviction. The scrupulous application of anti-fraud measures has had at least as much to do with placating the interests of those member states whose domestic production was most affected by the new concessions. However, it was reassuring that in 2005 the Commission issued a positive assessment on the extent to which the LDCs have benefited from EBA, and on the adequacy of rules of origin, anti-fraud and safeguards.

Conclusion

Both the EPAs and the EBA are ground-breaking agreements: the EBA went beyond any other WTO initiative and Cotonou's EPAs offered a fresh approach to development. While the European initiative was widely welcomed at the time, clearly developing countries would benefit further if these policies were replicated at the global level rather than limited to the EU's development framework. Of course, neither agreement addresses the non-tariff barriers that often restrict developing country exports from entering the EU market – or the supply-side limitations common in many developing countries that constrain their trade potential. The second decade of the twenty-first century may well see the application of environmental sustainability and climate change measures become progressively applied to the EU's global strategy. The post-Kyoto agreements since 2009 to provide financial assistance to help developing countries meet new carbon dioxide reduction targets provides an early indication of a possible new form of conditionality facing the developing world.

The record for implementing EPAs has been a disappointment for the Cotonou architects. What was presumed would be an appealing new trade and development paradigm has come to be viewed with increasing scepticism – except in the Caribbean – by the ACP states. Such an outcome should not have come as a great surprise to Europe as critical voices were plain to hear as early as 2002. The combined effect of the financial crises, global food shortages as well as the emergence of China as a development option substantially changed the international context of development, suggesting that the EPA philosophy was no longer in alignment with new expectations. The EU's commitment to integrating the developing world into the global economy via free trade remains the foundation of the current approach – embedded as it is in both Cotonou and the Lisbon Treaty and as an MDG mechanism. As a transparent negotiating partner the EU is unable to retreat from this position. Consequently, for the EPA project to be successfully completed in the future, the content of each agreement will need to match the individual development requirements of the ACP regions; flexibility respecting local requirements is needed, not any dogmatic 'one-size-fits-all' approach. The 2010 Cotonou review and the EPA experience to date suggest that while this is possible, future negotiation processes will continue to be drawn-out and an EPA based on a free trade formula is not in any sense a guaranteed outcome.

Without undermining the benign intent of the EBA, there continues to be concern among some developing countries that the EBA is in conflict with the broader development strategies of Cotonou. In an ideal world the reform process that led to the Cotonou Agreement would have developed in parallel with the EBA discussions – ensuring to some degree coherence, coordination and complementarity. However, the existence of two separate agreements with overlapping but not identical membership has presented the ACP with a potential dilemma. The least developed ACP countries are party to both agreements and have a choice of frameworks: the non-LDC ACP states, however, are excluded from the benefits of the EBA, and some remain concerned that the market access guaranteed by Cotonou will in practice be undermined by the more generous EBA provisions provided for non-ACP LDCs.

More significantly, the free access offered to the ACP LDCs seems to have nullified the necessity to enter into regional FTAs with the EU as outlined in the Cotonou Agreement. All potential ACP regional FTAs include LDCs, and as noted above in four of the five

African regions they constitute the majority of members. Why should any ACP LDC exchange non-reciprocal unlimited access to the EU market for a regional FTA that will give the EU free access to its markets and remove its ability to raise tariff revenue at its borders? The current level of implementation of even interim agreements would indicate that most LDCs are unconvinced of the added-value of free trade. Thus, unintentionally perhaps, the EBA has the potential to undermine the Cotonou Agreement objective of creating regional FTAs by 2020. In addition, the viability of the ACP as a coherent group has again been brought into question. And worryingly, the complexity of orchestrating a global approach to development policy at the EU-level that respects consistency, coherence as well as complementarity still presents significant policy implementation challenges. Even where consensus exists – as in the EU's adoption of the MDGs (see pp. 236–47) – the application of EU policy at the member state level remains varied. Adverse unintended consequences that characterized the Lomé experience continue to present a current danger to development policy in the twenty-first century.

Chapter 4

The Changing Institutional Setting: Policy-Making, Commission Reforms, ECHO, EuropeAid and the EEAS

In the context of EU evolution, development policy has historically been on the fringes rather than at the centre of debate. Reflecting perhaps its initial eleventh hour inclusion in the *projet européen*, none of the subsequent treaty reforms have taken the coherence of the Union's development policy as their starting point. This trend continued in the Lisbon Treaty which, while directed to the enhancement of the Union's role on the global stage, had as its focus the establishment of a single voice in CFSP, with development again somewhat of an afterthought. As a consequence of the apparent neglect, development has had to be squeezed into the policy frameworks and agenda, with institutional evolution the product largely of pragmatism than design. The consequential organizational tinkering and the impact of personalities that has been characteristic of EU development policy and practice must be read in this context.

We begin by outlining the formal mechanisms of EU development policy-making – the ordinary legislative procedure, and the roles of the Council, European Parliament and Commission. Against this policy-making context, we go on to consider the changing institutionalization of EU development and humanitarian policy and its implementation. Taking the organization of the 1995–99 Santer Commission as a starting point, we consider the administrative reorganization and policy evolution introduced by the Prodi Commission in 2000 and the emergence of the European Consensus on Development under the first Barroso Commission in 2005. Two of the Union's aid allocation institutions are then examined: ECHO, the Union's humanitarian aid and crisis response arm, and EuropeAid, responsible for the implementation of development assistance. We conclude by exploring the implications of the most recent wave of reforms – the 2009 Lisbon Treaty changes to the EU's external relations and development architecture introduced under the second Barroso Commission, paying particular attention to the emergence and scope of the EEAS in 2010 and the consequent changes to the Directorate-General for Development (DG-DEV).

Decision-taking in EU development policy

It is unnecessary here to go into the detail of the formal mechanics of decision-taking in the EU's development policy – these have been comprehensively examined elsewhere (see Keukeleire and MacNaughtan 2008). What follows, therefore, is a brief outline of the formal decision-taking framework within which development operates, and the actors involved in this process, in order to set the context for a more substantive consideration of specific structures for the implementation of EU development and humanitarian aid policy.

The ordinary legislative procedure

The core components of development policy are incorporated in Title III of the TFEU concerning 'Cooperation with Third Countries and Humanitarian Aid'. Specifically, Title III deals with the implementation of development policy (multi-annual programming of a country-specific or thematic nature) in pursuit of the EU's primary objective – the reduction and eradication of poverty – as well as the provision of humanitarian aid. The TFEU defines decision-taking within these fields as follows:

1. *Development Cooperation*: The European Parliament and the Council, acting in accordance with the ordinary legislative procedure, shall adopt the measures necessary for the implementation of development cooperation policy, which may relate to multiannual cooperation programmes with developing countries or programmes with a thematic approach. (Art. 209(1))

2. *Humanitarian Aid*: The European Parliament and the Council, acting in accordance with the ordinary legislative procedure,

shall establish the measures defining the framework within which the Union's humanitarian aid operations shall be implemented. (Art. 214(3))

As can be seen, as a Union competence, decisions on these aspects of development fall under the 'ordinary legislative procedure' (otherwise known as the 'Community method'), initially introduced under the Maastricht Treaty. Simply, on the basis of this procedure the Commission proposes (and subsequently implements), while the Council and the European Parliament make decisions jointly.

Complicating matters, beyond these core Title III development activities are to be found a range of tools which cut across the development framework. These include, for example, the negotiation of Cooperation Agreements, Association Agreements and trade agreements, all of which are mechanisms for engagement with the developing world. While still defined by the ordinary legislative procedure, decisions on these tools are more complex in their implementation, being subject to special provisions regarding the role and function of the central EU institutions (see Table 4.1).

Council

The Council is the mechanism through which member states retain oversight of the EU's development policy. Under the umbrella of the Council, two main frameworks exist for the consideration of development matters: (i) the Foreign Affairs Council (FAC); and (ii) Gymnich meetings of development ministers. The FAC and its counterpart, the General Affairs Council, were established under the Lisbon Treaty, which divided the functions of the predecessor General Affairs and External Relations Council between these two bodies. The FAC is tasked with overseeing the entirety of the Union's external action, including, along with development cooperation, the CFSP, the CSDP and external trade. Convened monthly, it brings together member state foreign ministers with the High Representative and members of the European Commission and, when considering development matters, member state ministers of development. Typically, development ministers will attend the FAC at least twice per year, assisting them in maintaining an overview of national policies with an eye to promoting coordination and complementarity.

Alongside the FAC, informal Gymnich style meetings of development ministers are also occasionally convened. These are usually also attended by the Commissioners for Development and Humanitarian Aid and the High Representative. Such meetings, while unable to adopt formal decisions, contribute to information sharing between member states on matters of development. In so doing they raise at least the possibility of avoiding duplication or indeed contradictory activity, though evidence of their success in either respect is lacking. These meetings also provide the framework through which member state ministers can contribute to progressing and steering development, allowing for dialogue on key issues within the EU development framework, though again the extent to which they are successful in this respect is a matter of conjecture.

Beyond the oversight function, the Council is also a key decision-taking institution under the ordinary legislative procedure. While legislation requires a formal Commission proposal (which the Council may itself request), the Council is, alongside the European Parliament, responsible for taking all decisions under Title III, including establishing overarching development policy, approving multi-annual programmes with developing countries or of a thematic nature, and establishing the framework within which the Union's humanitarian aid programme operates.

European Parliament

The European Parliament (EP) plays two primary roles in relation to Title III development policy: (i) monitoring; and (ii) co-decision. In this respect, the main actor is the EP's Development Committee (DEVE), comprising 30 members (and 30 substitutes), which is tasked with monitoring the EU's development policy generally and the EU–ACP relationship specifically. This is largely undertaken through the mechanisms of parliamentary questions and resolutions, own-initiative reports, and through meetings with key officials from the Commission and member states as well as external experts.

Beyond the monitoring function, under the ordinary legislative procedure the EP possesses a co-decision role alongside the Council in Title III matters. This provides it with the ability to shape the frameworks of development policy and humanitarian aid through amending Commission proposals as part of the legislative process. Beyond Title III development mechanisms, however, its role is more limited (see Table 4.1). Where Parliamentary consent is required,

TABLE 4.1 *Decision-taking procedures related to development*

	Commission	Council	European Parliament	Treaty basis (TFEU)
Title III: Cooperation with Third Countries and Humanitarian Aid				
Development Cooperation	Proposal	QMV	Co-decision	Art. 209(1)
Framework for Humanitarian Aid	Proposal	QMV	Co-decision	Art. 214(3)
Other Titles				
Interruption/Reduction of Economic or Financial Relations	Joint proposal with High Representative	QMV	Is informed	Art. 215(1)
Development and Cooperation Agreements	Commission (or High Representative for CFSP matters) recommends opening negotiations, and makes proposal for signing and concluding agreement	QMV (with exceptions)	Consultation or consent	Arts 207, 216–18
Association Agreements		Unanimity	Consent	
Trade Agreements		QMV (with exceptions)	Is informed	

Source: Modified from Keukeleire and MacNaughtan (2008: 105).

the possibility exists for the utilization of a veto or the threat thereof as a means for gaining influence, though this is regarded as a somewhat blunt instrument (Keukeleire and MacNaughtan 2008: 95).

The EP's role in development has been reinforced in two key ways. The first is through the conclusion of a series of framework inter-institutional agreements, most notably with the Commission. These agreements formalize the flow of information between the institutions, facilitate cooperation and provide a mechanism through which the EP can express a lack of confidence in specific commissioners. The second is through the Parliament's external engagement function, involving the sending of Inter-Parliamentary Delegations and representations to relevant international fora (coordinated by DEVE in the case of development policy), and participation in Joint Parliamentary Committees. Such engagement provides a means for representing the EP's positions to third parties (for example, on democracy and human rights), as well as the development of broader expertise which underpins and strengthens its engagement with the other actors in EU development policy – the Council and Commission (2000: 93–4).

Through the mechanisms outlined above, the EP has at times been able to exercise some influence over the shape and functioning of EU development. It has, for example, been key in embedding democracy and human rights into EU external relations (see pp. 194–7, 214), utilizing its budgetary powers over non-compulsory expenditure (of which development is one area) to leverage the creation in 1994 of the EuropeAid-administered European Initiative for Democracy and Human Rights. In this respect it has often also been a voice of conscience in the Union's external relations more generally, unwilling to forego moral imperatives on human rights in the face of the realpolitik of economic and trade negotiations.

Commission

While formal decision-taking authority within development policy lies with the Council and European Parliament, the Commission is responsible for the initiation and implementation of legislation. In this, four institutions have been particularly significant:

- *Directorate-General for Development (DG-DEV)*: responsible for development relations with the ACP through a contractual framework, the most recent iteration of which is the Cotonou Agreement, and the EDF funding instrument.

- *Directorate-General for External Relations (RELEX)*: responsible for relations with all regions of the world other than the ACP, as well as external relations more generally. RELEX's development role is funded through the DCI.
- *EuropeAid*: responsible for the implementation of development programmes established by DG-DEV and RELEX under their respective funding instruments.
- *ECHO*: The European Community Humanitarian Aid Office (now known as DG Humanitarian Aid and Civil Protection) is responsible for the administration of the Union's humanitarian aid.

As is discussed in greater detail below, these basic structures have undergone significant transformation in the wake of the Lisbon Treaty, with a reallocation of certain functions, the merging of DG-DEV and EuropeAid, and the emergence of the EEAS.

The Commission's exclusive right of initiative is already a powerful tool, but its latitude in Title III matters is further increased by the fact that EU development policy is a parallel competence exercised alongside, rather than above, those of the member states. As a consequence, there is no clear vested national interest in the design and structure of the policy, which gives the Commission significant additional room for manoeuvre in framing its policy suggestions. Beyond Title III, the Commission is also the institution responsible for the negotiation of agreements with third parties (the role of DG Trade).

Reforming development: from Santer to Barroso

Institutions matter in the EU, and the formal mechanics of decision-taking outlined above are insufficient to convey fully the evolution of EU development policy which represents a more complex institutional puzzle. Traditionally, the Commission (through DG-DEV) has taken the lead in setting the EU development agenda, even if member state and Council approval has remained an essential prerequisite. Yet within the Commission, development has been the subject of organizational redesign over the last two decades. In part these reforms have reflected a continual search for the most effective structure for the delivery of EU development policy; they also reflected, however, the changing dynamics between intergovernmentalism and supranationalism within the integration process, with ownership of development policy the objective of this tension. The Balkanization of development competences under the new External Action Service and its increasing complementarity with both CFSP and CSDP is the latest manifestation of this tendency.

The first full post-Maastricht Treaty Commission led by President Jacques Santer complicated the distribution of administrative responsibility for development issues. Whilst DG-DEV remained the focus for Lomé relations, three other DGs plus the autonomous ECHO were all involved in various aspects of development work. Friction between different Commission Directorates-General was particularly sensitive and much of the impetus towards free trade for the ACP can be traced to this institutional confrontation. This situation was further compounded by the competition within the College of Commissioners for seniority and policy dominance. The Santer Commission's administrative logic emphasized region rather than policy area in designating responsibilities. It was contentious at the time of introduction and proved, ultimately, to be flawed. Geographical differentiation was seen as an increasingly archaic perspective in the face of globalization. Policies were not country or regionally specific, but generalized. Indeed, the very existence of the WTO underlined the similarity of treatment between countries rather than their claim to uniqueness. Consequently, the Santer reform of Commission portfolios appeared inconsistent with contemporary trends and an inappropriate framework for addressing issues of complementarity, coordination and coherence (see Chapter 7).

To compound the problem there was a staff imbalance. As the 1999 Committee of Independent Experts report on Commission activities concluded, in some areas too few staff were often responsible for too large a budget. The notion of a burgeoning Brussels bureaucracy was never further from the truth. An earlier DAC Report was similarly critical of the EU's limited expertise. The number of specialist staff in key areas – such as women and development – was considered too limited. For example, in DG-DEV as late as 1998 there was just one designated advisor in gender policy and one individual working exclusively on poverty reduction policy – a rather sobering reality check for the soon to be adopted MDGs! The ambitions of the EU had raced ahead of the capacity of its permanent staff to implement such policies. In order to work, the EU's programme increasingly came to rely on the use of consultants to complement its limited core staff, further complicating efficiency and institutional responsibility. As one commentator concluded, both centrally as well as in the field:

> the administration of the Commission on development aid is badly organised as well as understaffed [which] has caused incoherence in the work, and has severely restricted the skill acquisition in the Commission. It is clearly not a sound policy for ensuring a competent development administration. (Reisen 1999: 54–5)

Both staffing issues and effective coordination were the subject of review in 1998. The proposed solution was the creation of a new grouping, the SCR. The SCR became operational in July 1998 with a mandate to develop greater policy coherence and utilization of staff resources and to manage all aspects (technical, operational, financial, contractual and legal) of EU aid. Somewhat paradoxically, it was also seen as a tool for introducing decentralization in the management of aid to third countries and promoting local 'ownership' of aid projects. Its geographic focus was global – not confined to just the ACP – and involved cross-cutting policy responsibilities. Food aid, environment, AIDS, democracy, human rights and CFSP, for example, were part of the SCR domain. The only exception was emergency humanitarian aid that remained exclusively under the direction of ECHO. As is discussed further below in the EuropeAid section, the SCR was ultimately unsuccessful and within a few years of its launch the new Prodi Commission was obliged to revisit the problem of development coordination.

The 2000 administrative reforms

The appointment of the Prodi Commission in late 1999 provided an opportunity for the EU to re-examine its general administrative structures, as well as address some of the publicly acknowledged shortcomings noted in the 1999 Committee of Independent Experts investigation into Commission fraud and mismanagement. The reforms applied to the development sector were the most radical in its history and were 'a bid to cut out waste and bring more coherence to its much criticized €9 billion aid budget' (Harding 2000). Institutionally, the EU's development policy had traditionally lacked a hierarchical structure and the policy autonomy retained by the different actors did little to promote coherence or coordination.

To a great extent, the reorganization was facilitated by the choice of Poul Nielson as a Commissioner and his appointment by Romano Prodi to the development portfolio. Whilst the Nice, Amsterdam and Maastricht Treaties had given the President of the Commission enhanced powers to organize portfolios and influence the composition of the Commission, it still remained the case that the member states retained the right to propose 'their' Commissioner, a situation that remains unchanged under Lisbon. Consequently, Prodi could only utilize the individual talents as moderated by the member states.

Nielson was proposed as a Commissioner by Denmark and had a strong record both as a committed European and in development, making him an appropriate choice for DG-DEV. The choice of Chris Patten as one of the then two allocated British Commissioners, and his appointment to External Relations, was also significant. The ambit of the External Relations Directorate-General was expanded considerably by Prodi and covered all countries other than the ACP, although its policy sphere did include responsibility for the SCR, human rights, democratization, multilateral organizations as well as CFSP. Consequently, many regarded the External Relations DG as the lynchpin of the Commission. Clearly, Patten's experience and international stature made him an influential political figure within the College of Commissioners. The appointment of Pascal Lamy, a protégé of Jacques Delors, as Commissioner for Trade was both a necessary political gesture and an effective choice.

From an administrative perspective, External Relations was only partially reintegrated. Nielson became Commissioner for Development in overall charge of development policy and humanitarian aid, including ECHO. Chris Patten was appointed as Commissioner for External Relations with control of the SCR as well as responsibility for external trade relations, delegations in all third countries, the coordination of external policies and the CFSP. Trade Commissioner Pascal Lamy had oversight of external trade and instruments of trade policy. His Directorate-General was involved in all trade-related matters, including GSP and the trading relations incorporated in the successor to the Lomé Conventions. DG-DEV continued to deal with only development issues in the ACP countries although its scope was expanded somewhat to include ECHO activities. Development relations with Asia, Latin America, the Mediterranean and elsewhere fell under External Relations, the domain of Chris Patten.

In early 2000 the Commission released proposals for the political guidelines for future EU development policy (Commission 2000g), together with a report on the reform of the management of external assistance (Commission 2000e). The priority given to this review by Commissioner Nielson was indicative of the EU's acknowledgement that the status quo could not continue. Nielson was frank in his assessment of past EU development policy that had suffered from 'over-rigid procedures, too little flexibility on the ground and a slowness to respond compared to the best donors'. In his view, the Commission's aid system was 'too complex and fragmented' and despite being the world's largest ODA donor the EU 'grossly under-exploited' its ability to influence development (Harding 2000).

The key elements of the new policy guidelines were familiar: to define a coherent global approach that combined trade, aid and political dialogues; to increase the impact and quality of the EU's development role internationally by seeking greater complementarity with the policies followed by the IMF, the World Bank and the OECD; and, at the core, a renewed commitment to fighting poverty and raising the standard of living of the poor. These policy objectives were informed by, and consistent with, those outlined at Maastricht: the alleviation of poverty and reintegrating the developing world into the global economy. However, the Commission proposal was equally sanguine about the EU's responsibility to increase its efforts to assist the poor and its ability to do so everywhere. Consequently, Commissioner Nielson floated the idea of a future EU development approach 'that focuses its attention on a limited number of areas' (Commission 2000c). EU activities would consequently be reduced or eliminated in some areas and core tasks would be identified where the EU offered a comparative advantage and added value in relation to poverty reduction. Six such core areas were identified:

1. trade for development;
2. regional integration and cooperation;
3. macroeconomic policies linked to poverty reduction;
4. food safety and sustainable development strategies;
5. strengthening institutional capacity;
6. good governance and the management of public affairs.

Cross-cutting issues (such as gender, environment and human rights) were to be incorporated within each of these core activities.

In response to criticisms presented by the EP, NGOs, civil society, several member states as well as those drawn from the EU's own experience and review of its development policy, new guidelines were proposed. First, it was recognized that a greater degree of 'ownership' of the development process was needed that facilitated participation by civil society and the poor in third countries. Second, despite successive treaty objectives, still greater coordination was needed between the development policies promoted by the EU, member states and multilateral agencies. Similarly, internal policy contradictions between development objectives and other EU policy sectors (such as trade or agriculture) still had to be reduced. And lastly, further institutional and procedural reforms were needed to simplify and speed up the delivery of development policy output. Clearly, many of these problems were familiar and their continued presence confirmed that treaty objectives in themselves are inadequate responses. What was equally clear was that development reform would be an ongoing process and one that would dominate the Development portfolio for the entire five-year term of the Prodi Commission – and beyond as experience has subsequently shown.

The Development Council meeting of May 2000 examined both these and other topics and in general all member states reacted positively to endorse the Commission's new guideline proposals. Not surprisingly, the Council affirmed both poverty reduction as the overarching objective of the suggested new EU policy and the emphasis on Europe's comparative advantage. It was agreed that a definitive Council position on the new policy framework would be adopted under the French presidency at the November 2000 Development Council meeting. It was agreed, however, that further steps were needed to increase complementarity between EU and member state development policies. The continuing problems of EU–member state coordination were again noted, and the aim of greater consultation and complementarity remained unfulfilled. A greater role for the EU in promoting macroeconomic reforms in the ACP, Latin America and Asia, consistent with structural adjustment, was advocated. In particular, the Council called on the Commission to focus on policies that reduced poverty, promoted regional integration and encouraged the creation of FTAs with the EU (Development Council 2000: 9). The proposals on European development policy were formally adopted in November 2000 in the form of a joint Council and Commission statement entitled *The European Community's Development Policy* (Council and

Commission 2000). The statement largely reflected the Commission's proposals, with a focus on poverty reduction and on the six areas of comparative advantage outlined above.

To coincide with the review of development policy, the Commission also issued a critical report on reforming the management of external assistance (Commission 2000e). This review was, in part, a response to the allegations of fraud and mismanagement made by the 1999 Committee of Independent Experts, and, in part, an obligation made by the Development Commissioner to the European Parliament during the confirmation hearings for the new Commission. The Commission's own analysis concluded that: 'performance has deteriorated over time to the point of undermining the credibility of its [the Commission's] external policies and the international image of the EU' (ibid.: 5). Consequently, it became a priority for the new Commission to overhaul what had become a dysfunctional system facing a crisis situation. This was to involve a complete overhaul of the SCR, only a few years after its introduction, and its transformation into EuropeAid (see discussion below).

The 2005 European Consensus on Development

Notwithstanding the administrative changes introduced in 2000, an array of initiatives at the global level during subsequent years quickly saw development-policy reform back on the European agenda. The Millennium Summit of September 2000, culminating with the ratification of the United Nations Millennium Declaration, led to the establishment of the MDGs and placed development firmly on the international agenda. This heightened global concern was reinforced with the convening of the International Conference on Financing for Development in March 2002 (producing the Monterrey Consensus), and the first High Level Forum on Aid Effectiveness in February 2003, leading, at the second Forum in 2005, to the Paris Declaration on Aid Effectiveness. Intrinsic to each of these initiatives was a refocusing of development, specifying key development targets in the case of the MDGs, and reforms to delivery in the case of the international conferences. In particular, the latter placed emphasis on conceiving aid relationships as a partnership between donor and recipient, and on the harmonization of international assistance, a particular concern in the context of European integration.

As a consequence, by the time the first Barroso Commission took office in 2004, European development policy again needed to be addressed. A review of the *The European Community's Development Policy* which had emerged from the 2000 reforms, though largely positive, highlighted the need to incorporate the recent initiatives that had emerged at the international level and to take account of the changed post-9/11 international environment which necessitated a development perspective on security and the greater integration of development policy into the EU's external relations (ECDPM, ICEI and ODI 2005: 7). This assessment was reinforced a matter of months later in the Commission's own communication on progress towards the MDGs, with a call for the EU to formulate 'a true European Development Strategy or a framework of guiding principles and rules to make its huge amount of aid more effective and genuinely "European"' (Commission 2005a: §3): in other words, to improve its coordination, coherence and consistency.

The initial draft document on EU development policy formulated by DG-DEV (Commission 2005d) failed, however, to garner universal support from member states. The proposal called for the harmonization of Commission and member state development assistance, with a more effective division of labour between the two. This attempted rebalancing towards the Union level proved, perhaps not unsurprisingly, to be controversial, with strong opposition from two groups: the UK, Denmark, Ireland and Sweden who were reluctant to accept the concept of a common EU approach, wanting instead to retain their policy autonomy (indicative of a strong intergovernmentalist policy trend); and Germany, the Netherlands and Finland who, while amenable to greater coordination at the Union level, were opposed to a Commission leadership role (Carbone 2007: 56). After negotiated compromises and the support of the vast majority of member states for at least increased coordination, the 'European Consensus on Development' (European Parliament, Commission and Council 2006) was subsequently adopted and signed by the Council, Commission and Parliament in December 2005.

The Consensus reiterated much of the earlier *European Community's Development Policy*, but for the first time designated achieving the MDGs as the primary objective of European development cooperation. Importantly, it defined insecurity and conflict as among the primary obstacles to achieving the MDGs (ibid.: §37), reflecting the security–development nexus as set out in the 2003 European Security Strategy. The Consensus established the goal of increasing member-state aid commitments to 0.7 per cent of GNI by 2015 (with an interim target of 0.56 per cent by 2010) (ibid.: §23), albeit four decades later than the original 1975 target set by the 1970 *UN Resolution on International Development Strategy*. By contrast, the CEECs who had not achieved a 0.17 per cent level by 2002 were given the more modest targets of 0.17 per cent by 2010 and 0.33 per cent by 2015. As argued in Chapter 8 (see Figure 8.1), much still needs to be done by member states if these levels are to be achieved within the specified time frame.

Nevertheless, by incorporating the MDGs, and applying the framework to instruments beyond purely development cooperation, the Consensus has given the Union a coherent vision around which to build its development practice. It remains, then, to explore the instruments of implementation – ECHO and EuropeAid – before moving on to the post-Lisbon Treaty reforms and the institutional implications that are raised by this latest iteration of the EU's global ambitions.

ECHO

The early years of the 1990s were a particularly turbulent period in world affairs and Europe found itself having to respond to a far greater range of humanitarian crises than before, including among others: a cyclone in Bangladesh; a cholera epidemic in South America; an earthquake in Iran; the Kurdish refugee crisis stemming from the Gulf War; civil war in Liberia; drought and civil war in Angola, Ethiopia, Mozambique and Somalia; and, of course, on the EU's doorstep, the onset of the civil war in Yugoslavia. As a consequence, the Community's humanitarian aid spending for 1990–91 was exceptionally high, reaching ECU 540 million – a figure exceeding that for the previous four years combined (Commission 1992: 19). Confronted by these increased demands, the European Commission was forced to reconsider its role in humanitarian aid and crisis response, and acknowledge that its existing arrangements were flawed. While humanitarian assistance had been provided since 1970, no formal mechanism or structure existed to oversee its allocation, with funding directed through various Directorates-General. In response, the Delors II Commission took the decision in November 1991 to establish a European Emergency Humanitarian

Aid Office (from 2005 the European Community Humanitarian Aid Office – ECHO) to 'manage all aspects of its emergency humanitarian aid' in the pursuit of 'speed and efficiency' of delivery (ibid.: 32).

Beyond the external demands of emergency response, the appearance of ECHO must also be situated within the specific context of the European project: ECHO was introduced at a time when the EU was undergoing one of its periodic attempts to undertake a *saut qualitatif* on the level of integration. Although neither ratified nor fully implemented until November 1993, the political decision to create an EU had already been taken at the intergovernmental level at Maastricht. The development of the CFSP, EMU and 'the hour of Europe' in the former Yugoslavia cumulatively presented the opportunity for the EU to redefine itself as an international actor and to assume a pivotal role in the post-Soviet power vacuum. The demands for greater and more frequent humanitarian interventions presented the fledgling EU with an obvious and practical opportunity to put these ambitions to the test.

At the time of its introduction, many development specialists were critical of the administrative and policy dichotomy. EU development policy remained governed by the Commission DGs, whereas humanitarian assistance became the exclusive domain of ECHO. It was argued, with some justification, that humanitarian assistance was more effective when it formed part of, rather than was divorced from, a wider and longer-term development policy approach. Indeed, this administrative and policy separation seemed implicitly inconsistent with the Maastricht goals of complementarity, coherence and coordination in development policy in general. These concerns notwithstanding, ECHO was a much-needed response to the pre-existing 1992 fragmented implementation structure.

ECHO began operating in 1992 and, reflecting its administrative separation, it was not included within any existing DG. In the absence of a Commissioner with a remit for humanitarian aid, ECHO remained functionally autonomous, being administered in its early years under the joint authority of its Director and the Commissioner for Development Manuel Marín. From 1995 when the Santer Commission assumed office, humanitarian aid and crisis response became a formal portfolio, allocated in that instance to Commissioner Emma Bonino alongside her responsibility for Consumer Policy. From the Prodi Commission in 1999 it became accepted practice to allocate the ECHO portfolio alongside that of Development generally (beginning with Commissioner Nielson), a situation that held until the Barroso II Commission saw its designation for the first time as the sole portfolio of a Commissioner, with Kristalina Georgieva being given responsibility for International Cooperation, Humanitarian Aid and Crisis Response.

The original autonomy of ECHO reflected a belief that the immediate needs of humanitarian aid were qualitatively and procedurally different from the more enduring policy perspectives demanded by development in general. The fact that after seven years' experience the decision was reversed suggests that the original dichotomy may well have been false and that the costs involved in applying a longer-term perspective are outweighed by the benefits of coordination. Of course, having a single Commissioner and dedicated staff did help to identify and distinguish initially the unique function of ECHO. This autonomy was also useful in enhancing the EU's capacity to take direct action as well as mobilize personnel and resources. Its independence was also a useful characteristic in coordinating EU-level humanitarian action and those operated bilaterally by the member states and other international agencies. Regardless, by the time the second Barroso Commission took office in 2010, questions of qualitative difference and organizational structure had been trumped by the exigencies of finding meaningful portfolios for the raft of new Commissioners who were the result of progressive Union enlargement since 1994. The reallocation of ECHO as a single competence separate from Development is perhaps best understood in these terms.

Role and operation

ECHO is operationally divided into three parts: Directorate A covers operations, Directorate B provides support to operations, and Directorate C covers policy and coordination. Directorate A is further divided into six geographic, thematic and administrative units:

A.1: Central Africa, Sudan and Chad;
A.2: East, West and Southern Africa, and the Indian Ocean;
A.3: Central and Eastern Europe, Newly Independent States, Mediterranean countries and the Middle East;
A.4: Asia and Latin America, and the Caribbean and Pacific regions;
A.5: Food Aid;
A.6: Information and Communication.

ECHO operates with only a small administrative core in Brussels: of its 254 staff, just over 100 are spread across 44 field offices in 36 countries (see Map 1.1). In addition, around 300 local agents are also employed in the field alongside ECHO staff (ECHO 2010a: 85; Human Resources and Security 2010: 1). ECHO's presence is highest in Africa (21 field offices), followed by Asia (11), Latin American and the Caribbean (five), the Middle East (five) and Europe (two).

Notwithstanding its formal establishment in 1992, ECHO did not gain legal status until the entry into force in June 1996 of 'Council Regulation No. 1257/96 ... Concerning Humanitarian Aid' (Council of the EU 1996), creating the necessary basis for a budget line. Under the Humanitarian Aid Regulation, which remains the governing instrument for ECHO, the organization's mission and mandate is defined as providing 'assistance, relief and protection operations on a non-discriminatory basis to help people in third countries, particularly the most vulnerable among them, and as a priority those in developing countries, victims of natural disasters, man-made crises, such as wars and outbreaks of fighting, or exceptional situations or circumstances comparable to natural or man-made disasters' (Article 1). This covers emergency humanitarian aid, emergency food aid, the mobilization of relief and personnel, disaster prevention and preparedness and the necessary coordination of funding and legal bases for action. More specifically, ECHO is governed by seven core objectives (Article 2):

1. saving and preserving life during emergencies and natural disasters and their immediate aftermath;
2. providing assistance and relief to those affected by longer-lasting crises as a consequence of fighting or war;
3. financing the transportation of aid, and the protection of humanitarian goods and personnel;
4. carrying out short-term rehabilitation and reconstruction work;
5. dealing with the consequences of population movements resulting from natural or man-made disasters;
6. ensuring disaster preparedness (including utilizing early warning and intervention systems); and
7. supporting civil operations to protect the victims of conflict.

Related activities include elements such as feasibility studies, monitoring humanitarian projects, the training of specialists, coordination of disaster prevention measures, anti-personnel landmine clearance operations, as well as the pervasive function of raising European public awareness of humanitarian issues and of the EU's leading international role. While institutionally separate, there are clear synergies between the activities of some post-2003 CSDP missions and ECHO's more immediate emergency function and role.

Importantly, ECHO's decisions on aid allocation are to be taken 'impartially and solely according to the victims' needs and interests' and 'not be guided by, or subject to, political considerations' (Preamble), a formulation explicitly positing humanitarian principles at the core of its operations and setting the organization outside of the framework of foreign policy instruments that the Union has developed. The centrality of such principles was subsequently reiterated in the 2007 'European Consensus on Humanitarian Aid' (Council of the EU 2008b), which gave formal expression in the EU context to the fundamental humanitarian principles of 'neutrality, impartiality and independence' (Article 10).

The Consensus was itself the product of two pressures. First, it was a European response to UN-led efforts to make the humanitarian aid system more effective. Second, it stemmed from European calls as far back as 1997 to establish a general policy document for the provision of humanitarian aid to stand alongside the operational framework established in the 1996 Regulation. In its 'Special Report 2/97 Concerning Humanitarian Aid' (Court of Auditors 1997), the Court of Auditors bemoaned the piecemeal approach to regulation bearing on humanitarian aid provision, which led to ambiguity and contradiction and, as a product, hesitancy in implementation both within the Commission itself and in cooperation with the Union's member states. The proposed solution was 'a general policy document, a kind of charter for humanitarian aid' (ibid.: §6.2). Commission reluctance meant that a decade passed before such a charter was implemented.

The centrality of 'needs' to the ECHO mandate structures its operating methodology. Need is determined using two frameworks: field level assessments and comparative analyses. Field level assessments are carried out by country desk staff and in field offices in cooperation with implementation partners. Such assessments determine areas of crisis at the local level and the scale and nature of humanitarian need. Comparative analyses across countries are utilized as a means for determining those countries that should at a general level be beneficiaries of ECHO aid. Two evaluation tools are used: a Global Needs Assessment (GNA) and a Forgotten Crisis Assessment (FCA) (ECHO 2010c).

The GNA establishes the vulnerability of each country utilizing readily available data, such as the UNDP's human development, human poverty and gender development indices, UNHCR figures on refugees and displaced people, World Health Organization (WHO) figures on malnutrition and mortality for children under five, UNDP and WHO figures on access to healthcare, Joint United Nations Programme on HIV and AIDS (UNAIDS) figures on the prevalence of HIV/AIDS, and the UNDP's Gini Index of individual and household income. The resulting Vulnerability Index (VI), which identifies countries with populations likely to suffer more than others in the event of humanitarian disaster, is subsequently mediated through application of a Crisis Index (CI) to determine whether these countries are actually in a crisis situation in which ECHO should intervene. Indicatively, the CI takes as its basis for measurement the existence of ongoing or recently resolved conflicts or natural disasters, or a large number of uprooted people, according greater weight to the event by its recency.

The FCA constitutes a unique characteristic of ECHO activity – dealing with crises that have effectively been forgotten by international donors. This again is a reflection of the centrality of 'need' to its operations, recognizing that effective solutions may be undermined by a lack of political will, and that crises often continue to affect populations long after they are of interest to the international media. The FCA is therefore calculated using the VI alongside statistical analyses of media coverage of crises undertaken by the European Joint Research Centre, figures on the amount of aid allocated to crises sourced from the UN's Office for the Coordination of Humanitarian Affairs and the OECD's Development Assistance Committee, and finally a qualitative assessment undertaken by ECHO desk officers. Utilizing this methodology, crises such as that of Sahrawi refugees in Algeria, the Rohingya persecution in Myanmar and the consequent refugee crisis affecting Bangladesh, and the plight of those affected by ongoing conflict between the Naxalite-Maoist insurgency and government forces in Indian-administered Kashmir, have remained on ECHO's agenda even as they have largely disappeared from that of others. Consequently, the EU remains the main donor in many of the forgotten corners of the world.

ECHO itself is a funding allocation rather than a project implementation organization, though the Humanitarian Aid Regulation did raise the prospect of a more hands-on role when it suggested the financing of Commission aid operations (Council of the EU 1996: Article 9). Indeed, a small number of direct operational interventions are identifiable. ECHO Flight, for example, established in 1994 and run from the Nairobi field office, provides air transport and freight services to humanitarian organizations operating in the Horn of Africa and the Great Lakes region. Initially launched for three years, the service is still operating, carrying around 1,500 passengers and 50 tonnes of cargo from 180 partners to 40 destinations each month.

ECHO funding is drawn predominantly from the general budget (approximately 93 per cent during 1993–2009) and to a much lesser extent from the EDF. Since 1993, its first full operating year, ECHO has been responsible for the allocation of over €11.2 billion in aid, with an implementation rate approaching 100 per cent (see Table 4.2). For 2009, the budget stood at just over €930 million, equivalent to 9.5 per cent of total external assistance administered by the European Commission. In contrast to other Directorates-General which have comparatively stable environments (in terms of financial commitments, policy development and project implementation), the very nature of humanitarian assistance has meant a less predictable context within which ECHO operates. One consequence is that the budget has been subject to significant fluctuation: for example, over one three-year period (1998–2000) the annual budget varied from €517 million in 1998, rising to €810 million the following year, before falling to €495 million in 2000.

ECHO's goals are achieved through funding relationships with more than 200 relief organizations falling into three main categories: (i) NGOs, (ii) UN agencies, and (iii) other international organizations (such as the International Committee of the Red Cross and the International Federation of the Red Cross and Red Crescent Societies). Interestingly, despite significant fluctuation in the comparative percentage of ECHO aid distributed by each of these three groups, including a peak flow to NGOs of 70 per cent of funding in 2000 (the end product of a decade in which NGOs were conceived as primary interlocutors in the democratization process in Eastern Europe), by 2007–09 the distribution had returned to roughly the levels of 1994, with 47 per cent going to NGOs, 39 per cent to UN agencies and 14 per cent to international organizations

Table 4.2   *ECHO budget, 1993–2009*

Year	Total (€ thousands)	General budget (%)	EDF (%)	Implementation rate (%)
1993	606,590	85.1	14.9	99.7
1994	762,970	65.4	34.6	100.1
1995	688,955	93.3	6.7	100.7
1996	669,850	98.4	1.6	98.0
1997	445,240	98.3	1.7	99.2
1998	517,600	92.8	7.2	100.0
1999	810,282	89.7	10.3	100.3
2000	495,310	99.4	0.6	99.3
2001	543,750	96.2	3.8	100.0
2002	539,320	96.8	3.2	99.7
2003	600,705	97.7	2.3	99.9
2004	570,412	90.8	9.2	100.0
2005	653,826	96.5	3.5	99.8
2006	671,350	95.8	4.2	99.9
2007	769,214	96.3	3.7	99.9
2008	938,748	100.0	0.0	99.8
2009	931,693	96.0	4.0	99.9
Total	**11,215,815**			**99.8**
Average 1993–2009	659,754	93.2	6.8	99.8
Average last 3 years	**879,885**	**97.5**	**2.5**	**99.9**

Source: Adapted from ECHO (2010a: 94).

in 2009 (compared to 49, 39 and 12 per cent respectively in 1994). Framework Partnership Agreements facilitate the disbursement of funds by outlining the procedures by which ECHO will grant financing and by defining the operational and financial accountability mechanisms for partners. Their provisions have, however, been criticized by the Court of Auditors (1997: §§4.11–4.21) for a lack of flexibility and inability to take account of the particularities of partners.

The 1996 Humanitarian Aid Regulation was also responsible for establishing the Humanitarian Aid Committee (HAC) (comprising member state representatives and chaired by the Commission), an important innovation dedicated to improving the central coordination of aid between donors. Where appropriate, ECHO drafts a 'global plan' for strategic action for a particular crisis or region with the objective of coordinating ECHO's strategy with those of other donors – the member states and the wider international donor community – which is then subject to HAC review and approval. This centralized attempt to promote complementarity and coordination is also reflected in the field: routinized and systematic procedures have been introduced to facilitate the regular exchange of information between all donor agencies. Conversely, the member states have agreed to use a uniform 14-point reporting system to inform ECHO of new bilateral aid initiatives. This information is also circulated via the online 'HOLIS 14 point' system to all concerned within 48 hours. This cumulative database on member state and ECHO aid has become an invaluable tool in realizing cooperation and effective complementarity.

Specific ECHO funding decisions are made under the 'comitology' process, with all decisions requiring approval from HAC. Approved decisions are passed to the European Parliament and, if no objection is forthcoming within one month, may then be formally adopted by HAC. Clearly, this process can take longer in cases where HAC or the Parliament raise objections or queries. Using the comitology principle, the Humanitarian Aid Regulation specifies three methods for allocating financing to humanitarian crises: the Emergency Financing Decision (Council of the EU 1996: Article 13), the Global Plan Financing Decision (Article 15.2), and the Ad Hoc Financing Decision (Articles 13, 15.2). Using the procedures for each of these decisions, typically ECHO funding can be authorized between ten days (for Emergency Decisions of up to €10 million and lasting not more than six months) and 3 months (for Global Plans of more than €30 million lasting up to 18 months, and where comitology requirements are more extensive) after the advent of a crisis (ECHO 2008: 4). Ten days, of course, can be a significant amount of time in a humanitarian emergency, and so in 2001 the Commission adopted an additional 'Empowerment Decision' financing procedure – the Primary Emergency Financing Decision – and a new emergency response mechanism for the Emergency Decision. Designed to cover the immediate needs of populations in disaster situations, the Primary Emergency Decision allows the Director-General of ECHO to allocate up to €3 million, typically within 72 hours, with ex post consultation with the HAC and European Parliament. Similarly, changes to the Emergency Decision allow the Commissioner of DG ECHO to allocate up to €10 million, again with ex post institutional involvement. The Empowerment Decision has significantly shortened ECHO's initial response times – for example, when the Asian tsunami struck on 26 December 2004, €3 million was allocated on the same day to provide shelters, non-food aid and medical supplies. This was followed on 30 December by a decision for €10 million for Sri Lanka and the Maldives, and on 31 December for a further €10 million for Indonesia (Court of Auditors 2006: §12).

As can be seen in Table 4.3, the allocation of ECHO funding by region over the last decade has largely mirrored the balance to be found in European development cooperation more generally. Africa has been the largest recipient of humanitarian aid, with the ongoing refugee crisis in Chad and the Sudan, a consequence of the Darfur Conflict, attracting a significant proportion of funding allocations. Often termed the 'forgotten crisis', ECHO's continuing engagement in the region demonstrates the significance of the FCA in determining aid allocations. In the first decade of its operations, however, ECHO funding was directed heavily towards its European neighbourhood – from 1992–98, 42 per cent of all aid went to areas affected by the conflict in the former Yugoslavia, reaching 55 per cent by 1999 (ICG 2001: 5). This skewing in favour of Europe, despite the fact that the majority of crises were occurring in sub-Saharan Africa (with the response to the Rwanda genocide receiving only 15 per cent of funding), raised accusations that ECHO was at odds with its own mission to deal with forgotten crises (ibid.: 6). Reflecting this distortion, in 2000 the European Parliament called for a reprioritizing of the distribution of humanitarian aid to 'achieve a better balance in favour of developing countries' (European Parliament 2000: §8).

ECHO has remained largely unaffected by the post-Lisbon reform process. The major change has been the incorporation of the civil protection units from DG Environment and its redesignation as DG Humanitarian Aid and Civil Protection. However, despite calls by the European Parliament as early as 1995 for the 'parallel management of emergency and development aid' (*Bulletin of the EU* 1997: §1.3.59) to create greater coherence between humanitarian

Table 4.3 *Relative percentage share of ECHO funding by region (including primary beneficiaries by region), 2001–09*

	2001	2002	2003	2004	2005	2006	2007	2008	2009
Africa	31.6	37.0	37.3	49.8	36.2	47.8	52.9	56.6	52.6
(Chad/Sudan)	(3.1)	(3.4)	(4.0)	(18.1)	(9.0)	(16.6)	(18.3)	(21.0)	(16.1)
Mediterranean and Middle East	11.1	11.9	24.0*	8.6	7.5	21.6	12.9	13.3	11.8
(Palestinian Territories)	(4.8)†	(6.5)	(6.3)	(6.5)	(5.2)	(12.5)	(7.8)	(7.8)	(7.1)
Europe, Caucasus and Central Asia	26.0†	15.5†	8.3	7.8	5.9	5.8	3.3	3.0	1.3
(Caucasus–Chechnya Crisis)	(7.4)	(5.2)	(4.3)	(5.0)	(4.0)	(3.9)	(2.7)	(1.2)	(0.6)
South Asia	14.2	16.8	12.3	11.8	12.9	8.4	11.4	10.1	16.9
(Afghanistan/Iran/Pakistan)	(10.1)	(13.6)	(9.3)	(6.2)	(10.4)	(3.5)	(3.5)	(3.9)	(11.6)
South East and East Asia	5.8	8.9	7.6	8.6	5.9	5.6	3.9	6.8	4.9
(Myanmar/Thailand)	(1.2)	(1.7)	(1.9)	(3.5)	(2.5)	(2.3)	(2.5)	(4.2)	(2.0)
Asian Tsunami (26 December 2004)	–	–	–	0.0	18.8	–	–	–	–
Latin America	7.4	5.1	2.3	3.2	3.4	3.7	5.2	3.6	3.0
(Colombia)	(1.8)	(1.7)	(1.3)	(1.5)	(1.8)	(1.8)	(1.7)	(1.3)	(1.3)
Caribbean	0.7	0.1	0.7	3.0	1.7	0.2	2.1	2.3	1.5
(Haiti)	–	(0.1)	(0.0)	(2.0)	(0.0)	(0.0)	(0.6)	(1.7)	(0.8)
Pacific	0.0	0.0	0.0	0.0	0.0	0.0	0.1	0.0	0.3
Other (e.g. Administration, UN Agencies)	3.2	4.7	7.5	7.2	7.7	6.9	8.2	4.3	7.7

* The peak in 2003 relates to the high level of funding (16.2% of all ECHO aid) directed towards Iraq to deal with the humanitarian consequences of the US-led invasion.

† The high level of funding in 2001–02 relates to the ongoing refugee problem in the Western Balkans, resulting from the Kosovo and FYROM crises of preceding years. This accounted for 15.3% of all ECHO spending in 2001 and 6.9% in 2002.

Source: ECHO Annual Report, various editions.

aid and development, ECHO remains institutionally independent of the EEAS and the newly named DG Development and Cooperation – EuropeAid. This differs markedly from state-level aid organizations (such as USAID, DFID and CIDA) which have tended to integrate policy, funding and implementation under a single roof. This separation may be explained by the humanitarian aid principles at the core of the Consensus, including most notably neutrality. The European Parliament in particular has placed a premium on the independence and impartiality of ECHO, as can be seen in its 2000 call for the 'Commission to take the appropriate steps to put a stop to the increased politicization of humanitarian assistance and the way this is taking the place of European Union foreign policy, because humanitarian assistance should essentially address the effects of crisis, be they the result of a natural disaster or a conflict, and not its causes' (European Parliament 2000: §12). Irrespective of the aims of Lisbon to link development and foreign policy more closely, the European Parliament is likely to continue to oppose any steps to bring ECHO into these structures, unwilling to realize greater coherence between development and humanitarian aid at the expense of politicizing the latter. An early indication of this tendency appeared to surface in 2011 when MEPs voiced concern about a suggested merger of the humanitarian aid budget with that for crisis management after 2013 – the latter instrument being seen as increasingly under the control of the EEAS (Willis 2011d). The spectre of greater politicization of humanitarian aid looks set to remain a contentious EU issue for the foreseeable future.

EuropeAid

The EuropeAid Cooperation Office was established in January 2001, the product of several years of ferment in EU development policy and practice. The nature and effectiveness of development assistance administered by the European Commission had become a matter of considerable debate by the mid-1990s, the product in part of the forthcoming renegotiation of the Lomé Convention and the less than spectacular results achieved in three decades of cooperation with the ACP. As noted already, a series of critical reports, including from the European Court of Auditors and the OECD's Development Assistance Committee, raised questions about the efficiency and functioning of the EU's increasingly large aid programme. In response, the June 1995 Development Council called for an evaluation of EU aid instruments and programmes globally; by May 1999 momentum had built for a comprehensive update of EU development policy.

A number of central weaknesses were identified in the Union's development assistance. First, inadequate staffing was highlighted, a consequence of the failure to expand development administration in line with the budget – by 2000, for every €10 million of aid committed there were 2.9 Commission staff, compared with 4.3 in the World Bank and between 4.0 and 9.0 in member states (Jones 2001: 426). One consequence of this under-staffing was a reliance on a network of 80 TAOs established to subcontract Commission programmes. The TAOs were widely criticized for excessive administrative costs (the annual cost of TAOs at €170 million was equivalent to 80 per cent of the administrative budget of the entire network of Commission Delegations) (Commission 2000e: 5), poor implementation, and generally substandard results.

Second, internal coordination between the various development budget lines and relevant Directorates-General was low. Aid management was characterized by slow implementation and weak programming, with the average time frames for completion increasing throughout the 1990s. During the five years from 1995, delays in the disbursement of funds increased from an average three years to four and a half, with some programmes experiencing backlogs of up to eight and a half years (ibid.: 6)! Finally, aid projects were seen to be poorly targeted and implemented, suffering from 'deficiencies in appraisal, preparation and monitoring and from delays in inputs and outputs which have considerably reduced their effectiveness', a product of the 'cumbersome management structure of this aid' (Court of Auditors 1999: 2). Central to these problems was the fragmentation in the administration of EU development assistance. The number of Directorates-General with an external relations competence had increased from two in 1984 to seven by 1997, producing 'a dispersion of human resources, a compartmentalisation of methods, a weakening of management capacities and a failure to define clearly the responsibilities of each service' (Commission 2000e: 6).

In response, and as previously noted, in 1998 a Common Service for External Relations was established to provide more coherence to EU provision of development assistance by separating responsibility for policy-making and project implementation. The SCR did have some success: by 1999, for example, aid disbursements reached record levels and progress was made in harmonizing contracts and tendering procedures (ibid.: 7). Overall, however, the SCR failed to deliver the substantive improvement in policy coherence and coordination envisaged, and despite certain improvements also worsened the situation in a number of ways. It failed, for example, to rectify the identified mismatch between aid volumes and administrative resources, while at the same time the streamlining procedures placed greater initial demands on these staff. It failed to clarify adequately the responsibilities of the SCR compared to other DGs. And it placed too much emphasis on correct procedure, rather than the speed of delivery or sensitivity to local needs (EuropeAid 2001: 163). Within a few years, therefore, the administration of EU development assistance was once more the focus of reform.

In May 2000 the *Reform of the Management of External Assistance* (Commission 2000e) was published by the Commission. This introduced a major set of reforms to the SCR, including its redesignation as the EuropeAid Cooperation Office and its upgrading to a full Commission Department under the control of a Board of four Commissioners (External Relations, Development and Humanitarian Aid, Enlargement, and Economic and Monetary Affairs) (EuropeAid 2001: 12). Subsequently, EuropeAid was upgraded to a full Directorate-General under the control of a single Commissioner.

Formally launched on 1 January 2001, EuropeAid brought together 1,200 staff to manage 80 per cent of the Commission development assistance programmes (Jones 2001: 427), though its component of the development budget compared with that administered by other DGs has since experienced an overall decline – from a share of 83 per cent of EU ODA commitments in 2001 (EuropeAid 2001: 155) to 74.3 per cent by 2009 (EuropeAid 2010: 174) – with a parallel decline in staffing levels to 1,019 by 2010 (Human Resources and Security 2010: 1). With the devolution of aid management to the Delegations, however, this figure is not necessarily indicative of a decline in importance.

Since EuropeAid began functioning there has been a notable increase in aid disbursement. In 2000, the year before EuropeAid officially began operations, the ratio of disbursement to commitments stood at 64.4 per cent for SCR administered funds, compared with 80.8 per cent for those administered by other Directorates-General and 69.3 per cent overall. Since 2001 this situation has improved significantly, with the disbursement ratio of EuropeAid funds at 84.6 per cent for 2001–09, higher than an average of 81.3 per cent for funds managed by other DGs.

Beyond the issue of disbursement of development assistance, coherence was pursued by broadening the role of EuropeAid in the programming process, extending it beyond simply implementation and evaluation to cover all elements of the cycle except the initial programming stage (in which overall country and regional strategies are defined), which was to remain the responsibility of the Directorates-General for External Relations and Development. Importantly, the establishment of EuropeAid has involved the elimination of the vast majority of TAOs. Nevertheless, the link with the local level has been maintained and made more effective: two-thirds of EuropeAid staff working on aid implementation are based in the field, and the devolution process has seen the management of external aid passed to European Delegations as a means for accelerating implementation and increasing responsiveness to local needs.

EuropeAid remains the implementation arm of EU development assistance – a position unaltered by the post-Lisbon Treaty reform process – responsible for an annual budget approaching €9 billion. The decision on 27 October 2010 to merge EuropeAid with the remainder of DG-DEV into a policy and implementation Directorate-General can only be seen positively, particularly in the context of the earlier merging for the first time of the DCI and EDF under a single structure. This brings to an end the division between policy and implementation of the majority of the EU's external assistance, now bringing the Union more into line with the organizational practice of its member states.

Lisbon Treaty reforms and development

The Lisbon Treaty, the successor to the failed European Constitution, was intended to complete the reform process necessitated by the eastern enlargement of the EU and begun with the Treaties of Amsterdam and Nice 'with a view to enhancing the efficiency and democratic legitimacy of the Union and to improving the coherence of its action' (Preamble to the Lisbon Treaty). Central to this process has been the establishment of the new High Representative of the Union for Foreign Affairs and Security Policy (combining the former roles of High Representative for CFSP and Commissioner for External Relations) and of an EEAS. The EEAS, first envisaged in the Constitutional Treaty, was seen as a necessary institutional support to the new High Representative. These innovations were seen as fundamental to ensuring the coherence and consistency in EU external relations, including its development policy. Indeed, as said by Valéry Giscard d'Estaing (former President of the European Constitutional Convention) shortly before the signing of the Lisbon Treaty, 'it would put an end to the duplication which exists between the current function of Mr Javier Solana, and that carried out within the Commission by Mrs Benita Ferrero-Waldner, in charge of the external assistance of the EU. One and the same person would therefore deal with problems and respond to the famous telephone calls of Henry Kissinger: "I want to speak to Europe"' (Giscard d'Estaing 2007).

Scope, function and the single phone number

The establishment of the scope and functioning of the EEAS has, however, proved less than straightforward, not least due to the array of external functions carried out by Commission Directorates-General other than DG External Relations, a situation which had, after all, been a key factor underlying many accusations of incoherence in the first place. When the second Barroso Commission took office in February 2010, for example, the number of Commissioners with an external relations competence increased from four to six. Alongside the High Representative (also a Vice President of the Commission) responsible at that stage for the CFSP and the CSDP, were Commissioners responsible for: Development; Enlargement and Neighbourhood Policy; External Relations; International Cooperation, Humanitarian Aid and Crisis Response; and Trade.

While the Lisbon Treaty outlined the need for the EEAS to assist the High Representative, it set out no framework of functions and competences, leaving this instead to be determined by a process of inter-institutional bargaining between the High Representative, the Council, the Commission and the EP. Inevitably, a certain tension was evident between the Commission and the new service over the retention of external competences. In this, the place of development policy and its associated budget loomed large, with the EEAS pushing for a greater development role as a means for delivering the 'consistency between its policies and activities' (Article 2F) demanded by the Lisbon Treaty, while the Commission fought to retain some control over these budget lines. In the event, the EEAS, established by Council Decision on 26 July 2010 (Council of the EU 2010), brought together the former DG External Relations with the Council-led CFSP, and elements of the Commission Directorates-

General for Development, and Enlargement and Neighbourhood Policy. The EEAS itself was established as 'a functionally autonomous body' (Council of the EU 2010: Preamble §1) existing independently of, but alongside, the Commission and the Council, an institutional innovation within the EU structure that remains somewhat of a work in progress.

The emergence of the EEAS and the reshuffling of the roles and functions of those Commission Directorates-General with external relations competences are expected to have far-reaching consequences for the operation of external relations generally and of development in particular. In terms of concrete structures, the new EEAS replaces the Directorate-General for External Relations, incorporating essentially its entire staff. Further, the network of more than 130 Commission Delegations, renamed European Union Delegations, has also been incorporated into the EEAS. These new EU Delegations, merging also the network of Council delegations, are now to function effectively as embassies, speaking for the Union as a whole rather than just the Commission. Finally, key elements of the DG-DEV have been integrated into the EEAS structure: DG-DEV's geographic desks – Directorates D and E covering the ACP – and elements of the general affairs Directorate C – those desks covering aid programming and management, as well as pan-African issues and institutions, governance and migration. For the first time, therefore, the European Commission's geographic units, previously divided between the Directorates-General for External Relations and Development, have been brought together in a single institution, finally removing the geographic division that had been promoted under the Santer Commission.

With the EEAS absorbing its country desks, the DG-DEV was initially transformed into a policy institution, though its retention of Directorate C3 responsible for economic governance and budget support did raise the prospect that a level of practical engagement would be retained, particularly given the increased significance of budget support in EU development. Nevertheless, under the new structure established by the Council Decision it was difficult to conceal the fact that Development had become very much a rump Directorate-General, an organization of leftovers which, given its reduced weight, ran the risk of having its policy advice ignored. As a consequence, and despite initial protestations to the contrary by Commissioner for Development Andris Piebalgs among others, a decision was taken by the Commission on 27 October 2010 to merge the remainder of the DG-DEV with EuropeAid to form a new Directorate-General for Development and Cooperation – EuropeAid (DG-DEVCO) (Commission 2010a: 2). As noted already, in so doing, the new Directorate-General will more closely resemble the structures of state-based development programmes, becoming both a policy and implementation institution, though with the notable absence of humanitarian aid and crisis response. From 1 January 2011, DG-DEVCO began operation under a transitional structure, with a final organizational framework in place by June (see Figure 4.1).

The reallocation of physical structures does not, however, provide the full picture. Intrinsic to the balance of power between the Commission Directorates-General and the new EEAS was control of relevant budget lines. Formally, all external relations budget instruments – the DCI, the EDF, the European Instrument for Democracy and Human Rights, the ENPI, the Instrument for Cooperation with Industrialized Countries, the Instrument for Nuclear Safety Cooperation, and the Instrument for Stability – are brought under the control of the High Representative and the EEAS through Article 9(2), a hangover from Ashton's initial, and far more centralized, proposals concerning the role and functioning of the Service. However, during negotiations in June 2010 the EP was able to leverage a range of concessions such that the formulation of annual spending programmes under the DCI and the EDF would be largely the responsibility of the DG-DEV (now DG-DEVCO), though operating in cooperation with the relevant sections of the EEAS (Article 9[4]). Further, thematic programmes are also to be prepared by relevant DGs under the authority of the Commissioner for Development. For the first time, therefore, the Commissioner for Development will be responsible for global development, rather than simply the ACP (with the Commissioner for External Relations responsible for 'the rest') as was previously the case.

Importantly, programming under the DCI and EDF is to be submitted jointly to the College of Commissioners by the Commissioner for Development and the High Representative, introducing the possibility of a veto by the latter. For other budget lines, the Commission also retains a role in the strategic policy and programming decisions at country and regional level that are now the responsibility of the EEAS – these must be prepared in consultation with relevant Commission DGs and utilizing Commission procedures, and require the endorsement of the College of

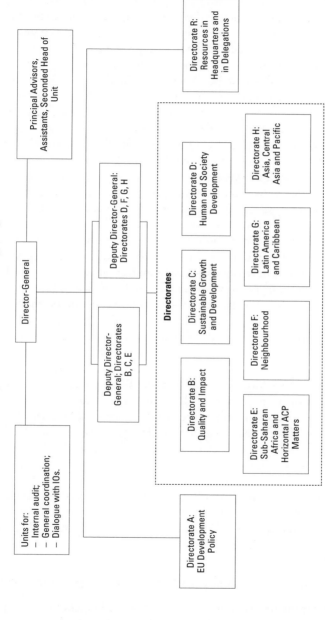

FIGURE 4.1 *DEVCO organogram*

Principal Advisors, Assistants, Seconded Head of Unit

Director-General

Units for:
- Internal audit;
- General coordination;
- Dialogue with IOs.

Deputy Director-General: Directorates D, F, G, H

Deputy Director-General; Directorates B, C, E

Directorate R: Resources in Headquarters and in Delegations

Directorates

Directorate D: Human and Society Development

Directorate C: Sustainable Growth and Development

Directorate B: Quality and Impact

Directorate H: Asia, Central Asia and Pacific

Directorate G: Latin America and Caribbean

Directorate F: Neighbourhood

Directorate E: Sub-Saharan Africa and Horizontal ACP Matters

Directorate A: EU Development Policy

Note: IO stands for International Organization.
Source: Adapted from DEVCO (2011).

Commissioners before they take effect, again introducing a potential veto. Given that EuropeAid itself was introduced in 2001 in part to remedy the fragmentation in the programming cycle, it can be queried whether these new processes represent a step back or a step forward.

Finally, harking back to the reform proposals of 2000, management of EU funds to be allocated through external assistance programmes falls to the EU Delegations. With the overall responsibility of the financial execution of these funds lying with DG-DEVCO, it can be presumed that the Delegations will be held accountable to DG-DEVCO in this area, even though they are accountable to the High Representative for all other aspects of their functioning. Practice and pragmatism will be essential attributes during the formative years.

With the above changes in mind, what remains unclear is precisely who speaks for Europe on development – the exact opposite of what the Lisbon reforms had originally promised. Is it the High Representative, responsible for the coordination of EU external action? Or is it the Commissioner for Development, responsible for the primary development-related budget lines, for policy and for implementation? Ashton's own early comments seemed to suggest a pre-eminent role for the High Representative, acting on the advice of relevant subordinates: 'I will rely on Andris Piebalgs and Stefan Füle for their advice on development and neighbourhood policy. The EEAS will follow their guidance when preparing the strategic programming. And I hope they will listen to my suggestions in the later stages' (Ashton 2010b). With the EP's subsequent successful intervention to shore up the role of the Commission, these hopes no longer seemed to be entirely realistic. However, events have since served to muddy the issue further. The granting in May 2011 of additional rights to the EU in the UN General Assembly (bringing it almost on to a par with sovereign states), including the physical inclusion of additional seats in the chamber for the High Representative and EEAS officials (Phillips 2011), again suggested the supremacy of the EEAS over its Commission counterparts. Whatever the case, it is clear that the problem of the single phone number has yet to be resolved.

Cooperation, collegiality and the place of development

While for the first time rectifying the historic but less than coherent compartmentalization of the developing world, evident in European external relations since the 1970s, the Lisbon reforms and the establishment of the EEAS nevertheless introduces its own peculiarities. The unification of geographic desks under the EEAS on the one hand, and the linking of the DCI and the EDF under the authority of the Commissioner for Development on the other, means that even while problems of geographic and policy coherence are to an extent rectified, responsibility for key development instruments is now institutionally separated from the geographic desks to which those instruments apply. Further, despite notionally bringing all aspects of the EU's external relations under one roof, it seems that the EEAS still maintains a clear division of labour and responsibility between general foreign policy and development instruments. Taken in conjunction with the overall coordinating role in EU external relations to be played by the High Representative, assisted by the EEAS, the ability of these institutions to operate collegially is central to the success of the project.

At the heart of collegiality and the coherent functioning of EU external relations lies the issue of establishing clear objectives and remedying inevitable tensions between foreign policy and developmental goals. This was confronted by the 2010 July Council Decision, under which the EEAS is charged with ensuring the 'unity, consistency and effectiveness' of the Union's external actions in pursuit of those goals established by Article 21 TEU (Council of the EU 2010: Preamble §4), with a particular emphasis on paragraph 2(d) to: 'foster the sustainable economic, social and environmental development of developing countries, with the primary aim of eradicating poverty'. It is further required to 'take account of the objectives of development cooperation' as established in Article 208 TFEU, the European Consensus on Development and the European Consensus on Humanitarian Aid. In this way, development has been placed at the heart of EEAS external action.

The question nevertheless remains to what extent developmental goals will condition or be conditioned by foreign policy goals more generally. Intrinsic to this is the increased politicization of development that has occurred in recent years, notable in the stronger links being drawn between security and development. This was first articulated explicitly in the 2003 European Security Strategy drafted by the former CFSP High Representative, Javier Solana. As examined in Chapter 3, the 2005 mid-term review of Cotonou saw the fight against terrorism and weapons of mass destruction incorporated into the agreement's Article 11, while in 2007 the Council adopted a set of Conclusions on security and development calling for the nexus between the two to inform EU strategy and policy (Council of the EU 2007). Such a linkage raises the prospect that strategic considerations rather than developmental need may shape future development-related decisions, a prospect further reinforced by the establishment of an EEAS formally designed to bring foreign and development policy closer together.

Beyond the politicization associated with the securitization of development, it also remains to be seen whether foreign policy decisions will impinge upon developmental programmes. To what extent, for example, will decisions taken to discipline third countries – the imposition of sanctions – lead to similar reductions in development assistance? To what extent, in other words, will the needs of populations be sacrificed to the realities of state-level political engagement? On a related note, while the Lisbon reforms attempt to address the foreign policy–development nexus, what of the developmental impact of EU trade policy? To what extent will the new structures be able to influence the Directorate-General for Trade, or will needs in this case be subject to the realities of market competition? The past experience of the influence of DG Trade on shaping the Cotonou debate does not auger well.

Finally, what part will the division between the geographic competence of the EEAS and the thematic competence of DG-DEVCO play? Indeed, it is in the thematic areas that much of the meat of the EU's approach to poverty reduction is to be found. DG-DEVCO's thematic focus, for example, on 'investing in people' is essentially about human development, prioritizing inter alia health, education, gender equality, employment, social cohesion, children's rights and so on. With the EEAS responsible for strategic programming on a geographic basis, the potential arises for such horizontal thematic issues to be marginalized. This concern was only reinforced with the circulation in-house of the first EEAS organogram from October 2010, which made no reference to development (Gavas 2010). Alongside administrative and military coordination structures, the EEAS was divided into five geographic divisions and one 'multilateral thematic' division. This latter incorporated some development-related issues (human rights, gender), but development itself was absent. By the official publication of the EEAS transitional structure in January 2011, however, this oversight had been rectified, with a Development Cooperation Coordination office established within the Global and Multilateral Issues division of the

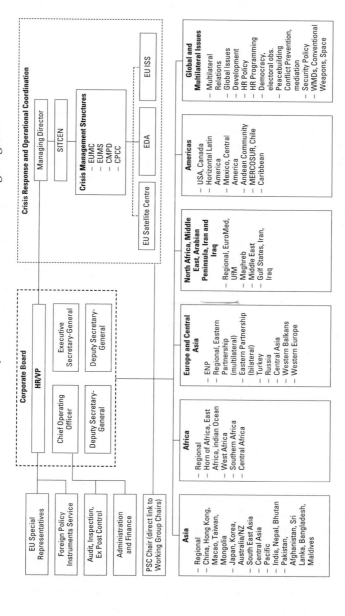

FIGURE 4.2 *European External Action Service organogram*

Note: ENP stands for European Neighbourhood Policy; UfM stands for Union for the Mediterranean.

now six-part structure. This shape and the place of development within it remained largely unaltered in the final iteration of the EEAS structure published in April 2011 (see Figure 4.2). Given the broad coverage of this division, the question remains as to how well development will be heard among a chorus of competing voices.

It is not yet clear how the centrality of development to external relations – established by the July Council Decision – will be realized. The initial structure established by the Council Decision involving as it did a rump DG-DEV raised the prospect that the development policy directorate would not possess the institutional weight necessary to make its voice heard in dialogue with the EEAS. The subsequent decision to link DG-DEV with EuropeAid will go some way in ensuring that its policy voice is not overshadowed in this way. To reinforce this influence, however, the transformation of DG-DEVCO could be taken a step further. As Santos (2009: 98) acknowledges, 'the World Bank enjoys a near-monopoly in intellectual debate on development, even though the Commission is well placed to put forward innovative ideas in this field and to strengthen the link between development research and policymaking'. Indeed, not since the early years of the Lomé Convention has the European Commission been seen as particularly innovative in its approach to development. With a significant step already taken in merging policy and implementation into a single DG, the time may also be ripe for further innovation. Having the ambition to transform the Directorate-General into an institution of excellence for development thinking would be a significant additional step in retaining its relevance, and in raising the profile of the EU as a global development actor.

Conclusion

This chapter has traced the institutional evolution that has structured EU development policy from the Maastricht to Lisbon Treaties and provides the necessary context against which the following geographically focused chapters can be better understood. The changing nature of the integration process over the last two decades has impacted significantly on both the institutional organization and priority given to development policy within Europe's external relations. While the treaties commit the EU to fostering global development – in the EU's words 'making the world a better place' – development policy has never taken central place in these successive reforms. Priorities closer to home – enlargement, the neighbourhood, monetary union, the single market – have shaped the nature of integration, and when looking outside the dominant paradigm has been CFSP. Consequently, development policy has had to adapt in order to remain relevant to the EU agenda. While it would be exaggerating to suggest the imminent demise of EU development policy, it would be equally foolhardy not to anticipate further changes in its nature and expression under the new and as yet largely untested environment of the Lisbon Treaty.

Chapter 5

Latin America: Exporting Regionalism

Despite the formalized relationship with the Caribbean, Latin America has always been on the fringes and marginal to Europe's mainstream development concerns. This distance is somewhat puzzling given the cultural, religious, historical and trading ties that exist. During the European Community's first decade Latin America was an equally important trading partner compared with Africa as a whole (and far more important than the Yaoundé states – accounting for roughly double the levels of imports and exports) (Holland 2002: 30). Many of the products that Europe sourced from Africa were available from Latin America, and supplies were arguably more secure. Further, Latin America seemed to provide a wealthier potential market for European export policy (Grilli 1993: 226–7). Why, then, the apparent neglect?

An explanation can be found in the historical context of the 1950s when the Community's evolving policies and interests were defined; and not in dispassionate economic analysis. Despite significant German and Italian migrant populations, the absence of a direct member state colonial heritage mitigated against creating a preferential-type framework. Consequently, largely on French insistence, Africa received initial preferential treatment. EU external relations in these formative years reflected, if on a larger scale, individual bilateral interests. A separate collective European perspective had not been established and in foreign relations priority was given to francophone concerns. As Chapter 2 outlined, the metamorphosis to wider ACP interests was, again, principally the result of a new bilateral concern, this time British. Similarly, the accession of Spain and Portugal to the Community in 1985 provided a new bilateral pressure, finally, this time for a more inclusive and formalized approach to European–Latin American relations.

Given the modest concessions originally given to the Yaoundé states the absence of a formalized cooperation agreement with Latin America should not be surprising. The first priority of the fledgling European Community was to generate internal economic cohesion and growth; external relations were very much of secondary importance and only given prominence if advocated by a leading member state – such as France. Italian attempts to promote relations with Latin America did not carry the same weight. For all third countries, the combination of a common EC external tariff and specific preferences for African states posed a real trading challenge. It has only been with the expanding ambitions of the EU to play an international role that a comprehensive approach to external relations has become evident. The 'neglect' of relations with Latin America – as well as with other regional groupings – was very much a consequence of the internal dynamics of European integration.

Furthermore, Europe's commercial intervention within the region was always confronted with the geopolitical reality of the USA. Even where South American states have sought to reduce their trade dependency on the USA, this reorientation has met with countervailing pressure from Washington. Consequently, asymmetry has typically characterized EU–Latin American relations: economic links have been underdeveloped compared to the greater importance given to political aspects of the relationship. As a result, during the 1980s Latin America was at the very bottom of the pyramid of privileges, outranked by the preferences offered to the ACP, the Mediterranean states, the Gulf and even ASEAN. In contrast, the 1980s process of democratization provided Europe with a platform on which to enhance a political relationship.

One reason why the EU was able to conduct a dialogue with the Yaoundé states was because they already had an institutional framework within which cooperation could be developed. In contrast, no such common institutional framework linked the various Latin American states together: a group-to-group dialogue did not exist. 'Latin America' as a term is not analytically that helpful, incorporating, as it does, some 17 states (Argentina, Bolivia, Brazil, Chile, Colombia, Costa Rica, El Salvador, Ecuador, Guatemala, Honduras, Mexico, Nicaragua, Panama, Paraguay, Peru, Uruguay and Venezuela). As the following discussion shows, the pan-continental approach is too unwieldy, with distinctions necessarily drawn between Central America, Southern America, the Rio Group and latterly MERCOSUR, which is discussed below. Whilst a number of initiatives have succeeded in establishing a framework for relations between the EU and regional subgroupings over the past two decades, almost all have failed to transform the relationship significantly. The inability of the Latin American countries themselves to agree on the principle of an FTA until the late 1990s was also an important impediment to institutionalizing relations. The following brief history focuses on the key developments.

Early relations

Italy was instrumental in initiating the EC's dialogue with Latin America. In 1969 the Commission issued its first-ever report on the relationship; and the so-called 'Brussels dialogue' began soon after (establishing regular meetings between the Latin American Ambassadors and EU officials in Brussels). The introduction of GSP provisions in 1971 also opened up the prospect of a fairer trading regime with Europe. More generally, 'the GSPs also marked the beginning of a rebalancing of the positions of Latin America and Asia in the hierarchy of trade privileges granted by the Community to developing countries' (Grilli 1993: 235). In contrast with this collective approach, bilateral relations with three Latin American countries – Argentina, Uruguay and Brazil – were established in the early 1970s. The mid-1970s also witnessed the introduction of European aid to the region (although historically per capita aid has mainly gone to Central American countries). However, these initiatives proved to be pyrrhic victories in the face of the signing of the first Lomé Convention in 1975. Whether rightly or wrongly, Europe gave the clear impression that Latin America was not to be included in their development strategy and could not expect preferential concessions. The accession of the UK reinforced Africa's privileged status, and by extending this favouritism to Latin America's Caribbean neighbours added insult to perceived injury.

A decade elapsed before a dialogue was effectively re-established and subregional frameworks created (subsequently the primary framework through which Europe would engage with the region). This signalled a renewed political interest in regional democratization as well as, obviously, the 1986 accession of Spain and Portugal and the consequent loss of privileged market access (thus mirroring the impact on Commonwealth countries of the UK's membership). Central to the European approach to the region in the early 1980s was a desire to establish a role distinct from that of the USA (Bretherton and Vogler 2006: 128), an approach embodied in the institutionalization in 1984 of the San José dialogue between the EU and the Contadora Group to promote regional conflict resolution. The San José process was significant for a number of reasons: it indicated the end of European acceptance of the Monroe Doctrine, it signalled a turning of the region towards Europe as a non-military and non-ideological interlocutor in Latin American affairs (Smith 1995) and it demonstrated a willingness to link political priorities with development assistance. An emphasis was subsequently placed on democratization and economic reform, but the most significant aspect has been European support for regional cooperation and integration. In many respects this is a reflection of Europe's belief in the benefits of regional integration for trade and particularly democratization – the entry of Greece (1981), Spain and Portugal (1986) and more recently the CEECs (2004–07) into the European architecture were all linked to the need to cement in place the democratic reforms that had just taken place in those countries.

The revitalization of the relationship was particularly evident during the 1990s as the idea of regionalism gained popularity across Latin America. The Treaty of Asunción establishing MERCOSUR brought together Argentina, Brazil, Paraguay and Uruguay in a project to create an outward-looking common market modelled on that of the EU, a stark divergence from the import substitution industrialization-based development models that had dominated the region during the 1960s and 1970s. MERCOSUR built on the earlier Treaty of Integration, Cooperation and Development which symbolized reconciliation between Brazil and Argentina and established the priorities of democratic consolidation and development. Alongside the launching of the Southern Common Market, the Andean Pact transformed in 1996 into the Andean Community and, following a two decade interregnum stemming from the 1969 'Football War' between Honduras and El Salvador, the Central American Common Market was relaunched in 1991. FTAs linking Colombia, Venezuela, Mexico and Chile were initiated and in 1998 the Andean Community and MERCOSUR completed a framework agreement with a view to creating a continental-wide free trade area. To supplement this, the EU concluded Association Agreements (incorporating FTAs) with Mexico in 1997 (which entered into force in 2000) and Chile in 2002 (which entered into force in 2005).

In terms of institutionalizing relations with the region, an initial cooperation agreement between the Community and the five Andean Pact countries (Bolivia, Colombia, Ecuador, Peru and

Venezuela) was signed in 1983 and extended into a more focused Framework Agreement of Cooperation a decade later. A Political Dialogue and Cooperation Agreement (covering familiar EU preoccupations such as good governance, immigration, transnational crime and terrorism) was subsequently signed in 2003, and updated in 2006 when Venezuela withdrew from the Andean Community, though this has yet to be ratified. Most recently negotiations for a comprehensive Association Agreement were launched in May 2007, organized around three pillars – political dialogue, cooperation and trade. Significantly negotiations were to go beyond issues covered in WTO talks, such as investment and intellectual property, and can be seen as an attempt to resurrect the 'Singapore Issues' advocated by the EU, Japan and South Korea but opposed by developing countries during the Doha Round negotiations (Allen and Smith 2008: 169). Negotiations, however, collapsed during the second half of 2008 and a new format was established as a mechanism for overcoming disagreements. Consequently, negotiations on political dialogue and cooperation are progressing at the regional level (updating the 2003 agreement) and separate multiparty trade negotiations were pursued with willing states – Colombia, Ecuador and Peru. These were concluded with Colombia and Peru in March 2010, with Ecuador having decided in July 2009 to suspend its participation in the process.

A similar array of interregional agreements has structured the relationship with the states of Central America (Costa Rica, El Salvador, Guatemala, Honduras, Nicaragua and Panama). A Cooperation Agreement with partner countries of the General Central American Economic Integration Treaty was signed in Luxembourg in 1985, specifically supplementing the San José priorities of conflict resolution, democratization and economic development with an emphasis on regional integration. This was superseded with the signing in San Salvador in 1993 of a Framework Cooperation Agreement. In 2003 a Political Dialogue and Cooperation Agreement was signed, though as with the Andean Community's this is yet to enter into force. Finally, negotiations for an EC–Central America Association Agreement were launched in June 2007, with Costa Rican and Panamanian participation dependent on their greater integration into the Central American Integration System. Negotiations were, however, suspended in 2009 prior to the scheduled eighth round in response to the removal of President Manuel Zelaya by the military and ongoing constitutional crisis in Honduras.

Of greatest regional significance was the 1992 Inter-Institutional Cooperation Agreement and the 1995 Interregional Framework Agreement signed with MERCOSUR, both of which were designed to strengthen regional political cooperation and lead to the progressive liberalization of trade (see discussion of MERCOSUR below). Cumulatively, these interregional developments symbolized Europe's 'rediscovery' of Latin America and underlined the region's efforts to liberalize, consolidate democratic institutions and embrace regional integration.

This consistent and progressive regional trend has helped to raise the profile and priority of Latin America from the EU's developing country perspective. However, MERCOSUR has increasingly become the EU's preferred framework for relations, arguably at the expense of the other Latin American cooperation agreements signed with the EU. MERCOSUR currently comprises 44 per cent of total EU exports to Latin America and 50 per cent of imports from Latin America (though this does represent a decline from 50 per cent of imports and 54 per cent of exports in 1996) (see Table 5.1). This has been accompanied by a significant decline in terms of the EU's balance of trade with the region from a surplus as high as €6.5 billion in 1998 to a deficit of almost €15 billion by 2008, though dropping to around €8 billion in 2009 as the financial crisis impacted on trade. The EU is MERCOSUR's main trading partner, accounting for 20 per cent of imports and exports in 2008, while MERCOSUR is far less significant for the Union, accounting for only 2.1 per cent of its imports and 1.8 per cent of exports in 2009 (making it the Union's eighth largest trading partner).

One consequence of this focus is that the EU's economic relationship with Latin America as a whole has mirrored the MERCOSUR relationship. The region's overall economic relationship at the end of the 1990s was comparatively fragile. Between 1990 and 1998, the percentage of Latin America's total exports going to the EU fell from 24 to 14 per cent and the EU share of Latin America's total imports decreased from 21 to 18 per cent. These figures have remained relatively steady since, with the EU accounting for 13.5 per cent of Latin American imports and 13.3 per cent of exports by 2009, compared with 33.9 and 36.8 per cent respectively for the USA. One consequence of this, again, has been a significant fluctuation in the balance of trade, from ECU 9.7 billion favouring Latin America in 1990 (Grisanti 2000: 6) to a peak flow of €13 billion towards the EU by 1998, and then, again, €19.2 billion in favour of

Table 5.1   *EU trade with Latin America, 1996–2009*
(€ billion)

	1996	1998	2000	2002	...	2007	2008	2009
EU imports								
CAN	4.6	4.9	5.1	5.9		10.3	11.3	9.3
Central America	2.3	2.9	4.3	3.8		4.7	5.3	4.6
MERCOSUR	14.9	18.1	23.6	24.1		42.6	48.2	35.1
Chile	3.2	3.5	5.1	4.8		12.5	11.3	7.4
Mexico	3.2	4.0	7.0	6.2		12.1	13.7	9.9
Venezuela	1.5	1.4	2.7	2.7		5.5	6.3	3.9
Total	**29.6**	**34.8**	**48.0**	**47.5**		**87.7**	**96.1**	**70.2**
EU exports								
CAN	3.7	4.5	3.6	3.9		5.8	7.0	6.0
Central America	2.4	3.1	3.7	3.8		5.3	5.1	4.2
MERCOSUR	18.6	24.6	23.9	18.3		28.2	33.5	27.2
Chile	2.7	3.3	3.5	3.1		4.8	5.1	4.5
Mexico	5.1	9.3	14.0	15.1		21.0	21.9	15.9
Venezuela	1.7	3.0	3.2	3.1		4.0	4.3	3.7
Total	**34.3**	**47.8**	**52.0**	**47.2**		**69.0**	**76.8**	**61.5**
Balance of trade								
CAN	−0.9	−0.4	−1.5	−2.0		−4.5	−4.3	−3.3
Central America	0.1	0.2	−0.6	0.0		0.6	−0.2	−0.4
MERCOSUR	3.7	6.5	0.3	−5.8		−14.4	−14.7	−7.9
Chile	−0.5	−0.2	−1.6	−1.7		−7.7	−6.2	−2.9
Mexico	1.9	5.3	7.0	8.9		8.9	8.2	6.0
Venezuela	0.2	1.6	0.5	0.4		−1.5	−2.0	−0.2
Total	**4.7**	**13.0**	**4.0**	**−0.3**		**−18.6**	**−19.2**	**−8.7**

Notes: CAN: Bolivia, Colombia, Ecuador, Peru; Central America: Costa Rica, El Salvador, Guatemala, Honduras, Nicaragua, Panama; MERCOSUR: Argentina, Brazil, Paraguay, Uruguay.

Latin America by 2008, dropping to €8.7 billion in 2009 as the financial crisis began to bite (Table 5.1). The conclusion of free trade Association Agreements with Mexico and Chile may potentially divert more trade from MERCOSUR, and evidence of this can already be seen – since 1996 Union exports to Mexico have increased from 15 per cent of the Latin American whole to 25 per cent, a period during which the MERCOSUR share has fallen from 54 to 44 per cent.

MERCOSUR

The delayed nature of the relationship with Latin America has meant that the debate on non-reciprocity that characterized Lomé has been bypassed in favour of adopting free trade as the starting point for discussion. The idea of establishing an EU–MERCOSUR FTA was first floated in 1994. The resultant 1995 Interregional Framework Cooperation Agreement paved the way, if cautiously and at a measured pace, for the debate on gradual and reciprocal trade liberalization with a view to creating an eventual free trade zone. It led in 2000 to the launching of negotiations for an ambitious EU–MERCOSUR Association Agreement, the centrepiece of which is a comprehensive FTA. The realization of an FTA was envisaged as a relatively long-term process with implementation commencing in 2005 at the earliest, with the prospect of 10–15 year transition periods for selected products (in line with WTO practice), though these expectations proved overly optimistic. This prolonged transition would also allow MERCOSUR to mature institutionally and for other frameworks for South American regional integration to emerge, as well as provide the EU with a further breathing space before implementing the required CAP reforms (Dauster 1998: 448). More generally, relations with MERCOSUR provide the EU with another avenue through which it can begin to extend and define a coherent global external policy (Bessa-Rodrigues 1999: 85): relations with Latin America (as well as those with Asia) constituted the key missing elements in the EU's international actor profile.

The economic arguments in favour of an FTA had been building throughout the previous decade during which time the EU had become MERCOSUR's largest trading partner and supplier of foreign direct investment (FDI), supplanting the USA's economic dominance in the Americas. For the EU, the proposed Latin American FTA did not signify any departure from the dominant economic philosophy of the 1990s: free trade is consistent with its global approach and international rivalry with the USA for trading dominance. Indeed, the prospect of a USA-led Free Trade Area of the Americas (FTAA), composed of a 34-country group from north to south proposed for the year 2005, was an additional motivation for the Europeans, who feared the diversionary trade impacts of such an arrangement. The FTAA concept has however been moribund since the last summit meeting in Argentina in 2005, having collapsed under the weight of disagreements over trade in services, intellectual property rights and agricultural subsidies (mirroring disagreements within the Doha Round).

For the five Latin American states, arguably, the FTA with the EU has a number of advantages. First, it provides a new economic option to the historical dependency on trade with the USA. Second, and consequentially, balance and diversity in the region's external relations may be enhanced. And third, such cooperation provides a further incentive towards the longer-term objective of South American regional integration.

Intentionally, no timetable deadline was set for completion of negotiations other than that implied by the parallel WTO discussions: the new Doha Round of global liberalization was initially set as a precondition for the FTA proposal. Yet WTO negotiations have been beset by disagreements between developed and developing nations, primarily concerning agriculture and intellectual property, meaning that the negotiations that were initially planned to conclude in December 2005 remain ongoing.

Progress towards the Association Agreement and consequent FTA has been slow. Particularly evident has been French reticence stemming from the possible agricultural implications of any such FTA for Europe's farmers. As the protracted discussions over an earlier South African FTA had shown, the CAP constitutes an impediment that often makes the EU an inflexible negotiating partner. The French government seems likely to weigh any global concessions made in the WTO context against any further special concessions towards South American free trade.

Impeding progress has not been the exclusive domain of European member states however. As FTA negotiations progressed, the MERCOSUR states, particularly Brazil, have themselves proved an obstacle to agreement, believing that the Doha Round offered better opportunities to liberalize trade in a form more tailored to their advantage (Vasconcelos 2007: 177). Further, the structure of

MERCOSUR, with integration that remains only shallow, undermines the ability to negotiate such ambitious agreements as strong member state priorities, combined with weak cooperative structures, limit the ability to define collective goals to be pursued in interregional negotiations (Doidge 2011: 155).

Under the weight of these ongoing disagreements, EU–MERCOSUR negotiations were suspended in 2004. Proposals for progressing discussions were put forward by both sides in November 2006, followed by suggestions that negotiations would resume in late 2007 (*La Prensa Gráfica* 2007); these were subsequently delayed again until May 2008 (*O Estado de S. Paolo* 2007), and by the end of 2009 negotiations had still not resumed. In mid-2009, however, there was again movement on the issue – following the lack of success in Doha Brazil became re-energized on the question of an EU–MERCOSUR FTA, though feared that failure to date in the WTO would translate into greater demands from the EU in interregional negotiations (Leo 2009) – and in May 2010 a decision was taken to officially restart negotiations. The question remains, however, as to whether the apparent failure of Doha will give added impetus to EU–MERCOSUR negotiations from 2010 onwards, leading to a successful conclusion of an FTA.

EU interest in MERCOSUR, however, goes beyond free trade to a greater partnership in the broader multilateral system. The two organizations share much of their basic DNA, the open integration process in MERCOSUR having been modelled on that of the EU. One consequence is that MERCOSUR is viewed by the European Commission and a number of member states as a potential political ally in the context of an increasingly multilateral global system (Teló 2007: 140), sharing many of its ideals on multipolarity, democracy, human rights, security and the environment. A strong interest therefore exists in consolidating and extending integration within MERCOSUR (see Doidge 2011: 156–9), enabling it to be a useful partner of the EU in the construction of the regime of rules, norms and institutions governing the global system, and to stand as a strong pillar within a multipolar structure. While the conclusion of a comprehensive Association Agreement, founded upon an FTA, can only strengthen such interregional political engagement, what remains unclear is the extent to which such an envisaged relationship can progress in its absence. Europe's focus on integration and capacity building in the region (see discussion below) must be understood in this context.

In summary, interregional cooperation between the EU and Latin America remains a long-term objective reflecting both a desire for liberalized market access and a degree of 'parity' with the USA regionally (Allen and Smith 1999: 102). While there is now an established cycle of formal meetings (with the San José Group, the Rio Group and Andean countries for example), one cannot but be struck by the comparative limitations of the relationship rather than its substantive impact, with fundamental disagreement over trade issues effectively undermining economic cooperation. In contrast with the architectural clarity of the EU–ACP relationship, the multiplicity of institutional frameworks also distracts from the coherence of EU–Latin American relations.

The aid dimension

Latin America has historically also been a low priority in the EU's aid framework. Not included among the associated OCTs referenced in the Treaty of Rome, or in their subsequent iterations as the Associated African States and Madagascar (under the Yaoundé Convention) and the ACP states (under Lomé and Cotonou), from 1974 Latin America became part of a new residual grouping known as the ALA, a bureaucratic invention that was initiated as a response to the acknowledged gap in European relations with non-ACP developing countries. This approach appeared to defy logic by grouping together a wide range of geographically and economically diverse recipients in Asia and Latin America under a single category, and is understandable only for what it was – a collection of the leftover developing countries. For the very worst reasons pertaining to Eurocentric administrative compartmentalization, it initially combined eight Central American states, ten from South America, six from South East Asia, six from South Asia, four from the Middle East, Central and East Asia, and three from Africa.

Evolution of the aid relationship

The EC's aid relationship with Latin America preceded formal development relations with the region. This took the form of food aid, one of the few Community development aid instruments (alongside disaster relief) that could be applied to non-associated developing countries. EC food aid was first provided under the 1967 Wheat Trade Agreement signed in Rome after the Kennedy Round of

GATT, part of the response to the ongoing food crisis in the developing world. With an initial budget of US$20 million, the Community's commitments had increased to US$273 million by 1975, with the majority of aid going to Asia. Of the 1.8 million tonnes of cereals distributed between 1968 and 1974, for example, 44.5 per cent went to Asia, with only 4.5 per cent finding its way to Latin America, compared with 16.2 per cent for Africa (Commission 1974: 28). India and Bangladesh were the primary recipients of food aid, receiving 6.5 and 6.4 per cent, while no state from Latin America ranked in the top ten (Cox and Koning 1997: 6).

While allowing the Community to expand its assistance beyond the associated states, the food aid programme suffered from the problems of short-termism (being dependent on European agricultural surpluses) and an acknowledged lack of policy coherence (Commission 1971: 14), one of the factors that led to calls for reform of European relations with the developing world. From 1971 to 1972, the piecemeal nature of the Community's international assistance, including the exclusion of Latin America, Asia and the Mediterranean, became the subject of discussion within the Commission, with the publication of the 'Memorandum on a Community Policy for Development Co-operation' (Commission 1971) as well as a *Programme for Initial Actions* (Commission 1972). Debate subsequently took place in the EP and the Council – the first such meeting of development ministers in EC history – before the Paris Summit of October 1972 lay down a set of general policy directives providing the political basis for an EC development policy.

Among the first direct outcomes of this process was the introduction of annual programming alongside ad hoc policy formulation in the aid relationship with non-associated developing countries, financing directly from the EC budget and an emphasis on humanitarian (especially emergency) aid. This led to increases in the quantity of food aid, of which Asia remained the primary beneficiary, though with an increasing proportion going to Latin America – by the 1980s, Nicaragua, Bolivia and Honduras had joined Bangladesh, India and Pakistan as the main recipients.

Of significantly more importance for Latin America, the reform process begun by the 1972 Summit Declaration also led to the establishment of a programme of Financial and Technical Assistance to the ALA states. This was formally launched in July 1974 with the passage of a Council Resolution confirming the principle of extending Community assistance to non-associated developing countries.

In 1975 the Commission presented to the Council an action programme on financial and technical assistance to non-associated developing countries, identifying potential areas of activity in food production and rural development, trade and emergency aid. Already clear at this early stage was the priority to be accorded to measures supporting and promoting regional integration, with the action programme placing emphasis on this. Initially, however, assistance (given in the form of grants) was something of a token gesture, with an endowment of only 20 million EUA (Grilli 1993: 254). In 1977, a draft regulation defining the core principles under which the Financial and Technical Assistance programme would operate was proposed by the Commission and provisionally accepted by the Council. These were:

- improving the living conditions of the poorest;
- a focus on rural development, and particularly food production;
- encouraging regional projects; and
- the allocation of a proportion of aid to deal with humanitarian crises and disaster relief.

From 1978, financial and technical assistance was carried out in accordance with these core principles, though they were not formally adopted until passage of the 1981 *Council Regulation on Financial and Technical Aid to Non-Associated Developing Countries* (Council 1981).

Between 1976 and 1991, the budget allocation for financial and technical assistance to the ALA states rose from its initial 20 million EUA to ECU 357 million, with a total of ECU 2.9 billion being allocated over the entire period. This is to be compared with the total development aid allocations to the ALA of ECU 5.5 billion (with total ODA rising to ECU 6.4 billion when economic cooperation and humanitarian aid are included). Financial and technical assistance therefore accounted for more than 50 per cent of development aid allocations to Latin America and Asia (45 per cent of all ALA aid allocations), with the remainder comprised of food aid and support given to NGOs operating in the regions (Commission 1994: 29). Latin America accounted for 29.7 per cent of allocations for ordinary projects during this period, with 67.8 per cent going to Asia and 2.5 per cent to other countries in Africa and the Middle East. Nevertheless, the Latin American quota was on the increase towards the end of the period, rising from 30 per cent in 1987 to 41 per cent by 1991.

Assistance was given to 13 Latin American states between 1976 and 1991: five South American states (Bolivia, Colombia, Ecuador, Paraguay and Peru), six from Central America (Costa Rica, El Salvador, Guatemala, Honduras, Nicaragua and Panama) and two Caribbean island states (Dominican Republic and Haiti). Bolivia was the main beneficiary, receiving 3.4 per cent of overall assistance to the ALA states, followed by Peru (3.0 per cent), Honduras (2.2 per cent), Nicaragua (1.8 per cent), Guatemala (1.4 per cent) and Costa Rica (1.2 per cent). The remaining Latin American states received less ALA financial assistance than did the single African state of Mozambique (1.1 per cent). Broadly speaking, commitments corresponded to the Commission's prioritizing of the poorest countries, though with some notable exceptions: Haiti, the poorest of the 13 (with a GNP per capita of only US$370), fell in the middle of the group as far as assistance received, with ECU 3.9 per capita, while Costa Rica, one of the wealthiest (with a GNP per capita of US$1,850), received some of the highest assistance at ECU 10.6 per capita.

The sectoral distribution of assistance to Latin America conformed to the priorities elaborated in 1977. The agricultural sphere was the focus of the majority of financial commitments over the 1976–91 period. Nevertheless, also evident was a gradual move away from this initial focus as beneficiaries increasingly made their wants and needs known, and as the EC increasingly tried to respond to emerging priorities (e.g. those associated with the emerging neoliberal economic consensus). Between 1976 and 1987, 75 per cent of commitments were directed towards agricultural projects. By 1991 this had dropped to 45 per cent. Increasingly prominent was institutional development, credit for agro-industrial activities, fisheries, support for economic restructuring, and rural microprojects (rather than the rural infrastructure, irrigation and development projects that had previously dominated) (Commission 1994: 14).

Also particularly notable in financial and technical assistance to Latin America was the emphasis on regional coordination. As the Commission acknowledged, 'in Latin America, the largest beneficiary countries are the ones associated in some form of integration because of the EEC special concern with that policy' (Commission 1990: 14). Around 40 per cent of financial and technical assistance to Latin America and 34 per cent of economic cooperation (a combined total of 26 per cent of all ODA to Latin America) was targeted at regional projects and institutions, most notably the Andean Pact and the Central American Common Market. This is to be compared with Asia where only 4 per cent of financial and technical assistance, though 25 per cent of economic cooperation, was committed at the regional level (3.7 per cent of all ODA). Resources were particularly targeted at strengthening regional institutions such as the Secretariat of the Andean Community, increasing its capacity to perform those functions allocated to it (potentially leading to spillover effects and further integration according to neofunctionalist explanations).

On 25 February 1992 a new Council Regulation on Financial and Technical Assistance to, and Economic Cooperation with, the Developing Countries in Asia and Latin America was adopted. It reflected both the range of priorities incorporated into the new Maastricht Treaty and subsequent Council Resolutions which sought to prioritize and expand ALA aid in line with other EU development activities, and responded to a range of identified shortcomings in ALA assistance to date, including the short-termism associated with annual programming, the ad hocism and lack of strategy in sectoral allocations of assistance, the lack of a sense of ownership of programmes by recipient states, the need to recognize the variation between ALA states, and the new developmental context in which these states found themselves. In particular, the 1992 Council Regulation broadened aid objectives to include human rights, gender, democratization, good governance and environmental issues in the main policy objective of poverty eradication, and placed a far greater emphasis on economic cooperation. In addition, supporting regional integration was again defined as a priority area for financial and technical assistance. Two strands of assistance were now envisaged under the ALA Regulation: (i) development aid to assist the poorest peoples and countries; and (ii) economic cooperation for those countries and regions with the potential for economic growth (Commission 1994: 4). Further, the ALA regulation introduced five-year programming cycles, embodied in the new Country Strategy Paper. Since 1992 significant effort has been directed towards engaging recipient states in the preparation of these strategy papers, a reflection of increased emphasis on participation and ownership in development more generally.

Despite the relatively low priority afforded the region, EU commitments to Latin America increased steadily during the 1990s, rising from just over €220 million in 1990 to around €500 million by the end of the decade. This must be taken in the context of the pressures on external aid programmes experienced by developed states in the years following the end of the Cold War as domestic publics demanded reductions in spending. Between 1990 and 1999, for example, assistance from EU member states to Latin America fell some 35 per cent from €1.7 billion to €1.1 billion. Unlike the member states, Commission budget allocations seem to have been somewhat insulated from public opinion, a side-effect perhaps of the lack of popular engagement with the integration process in general. This relatively positive picture of EU assistance, however, was undermined by ongoing problems of disbursal. During the 1990s, payments averaged only 67 per cent of commitments, an issue that was to become increasingly highlighted in evaluations of EC aid performance.

Commitments to Latin America dropped significantly in 2000 to only €352 million, with shrinking funding and implementation problems leading to questions being raised in the EP concerning the apparent scaling down of cooperation with the region (*Official Journal* 2001). In the following years commitments recovered to the levels of the late 1990s, before dipping again in 2004 (Table 5.2). ODA allocations continued to be broadly in-line with the Commission's prioritizing of the poorest countries, though still with notable exceptions. From 2000 to 2006, Uruguay and Panama, among the top third of Latin American countries in terms of GNI per capita (on a purchasing power parity – PPP – basis), were also among the top half of recipients of EC ODA per capita (receiving €9.8 and €8.3), while Paraguay, among the poorest, was in the bottom half of recipients (€7.3 per capita). Uruguay and Panama also rank highly in terms of HDI, being among the top six Latin American states. Brazil, which falls in the upper half of the range for GNI per capita – but which is characterized by massive income disparities, a fact highlighted by the Commission in its 2000 communication on *The European Community's Development Policy* (Commission 2000g: 19) – was at the bottom of the ODA list, receiving only €0.5 per capita. Overall, North and Central America benefited to a greater extent than the South, receiving €5.9 per capita compared with €2.9, despite having a higher PPP GNI at $10,666 compared to $9,293 (Table 5.3).

Table 5.2 *EU ODA commitments and disbursements to Latin America (managed by EuropeAid and other DGs), 2000–09 (€ million)*

	2000		2002		2004		2006		2007		2008		2009	
	Com.	Dis.	Com.	Dis.	Com.	Dis.	Com.	Dis.	Com.	Dis.	Com.	Dis.	Com.	Dis.
North and Central America (bilateral)	72.7	113.7	104.9	129.3	100.4	142.1	169.9	163.3	57.5	151.1	99.3	108.5	152.1	110.6
South America (bilateral)	137.5	132.5	223.8	158.6	196.7	138.5	202.4	228.7	260.7	275.6	279.7	259.2	219.3	290.9
Regional	146.9	45.7	337.5	87.4	79.0	117.7	102.4	95.5	234.2	138.6	105.3	141.8	99.8	106.5
Latin America total	**352.3**	**289.6**	**540.7**	**338.4**	**368.4**	**393.0**	**425.6**	**477.6**	**486.3**	**518.2**	**401.6**	**458.9**	**446.3**	**474.2**
% dispersal		82.2		62.6		106.7		112.2		106.6		114.3		106.3
EU ODA Total (€ billion)	7.1	4.0	6.5	5.9	7.5	6.9	9.8	8.1	9.9	8.5	12.0	9.2	11.8	9.9

Notes: North and Central America: Costa Rica, El Salvador, Guatemala, Honduras, Mexico, Nicaragua and Panama; South America: Argentina, Bolivia, Brazil, Chile, Colombia, Ecuador, Paraguay, Peru, Uruguay and Venezuela.
Source: EuropeAid Annual Report, various editions.

The precise sectoral allocation of assistance in the post-1992 period reflected the changed emphasis of the ALA Regulation with a focus on long-term and sustainable development and economic modernization. Evident, for example, was a new focus on food security rather than food aid, a result of the new Food Aid Regulation of 1996 which introduced greater flexibility into funding allocations. Financial and technical assistance was increasingly targeted at urban projects (particularly the informal sector), gender rights (including the full participation of women in development), education and training (most notably capacity building for regional institutions and university exchanges) and environmental protection (the ALA Regulation having set aside 10 per cent for environmental projects for the 1991–95 period) (Commission, 1995). Economic cooperation reflected to a greater extent than previously the interests of Latin American countries, with the emergence of programmes targeted at small and medium enterprises (AL-Invest) and closing the digital divide (@las). Of particular note during the lifetime of the 1992 ALA Regulation has been the greater commitment of assistance to projects aimed at improving social cohesion, Latin America having remained the most inequitable region in the world. By 2004, social cohesion funds accounted for 60 per cent of total commitments to the region (EuropeAid 2005: 80). Regional projects also remained at the core of the EU's approach to Latin America. While regional allocations dipped in the early 1990s, they had recovered by the end of the decade, accounting for 23 per cent of all commitments in 1998 and 19 per cent in 1999 (Commission 2002a: 33–4) (see discussion below).

Since the turn of the millennium, the aid relationship with Latin America has again undergone significant transformation, a response to the debates on effectiveness and coherency that had emerged from the mid-1990s as Lomé was undergoing renegotiation. In June 1995 the Council of Ministers ordered an evaluation of EU assistance to the ALA states, with the final report received in 1999. In-line with assessments of ACP and Mediterranean programmes, the report highlighted problems with project implementation – particularly delays and poor project management – often traceable to the inflexibility of financing agreements, ongoing project sustainability, transparency and accountability, and with the Maastricht Treaty principles of coordination, complementarity and coherence (Commission 1999).

The subsequent reform process that took place during 2000–05 culminated for the ALA states in the 2006 Financing Instrument for

Table 5.3 GNI, HDI and ODA commitments to Latin America, 2000–09

	GNI		GNI (PPP)		HDI	Cumulative total 2000–06 (1992 ALA Regulation)			2007–09 (2006 DCI)		
	(US$ billion)	Per capita (US$)	(US$ billion)	Per capita (US$)		ODA (€ millions)	ODA per capita	Ranking of ODA per capita	ODA (€ millions)	ODA per capita	Ranking of ODA per capita
North and Central America											
Costa Rica	27.5	6,060	49.6	10,950	0.846	34.42	6.9	10	8.72	1.7	12
El Salvador	21.4	3,480	40.9	6,670	0.735	135.72	22.6	3	51.48	8.6	5
Guatemala	36.6	2,680	64.2	4,690	0.689	130.66	9.3	6	66.74	4.8	8
Honduras	13.0	1,800	28.0	3,870	0.700	203.90	29.1	2	81.00	11.6	1
Mexico	1,061.4	9,980	1,517.2	14,270	0.829	67.370	0.6	16	21.35	0.2	16=
Nicaragua	6.1	1,080	14.9	2,620	0.710	270.10	45.0	1	68.87	11.5	2
Panama	21.0	6,180	39.5	11,650	0.812	24.89	8.3	7=	10.74	3.6	9
Total	1,187.0	8,074	1,754.3	11,934		867.06	5.9		308.90	2.1	

Cumulative total

	GNI		GNI (PPP)		HDI	2000–06 (1992 ALA Regulation)			2007–09 (2006 DCI)		
	(US$ billion)	*Per capita (US$)*	*(US$ billion)*	*Per capita (US$)*		*ODA (€ millions)*	*ODA per capita*	*Ranking of ODA per capita*	*ODA (€ millions)*	*ODA per capita*	*Ranking of ODA per capita*
South America											
Argentina	287.2	7,200	559.2	14,020	0.869	76.07	1.9	15	19.46	0.5	15
Bolivia	14.1	1,460	40.1	4,140	0.695	222.90	22.3	4	112.32	11.2	3
Brazil	1,411.2	7,350	1,932.9	10,070	0.800	102.54	0.5	17	37.99	0.2	16=
Chile	157.5	9,400	222.4	13,270	0.867	57.61	3.4	13	25.50	1.5	13
Colombia	207.4	4,660	379.1	8,510	0.791	271.37	6.0	11	100.44	2.3	11
Ecuador	49.1	3,640	104.7	7,760	0.772	108.05	8.3	7=	85.24	6.6	7
Paraguay	13.6	2,180	30.0	4,820	0.755	43.65	7.3	9	63.26	10.5	4
Peru	115.0	3,990	230.0	7,980	0.773	110.99	3.8	12	100.08	3.5	10
Uruguay	27.5	8,260	41.8	12,540	0.852	29.22	9.8	5	20.78	6.9	6
Venezuela	257.8	9,230	358.6	12,830	0.792	75.27	2.7	14	20.91	0.7	14
Total	2,540.4	6,632	3,898.8	10,180		1,097.67	2.9		585.98	1.5	

Sources: EuropeAid Annual Report (various editions), UNDP (2009), World Bank (2010b).

Development Cooperation. This constituted a significant rationalization of the EU's financing instruments for development, with external assistance now governed by only three – the ENPI (managed by DG External Relations) for Eastern Europe and the Mediterranean, the EDF (managed by DG-DEV) for the ACP states, and the DCI (managed by DG External Relations) for all non-associated countries – rather than in excess of 30 legal instruments as had previously been the case (EuropeAid 2005: 25) (of course, as discussed in Chapter 4, responsibility for these funding instruments has again been the subject of debate during the establishment of the EEAS). The DCI's stated priorities are promoting social cohesion and regional integration.

Also important has been the emergence of Budget Support into the EU's development assistance to Latin America, beginning with Nicaragua and subsequently also applied to Bolivia, El Salvador, Honduras and Paraguay. From 2003 to 2007 such support averaged €67million per year, with €166 million allocated in 2008 (EuropeAid 2009: 109) and €158 million in 2009 (EuropeAid 2010: 98). Indeed, the Commission is now defining the approach as 'the preferred instrument of cooperation with Latin America' (EuropeAid 2009: 109). This constitutes a significant transformation in aid delivery, involving the transfer of assistance directly to the general or sectoral budget of the recipient state. Such a process has gained increasing prominence in the development community over recent years, being seen as a means of reducing fragmentation of aid activities and increasing project sustainability, accelerating the disbursal of funding, promoting policy coherence, reinforcing recipient financial and bureaucratic structures and increasing their accountability to domestic publics, and enhancing country ownership of development projects. While no specifically European evaluation of general budget support programmes has yet been undertaken, the Commission participated in a joint evaluation with other bilateral and multilateral donors in 2006 which delivered an overall positive outlook, citing budget support as having been 'a relevant response to certain acknowledged problems in aid effectiveness' (IDD and Associates 2006: 15).

It is still too soon to make an assessment of the impact of the changes introduced in the DCI and the emergence of budget support on the provision of assistance to Latin America, though one positive point may be noted. While the ratio of payments to commitments for 2000–06 was relatively high at 88 per cent, for 2007–09 it stands at 109 per cent (a trend traceable back to 2005). Is this a turning point in the administration of Community aid, or is it, as seems more likely, simply the follow-on effect of a general decline in aid commitments to the region since 2002 and the logical process of catch-up in disbursements as allocated funding makes its way through the system?

Integration

While regional projects have always been a major component of Europe's aid programme with Latin America, evident since 2000 has been a preference for programmes targeted more directly at promoting and reinforcing regional integration itself, exporting the EU's own model. Here, the striking contrast is with Asia where perspectives on regional integration consciously distance themselves from following the EU model, preferring instead to use the European experience as an informative reference point from which to draw both positive and negative lessons. Successful integration arrangements in Latin America are increasingly seen as instrumental to the political and economic policy objectives of the EU.

From 2000, in-line with the strategic partnership decisions taken at the first EU–Latin American and Caribbean (EU–LAC) summit convened in Rio de Janeiro in 1999, regional projects garnered an increased share of ODA commitments (Table 5.2), accounting for 36 per cent of all assistance to Latin America between 2000 and 2006 (peaking at 61 per cent in 2002). Particularly evident has been an overt engagement in capacity building and training as a means for supporting and promoting integration in Central America, the Andean Community and MERCOSUR.

At the EU–LAC summits in Madrid in 2002 and Guadalajara in 2004, the Union explicitly linked the conclusion of an EU–Central America Association Agreement with progress in regional integration. In keeping with this objective, Regional Strategy Papers for 2002–06 and 2007–13 have defined supporting the integration process as their primary objective. As a consequence, while only 5 per cent of assistance to Central America between 1984 and 2000 directly supported integration, the allocation for the 2002–06 period was 60 per cent. Projects included a Customs Union Support Programme in 2001, a Programme of Support to Central American Integration (PAIRCA) in 2003 to build the capabilities of regional institutions (with PAIRCA II launched in 2008), and a Programme of Support to the Design and Application of Central American Common Policies in 2005, among others. The indicative work programme for 2007–13 allocates approximately 25 per cent of funding to strengthening regional institutions, 60 per cent to consolidating the customs union and common policies, and 15 per cent to regional governance and security matters.

Supporting integration is also at the core of regional strategies for the Andean Community, though more limited in scope than with Central America, with a lower level of funding being allocated to regional cooperation, and other sectoral issues – such as the trade in illicit drugs – attracting attention. Resources have been directed to technical assistance and institution building in the Andean Secretariat, and to a lesser extent the Court of Justice and other associated institutions. Of particular importance has been assistance directed towards the establishment of an Andean common market, including programmes for customs cooperation (Granadua), common standards and technical regulations (Calidad) and the harmonization of competition rules (Competencia). More recently, in 2008 the EU launched a Regional Economic Integration Programme for the Andean Community to harmonize border controls on intra-regional trade. The shallowness of Andean integration is increasingly seen to have limited engagement between the two regions, with the Union now recognizing that if cooperation is to progress, and the Andean Community is to be a useful partner for the EU, then its level of integration needs to be significantly advanced.

MERCOSUR, too, is the focus of EU integrative efforts, with institutional and market integration at the heart of the Union's strategy. From 1992 to 2002, 56 per cent (approximately €28 million) of assistance to the region was targeted at economic integration, intra-regional cooperation and institution building, with the remainder going to trade promotion. Notably, this included capacity building for the MERCOSUR Secretariat, seeking to transform the institution from a purely administrative organization into one capable of a technical policy role, thus moving it one small step along the path of the Commission model. From 2002, emphasis was placed on further integration and the creation of a common market as being preconditions for a future Association Agreement with the EU. A slight shift in funding was evident, with 70 per cent (around €33.5 million) for 2002–06 targeted at support and promotion of integration, and the remainder going to civil society engagement. This level of funding remains largely unchanged for 2007–13 with priorities being promoting the further institutionalization of MERCOSUR and the completion to the common market.

Conclusion

To summarize, the EU's development relationship with Latin America has undergone profound changes since its inception. Initially an afterthought, the relationship between the two has slowly evolved as the Union has attempted progressively to remedy evident shortcomings. The introduction in 1971 of GSP provision introduced greater balance into the place of Latin America (and Asia) in the Community's relations with the developing world, though Commission proposals in 2011 to halve the number of GSP recipients will impact on Latin American countries greatly, with Brazil evidencing particular concern (Willis 2011a). Beyond this, the launching of a programme of Financial and Technical Assistance in 1974 (codified in the 1981 FTA Regulation) established a formal basis for the aid relationship, though it still suffered from short-termism, lack of ownership and the absence of a clear strategy, with assistance disbursed over a wide range of sectors. The 1992 ALA Regulation subsequently introduced five-year programming cycles to provide a longer-term view and defined development priorities in line with the Maastricht Treaty. Nevertheless, it too suffered from continuing problems with aid disbursal, project implementation and the familiar three 'Cs' of coordination, coherence and complementarity. Most recently, the 2006 DCI, with its rationalization of financing instruments, accompanied by the move towards budget support, have sought to rectify these problems.

Also evident, particularly since 2000, has been the increasing use of aid to support specific foreign and economic policy objectives of the EU in Latin America. This has been tied intimately to the push towards ambitious regional Association Agreements anchored on free trade. After an initial period of frantic activity at the turn of the millennium, progress with each of the three regions subsequently stalled. The EU's strategy towards Latin America is constrained both by the level of integration in MERCOSUR, Central America and the Andean Community, and by the willingness of the sides to make concessions on matters such as agriculture and intellectual property rights. This situation is likely to continue until capability catches up with ambition. The refocusing of regional assistance, therefore, on projects designed to address precisely this issue, encouraging and promoting deeper integration modelled on the EU's own experience, may be seen as an investment in the future of EU–Latin America relations. Whether integration can progress, or whether conflicting viewpoints among Latin American states will undermine this possibility, remains to be seen.

Chapter 6

Asia: From Development to Dialogue

As with Latin America, development has been a low priority in EU relations with Asia. Rather, economic considerations have predominated – the exigencies of trade and competition have historically trumped all other issues, including development. Reflecting this, the Union's relations with the region have primarily focused on East and South East Asia, structured largely through the frameworks of the EU–ASEAN relationship and the ASEM process. What follows is an overview of the emergence and content of these structures and the apparent recent inclusion onto the ASEM agenda of a new development focus. Finally, consideration is given to the aid dimension in EU–Asia relations, the poor cousin to the economic relationship.

Asia: beginning a dialogue

In keeping with the EU's peculiar segmentation of the developing world, it is revealing that the ASEM, which established a regular forum for dialogue, was only established as late as 1996. Prior to this, in comparison with the ACP states and even Latin America, Asian development was not a policy priority and was accorded little recognition. This peripheral relationship was all the more puzzling given that Asia has a shared colonial history with many other parts of the developing world. France, Great Britain, Portugal, Spain and the Netherlands all had post-colonial links to the region, creating a network of interests that straddled India, Indochina and Indonesia. In addition to the shared cultural aspects of language, much of Asia could also provide a similar range of agricultural and tropical goods that were originally supplied by the Yaoundé and latterly ACP states. Contrary to the evidence of hindsight, from the perspective of the 1950s, Asia seemed a less appealing partner than Africa or Latin America. It was geographically remote, generally poor, comparatively diverse, and regarded as a less reliable supplier of the raw materials needed by Europe (if largely because of the Cold War context of Soviet and Chinese regional influence). The original six members of the 1957 EEC considered the influence of the UK in the region as a further disincentive. Commonwealth ties and the pervasive influence of the English language served to convey the impression that many parts of Asia remained British domains. At the simplest level, it came down to a question of priorities. The fledgling Community had modest resources and limited external ambition. The importance of francophone Africa initially precluded all other options, including ties with Asia. By the time of UK membership, the Asian context had changed considerably and it was already becoming apparent that Asia had become an export competitor for Europe rather than a dependent partner in need of assistance. Thus despite the strong ties between the UK and the Indian subcontinent in particular, no Asian country was permitted to join the Lomé Convention. This missed opportunity essentially confined Asia–EU relations to the lowest of priorities for the next two decades.

During this period European policy became fragmented and lacked any clearly articulated overall Asian strategy other than a rationale based around a particular economic advantage, a situation that continues to influence relations today. In a sense, this was an inevitable and appropriate response and reflected the increasingly disparate nature of Asia as an economic grouping. Europe's relations could be located along a continuum running from benevolent humanitarianism to competitive disinterest along which three distinct groups could be identified. To the one extreme, South Asia (including India, Pakistan and Bangladesh) remained economically underdeveloped and eligible for European humanitarian aid but not for preferential trade arrangements. Towards the middle of the continuum were those countries (largely the then ASEAN group of Indonesia, Malaysia, Thailand and the Philippines) that had begun to develop complementary economies to Europe and who shared a broad political (anti-communist) agenda. To the other extreme the newly industrialized countries (NICs) of East Asia (such as Taiwan, Hong Kong, Singapore and South Korea) began to pose a real and increasingly competitive threat to key areas of European production. This economic growth made the NICs incompatible with the non-reciprocal philosophy that shaped Lomé in the early 1970s (Grilli 1993: 271–2). During the 1970s and 1980s this continuum became polarized as a larger number of countries progressed to the

NIC camp. Consequently, these states were largely excluded by definition from Europe's development perspective and, without any
issues of conflict or strong advocates to promote their cause,
Europe–Asia relations largely continued in the form of benign
neglect.

Although pragmatism was a common link in European attitudes
towards these three Asian groupings, there were policy differences
in Europe's relations with South Asia, ASEAN and the NICs. Grilli
(1993: 276) characterized Europe's posture towards South Asia as
'mildly sympathetic ... with minimal effective involvement in terms
of economic assistance'. Under the 1971 GSP regime three South
Asian states were categorized as least developed and gained the best
market access – even if their export potential meant that they could
take little advantage of the concessions. Other bilateral commercial
cooperation agreements were subsequently signed during the 1970s
with India, Sri Lanka, Pakistan and Bangladesh – but only on the
MFN basis giving no special preferences. Of course, direct aid was
provided outside these agreements for rural development to
promote both food supply and food security. The bulk of European
aid to Asia was concentrated on South Asia within which India
increasingly dominated. However, aid to South Asia only represented around 7 per cent of the total European aid budget, and in
absolute and relative terms bilateral aid from member states was
more important. As Grilli noted, 'with more than two and a half
times the population of sub-Saharan Africa and a substantially
lower per capita income, South Asia received five times less financial
aid from the Community during 1976–88' (ibid.: 280). Given the
concentration of the world's poor in South Asia it remains to be seen
how the EU's renewed MDG priority of poverty alleviation can be
directed towards the region without diminishing efforts made elsewhere, especially in Africa. However, unless poverty eradication in
Asia is given the same priority as it is in EU–Africa relations, the EU
is unlikely to meet its self-imposed treaty obligations or persuade
many that its policy framework is either appropriate or effective.

The Association of Southeast Asian Nations

Origins and indifference

Launched with the signing of the Bangkok Declaration in 1967,
ASEAN had by 1999 grown from its five original members to

include all ten South East Asian countries, with the potential inclusion of an eleventh – East Timor – in the coming years (it was recognised as an ASEAN Observer in 2002, joined the ASEAN Regional Forum in 2005, acceded to the Treaty of Amity and Cooperation in 2007 and expects to become a full member by 2012).

The emergence of ASEAN foreshadowed a shift in relations between Europe and South East Asia from bilateralism to an interregional basis, a process that was eventually initiated by the Association at their Fourth Ministerial Meeting in 1971. The ASEAN move was a response to the pending accession of the UK to the EC which would lead to the effective dismantling of the Commonwealth system of trade preferences of which Malaysia and Singapore were beneficiaries. After a decade of discussions concerning the structure the relationship should take, EC–ASEAN links were finally formalized in 1980 with the conclusion of a region-to-region agreement, the EC–ASEAN Economic and Commercial Cooperation Agreement. In terms of institutional structures, annual Joint Cooperation Committee meetings are held and every 18 months ministerial-level political dialogues are convened. The major contemporary focus for political dialogue is through the ASEAN Regional Forum that was established in 1994 to promote regional peace and stability. It remains Asia's only collective security arrangement and the EU participates as a full member. Nevertheless, the EU–ASEAN relationship has been primarily economic, dominated by issues related to trade and market access. Development, so far as it has been considered, was very much an adjunct of the economic relationship, with the underlying assumption that poverty was best tackled through economic growth.

The formalization of the EC–ASEAN Cooperation Agreement disguised the fact that little substantive change was initially implemented and normal GSP levels remained the extent of preferential treatment (McMahon 1998: 235). A number of ASEAN countries began to lose even this advantage for specific products as they were 'graduated' out of the system during the 1990s. For most tropical agricultural products, however, ASEAN exports remained disadvantaged by pre-existing Lomé preferences. The signing of a series of bilateral trade and cooperation agreements between 1982 and 1987 with Indonesia, China, Thailand, Singapore, Malaysia, South Korea and the Philippines, and with Vietnam in 1994, largely served to confirm the status quo (van Reisen 1999: 138). However, the value of EU–ASEAN two-way trade continued to increase annually, from a low of ECU 22.4 billion in 1988 to more than three times this figure at ECU 71.3 billion by 1995. The EU had become ASEAN's second largest export market and third largest trading partner (after Japan and the USA). This, however, was attributable to ASEAN's export-oriented development strategy (and consequent high growth rates) and a favourable business climate, rather than to any value-added from the EC–ASEAN relationship. Indeed, relations between the two in this period have been characterized as one of 'asymmetrical indifference' (Rüland 2001a), an indifference characteristic of the EU approach to the broader Asian region.

This history of European indifference ended with the 1994 Commission document *Towards a New Asia Strategy*. The motivation was both internal and external, but again primarily economic. Clearly, Asia represented a striking omission in the EU's profile as the world's leading trading power. There was also a 'credibility gap' in EU relations with Asia that the strategy document sought to address. The economic opportunities that Asia presented, especially in the post-1989 context, were consistent with the EU's global economic agenda and newfound devotion to trade liberalization, if admittedly they were primarily motivated by the fear that Europe stood 'to lose out on the economic miracle taking place there because of the strong competition from Japan and the United States' (Commission 1994b: 17). A more coherent and regionally sophisticated European response to Asia was long overdue. The policy objectives were to increase the EU's economic presence in the region, develop and extend the political dialogue and to assist in reducing Asian poverty levels. In keeping with the tone of the mid-1990s, Europe's role in promoting democracy, good governance and the rule of law was given equal importance with economic gains (van Reisen 1999: 139).

For the purposes of the Commission document Asia was recategorized into three regions – South Asia, East Asia and South East Asia – though the clear focus of the *New Asia Strategy* was East Asia, leading to the creation of the ASEM (see below). Direct bilateral partnership agreements with individual countries were concluded where possible (with India and Bangladesh for example). Despite recognizing ASEAN as the 'cornerstone' of the EU's dialogue with Asia, the *New Asia Strategy* was notably quiet on EU–ASEAN cooperation, raising questions as to the EU's commitment to this partnership. It was in part to answer such criticism that the Commission published its 1996 communication *Creating a New*

Dynamic in EU–ASEAN Relations, a document that failed to live up to its title, and did little to allay concerns about the future of the relationship. The *New Dynamic* noted the lack of vision in the relationship, and went on to argue that should the new ASEM framework successfully lay the 'foundations for a modern concept of Europe–Asia relations, the links between Europe and ASEAN should reflect and amplify this insight within a specific framework' (Commission 1996: 8), raising the issue of the marginalization of EU–ASEAN in favour of ASEM.

Crisis, deadlock and the rise of integration promotion

By the late 1990s, the EU–ASEAN relationship was under strain. The 1997 Asian financial crisis distorted the normal EU–ASEAN balance of trade to the extent that from 1998 onwards Europe has experienced a significant trade deficit (see Table 6.1). It should be noted, however, that the European states contributed significant financial assistance through the IMF to aid the recovery of affected states, surpassing the USA in this respect (Moeller 2007: 468). Nevertheless, expansion of the trade relationship continued, and by 2006 the EU had become ASEAN's second largest trading partner and export market (after the USA). In 2008, total trade with ASEAN had reached €135.4 billion, though this included an ongoing trade deficit of €24 billion.

In addition to the undermining of the economic relationship as a consequence of the Asian financial crisis, the late 1990s also saw the virtual breakdown of relations with ASEAN resulting from political disagreements. With the entry into force of the Maastricht Treaty in 1993, the promotion and protection of human rights and fundamental freedoms was given legal basis as an objective of the new CFSP (Article 11 TEU). As noted above, this emphasis was restated in the context of Europe–Asia relations in the *New Asia Strategy*: it was this introduction of political goals into a primarily economic relationship that was to prove an impasse in EU–ASEAN relations. Sparked initially by their inclusion in discussions at the ninth Ministerial Meeting in 1991, the issue of human rights became a fully fledged conflagration following the accession of Myanmar to ASEAN in July 1997. A concerted campaign by the EU and the USA to prevent the accession had failed (indeed it may even have accelerated the process as the Association drew together around the principle of non-interference), and in the aftermath the Union refused to

Table 6.1 *EU trade with ASEM, 1996–2009 (€ billion)*

	1996	1998	2000	2002	...	2007	2008	2009
EU imports								
China	30.0	42.0	74.6	90.2		232.7	247.9	214.8
Japan	52.6	66.0	92.1	73.7		78.5	75.1	55.8
S. Korea	11.1	16.0	27.0	24.6		41.4	39.6	32.1
ASEAN	38.7	52.3	75.4	68.1		80.6	79.7	67.8
Total	**132.4**	**176.4**	**269.1**	**256.5**		**433.2**	**433.2**	**370.5**
EU exports								
China	14.8	17.4	25.9	35.1		71.9	78.4	81.6
Japan	35.8	31.6	45.5	43.5		43.7	42.3	35.9
S. Korea	14.4	9.1	16.7	17.7		24.8	25.6	21.5
ASEAN	41.0	30.5	41.8	40.6		54.5	55.7	50.2
Total	**105.9**	**88.6**	**129.9**	**136.8**		**194.9**	**202.0**	**189.2**
Balance of trade								
China	−15.3	−24.6	−48.8	−55.1		−160.8	−169.5	−133.2
Japan	−16.8	−34.5	−46.6	−30.2		−32.5	−32.8	−19.9
S. Korea	3.3	−6.9	−10.2	−6.9		−16.6	−14.0	−10.6
ASEAN	2.3	−21.8	−33.6	−27.5		−26.1	−24.0	−17.6
Total	−26.6	−87.8	−139.2	−119.7		−238.3	−231.2	−181.3

Source: Eurostat Database.

extend the Cooperation Agreement to cover ASEAN's newest member. Further, the institutional structure of EC–ASEAN cooperation was interrupted, with the annual Joint Cooperation Committee and the 18-monthly ASEAN–EC Ministerial Meeting (AEMM) delayed until May 1999 and December 2000 respectively, nearly four years after their preceding meetings. And when held, these were given a lowered priority on the European side – the most senior attendees were the Deputy Prime Minister of Sweden and the French Minister of Cooperation and Francophony. While these political differences remain and pose a significant obstacle to political relations, both sides have worked to prevent this undermining other elements of the relationship. However, the EU–ASEAN dialogue has in many ways become little more than a consultation mechanism, with little substantive cooperation on issues of political import.

Since the restarting of EU–ASEAN dialogue, relations have continued much as they had previously, with the economic relationship of primary importance. Grandiose statements of intent, such as the *New Dynamic*'s call for the creation of an 'active partnership', were accompanied by little in the way of substantive cooperation. EU assistance has been provided for a range of projects in ASEAN to promote, among other things, technical training and cooperation, though with no underlying strategic focus determining funding arrangements. Rather, as one Commission official commented, the EU has been 'more or less giving in to the shopping-list of wishes on the ASEAN side' (Doidge 2008: 45).

In common with Latin America, what has become increasingly evident is an emphasis on promoting regional integration within ASEAN as a path to economic growth and stability and, consequently, in the EU's view, poverty alleviation and sustainable development and, in the post-9/11 world, combating terrorism. Initially raised at the tenth AEMM in 1992, European support for ASEAN integration has become an integral element of the dialogue (see Doidge 2011: 93–6). Consequently, the €580,000 Institutional Development Programme for the ASEAN Secretariat was launched in 1995, followed by the €4 million ASEAN Programme for Regional Integration Support (APRIS) in 2004 and its €8.4 million (including a €1.1 million ASEAN Secretariat contribution) successor, APRIS II in 2006. As was clarified in the 2003 *A New Partnership with South East Asia*, deeper regional integration of ASEAN is seen as a foundational element in the promotion of the EU's economic, political and developmental goals in the region. In line with this regional approach, the Transregional EU–ASEAN Trade Initiative was launched in 2003, establishing a system of regulatory cooperation to facilitate trade flows and market access, and reinforcing ASEAN's own economic integration initiatives. This was taken further in May 2007 when agreement was reached between the EU and ASEAN to launch negotiations on an FTA, linking the EU with the ASEAN Free Trade Area. Potential exists for a successful FTA to produce greater cooperation between the EU and ASEAN on the global stage on economic and trade matters, which in turn could act as the foundation for deeper dialogue and greater cooperation at the global level on those political matters that have to date proved so problematic.

The Asia–Europe Meeting

Key to the EU's approach to Asia since the mid-1990s has been the emergence of the Asia–Europe Meeting. Following the *New Asia Strategy*'s call for a deepening of Europe–Asia relations, and in the wake of initial scepticism concerning an earlier proposal from Singaporean Prime Minister Goh Chok Tong for an Asian–European Summit, the inaugural ASEM Heads of Government meeting was convened in Bangkok in 1996, bringing together the Fifteen plus the Commission and ten regional states – Brunei, China, Indonesia, Japan, South Korea, Malaysia, the Philippines, Singapore, Thailand and Vietnam. Clearly, three of these (Brunei, Japan and Singapore) do not fit even the most generous definition of development and a further three states (Japan, China and South Korea) were not part of ASEAN. Rather, they reflect the reality of the EU's primarily economic interest in the region (particularly a perceived need to counter US economic engagement), with development largely an afterthought. To an extent ASEM mirrors a European constructed reality (in the same way that the ACP only exists within an EU context). Thus although ASEM is an important part of the EU's overall development approach, it provides neither an exclusive nor comprehensive approach to Asian development issues.

When launched, ASEM offered three important attractive features to the EU. First, it offered an alternative to the deadlocked ASEAN dialogue, excluding as it did Myanmar, the main focus of disagreement with ASEAN on issues of human rights, democracy and the rule of law. A compromise was reached on membership whereby, while each side was to choose its own members, the accession of new candidates would be subject to approval by all ASEM states – the so-called 'double-key' approach. Second, the EU's broader global economic interests beyond mere development policy were potentially better served by the ASEM process rather than by ASEAN, facilitating a redefinition of Europe's ties with the region. Given, as the *New Asia Strategy* acknowledged (Commission 1994b: 3), that the main thrust of EU policy in Asia was economic, it was seen as advantageous to be involved in a grouping that included the Asian economic powers of China, Japan and South Korea. Additionally, the inclusion of China was seen as a means of socializing the emerging superpower into the web of global rules, norms and values that the ASEM process was expected to advance.

From the Asian perspective, the expansion of the EU Single Market and the lingering suspicions about 'fortress Europe' suggested the necessity for dialogue. Third, the global context of accelerated regionalization served further to underline the vacuous nature of existing EU–Asia relations and provided added incentive to create at least a dialogue, if not a set of institutions. ASEM, in many ways, appeared to provide the 'missing link' in the global economic triad, providing an alternative to the Asia–Pacific Economic Cooperation (APEC) process that the USA had engineered in 1993. Fearing Europe's further marginalization by its exclusion from APEC membership or even observer status, ASEM was the EU's answer to this perceived American unilateralism and special relationship with Asia (Köllner 2000: 7).

The first decade

Economically, EU–ASEM relations are of significance, particularly when compared with the declining economic importance of the ACP states. Table 6.1 provides import and export data for the 1996–2009 period. During this time the overall volume of EU–ASEM trade increased by around 140 per cent, despite the significant decline from 2008–09 as the financial crisis affected trade. Of particular note is China, which provided the most significant increase during the period (from €30.0 billion to €214.8 billion), replacing Japan by 2001 as the single largest exporter to the Union. EU exports to ASEM countries stagnated as a result of the reduced demand caused by the Asian economic crisis of the late 1990s, but nevertheless demonstrated a significant increase over the whole period (though to nowhere like the level achieved by the ASEM states). Consequently, the balance of trade has increasingly favoured the ASEM partners: the EU has been a much more important export market for ASEM than East Asia has been for the EU. Prior to the Asian financial crisis the balance of trade favouring ASEM was generally stable at €25–30 billion, with this level tripling by the end of the 1990s and going on to reach €238.3 billion by 2007 before declining to €181.3 billion in 2009. Correcting this imbalance will need to be a priority if the ASEM process is to be maintained and developed.

The perspective for FDI is somewhat different and in part compensates for the imbalance in trade flows. Globally, the EU is regarded as the world's largest investor – both for outward investment and as an FDI recipient. In 2008, the EU accounted for 60.8 per cent of outward FDI flows and 43.9 per cent of FDI inflows: in comparison the total combined FDI figures for the USA were 13.7 per cent, and for ASEM 3.5 per cent.

However, the developing countries of Asia rank well below the USA and Latin America in terms of their share of the EU's FDI, with 37.7 per cent of extra-EU FDI outflows in the period 1995–2008 destined for the USA (with a peak of 61.8 per cent in 1999), 8.1 per cent to Latin America (peaking at 16.2 per cent in 1997) and 2.8 per cent to the ASEAN states (peaking at 5.8 percent in 1996). Intra-EU FDI remained by far the most important market, totalling 58.9 per cent of all outflows in the period 1995–2008 (peaking at 71.7 per cent in 2002). Despite this lower priority, the EU's share of FDI outflows within the broader ASEM region stood at 12.3 per cent by the time of the launch of ASEM in 1996, though subsequently this level declined and did not exceed the 1996 percentage again until 2002: however, recently the downward trend has resumed and in 2008 the EU share had fallen to just 8.9 per cent. Interestingly, despite significant increases in the level of EU–China trade, the flow of FDI remains modest, averaging just 1.5 per cent of extra-EU outflows from 2000 to 2007, and standing at 1.4 per cent (€4.7 billion) in 2008. (All the above statistics were calculated from the Eurostat Database.)

ASEM was originally conceived as a comprehensive platform for dialogue and cooperation reflecting the emergent role of Asian economic 'Tigers' and Europe's somewhat marginal involvement in the region. After the various enlargements of both ASEM (2010) and the EU (2007), the current total ASEM Asian member states' population stands at 3,385 million (almost seven times that of the EU) with a combined GDP per capita of US$3,688 compared with the EU's US$34,925 (although the respective PPP figures are closer at US$5,990 and US$30,677 respectively). Particularly noticeable has been the trend in Asian ASEM post-1996 membership towards developing countries and, as a consequence, the increase in overall poverty within the Asian grouping, a function largely of the inclusion of Cambodia, Laos, Myanmar and, more recently, India, Mongolia and Pakistan. Indeed, the six most recent Asian accession states to ASEM are the Asian states with the lowest HDI and (accompanied by Indonesia) the highest Human Poverty Index rankings (UNDP 2007).

The inaugural ASEM meeting was convened in Bangkok in 1996.

The objectives of the meeting were intentionally modest: its value was less to do with producing groundbreaking initiatives than establishing mutual confidence in, and the purpose of, the process. The general conclusion – from both the European and Asian participants – was that ASEM-1 achieved its modest goals and a more substantive expectation for future cooperation was established (Dent 1997). This first meeting shaped the key characteristics of ASEM: these have been defined as informality, multi-dimensionality, partnership and a high-level focus. And, as explained by the then external trade Commissioner, somewhat disingenuously given the factors underlying the Union's push to extend its ties with Asia, the contrast with APEC was an important motivation:

> Unlike APEC, ASEM is not confined to economic and commercial matters – although they do play an important part, as is inevitable given that the European Union and its Asian partners in ASEM together make up around half of world GDP – ASEM also includes a cultural and people-to-people dimension and a substantive political dialogue. One of its key features is its informality. (Quoted by Schmit in Fangchuan and Niemann 2000: 106)

Thus, the basis of cooperation was to be primarily informal rather than institutionalized, although biennial summits and meetings for foreign, economic and finance ministers plus Senior Officials Meetings (SOMs) are convened in the intervening years. This approach was seen as complementary to the other formal structures for dialogue (such as ASEAN) that already existed. Theoretically at such meetings there is no official agenda (conforming to an Asian rather than a Eurocentric style) with participants free to discuss whatever issues they choose (provided that there is no strong opposition to a specific topic). The 1996 Summit reflected this multi-dimensionality and set itself wide-ranging tasks including a new Asian–EU partnership to promote growth, as well as joint action to support global peace, stability and prosperity! Areas for practical collaboration were also outlined. These covered environmental issues, international crime and drugs, as well as less sensitive initiatives covering economic, scientific and cultural collaboration and an enhanced level of political dialogue. The two sides did not necessarily share the same expectations from ASEM-1. Human rights were a European concern whereas the Asian participants preferred an exclusive focus on trade. Remarkably, and perhaps revealingly, the ASEM agenda did not envisage any meetings for Development Ministers, and indeed development remained largely absent from discussion for the first decade of dialogue. Reminiscent of Europe's relations with the ACP, the notion of partnership rather than dependency was the motivating factor: however, in contrast to the Lomé experience, Asia appears to have been more successful in asserting the equality of the partnership. And finally, and as outlined above, the process is focused intentionally at the level of political elites. However, it would be hard to characterize the ASEM process as intense since personal relationships at the Heads of Government level are difficult to sustain, especially on a biennial basis and where attendance at the summits has been mixed.

The degree of informality is, of course, underpinned by regular bureaucratic contact. The responsibility for coordination is with the Foreign Ministries, with two representatives for ASEM and two for the EU (the presidency and the Commission). The SOMs play a role similar to that of the Committee of Permanent Representatives (COREPER), bringing together foreign affairs officials from both sides to discuss the political dialogue informally. It performs an essential function in ensuring that the actual ASEM Summit can be productive. A similar role in preparing the economic agenda is played by the SOM on trade and investment and to a lesser extent that of the meeting of finance officials. Less regular contacts are maintained in the area of customs and science and technology. ASEM has also undertaken a number of initiatives to promote business, cultural, trade and investment contacts outside government. Among these are the Asia–Europe Business Forum; the Asia–Europe Foundation; and the Asia–Europe Environmental Technology Centre.

Cooperation over the following decade remained steady rather than innovative, with the agendas of ASEMs-2–4 being determined to a great extent by external events, impacting upon the ability to make substantive steps in cooperation. The second ASEM meeting, held in London, was overshadowed by the 1997 Asian economic crisis – the source of a thinly veiled *Schadenfreude* among those Europeans who had taken offence at the hubris of Asianists in the preceding years (Rüland 2001b: 63) – that effectively stalled many of these joint proposals and posed new challenges for the EU–Asia relationship. ASEM-3, convened in Seoul in 2000, was impacted on by the rapprochement on the Korean Peninsula. The fourth ASEM was held in Copenhagen in 2002, little more than a year after the 9/11 terror attacks, and the shadow of these events hung over the proceedings – the themes of the summit, as Danish Prime Minister Anders Fogh Rasmussen noted, could be summed up in two words – globalization and counter-terrorism (Sun 2002).

The focus of cooperation during the first decade was largely economic and, whilst the Commission priorities were not antagonistic to development issues, the emphasis was very much on the role of business and trade. A common approach to strengthening the rules-based multilateral trading agenda of the WTO in the wake of Seattle was seen as a high-level priority. In line with this, alongside a range of public and private linkages and business dialogues between the two regions that grew over the years, ASEM-2 saw the launch of two joint plans – the Trade Facilitation Action Plan and the Investment Promotion Action Plan. The focus of the trade plan – only non-tariff barriers were to be examined – symbolized the modest, cautious and non-controversial nature of the ASEM agenda. Challenging and divisive economic issues (let alone political ones) were avoided. The most significant of these was the EU's application of anti-dumping regulations against particular Asian exports. Six ASEM countries were among the top ten countries for violating the EU regulation, with China being the worst offender with 34 violations from 1990–98 (van Reisen 1999: 147). One can seriously question the real motivations behind the EU actions. After all, it is the low labour costs that gave China, India and other Asian countries one of the few areas of comparative advantage in the global economy. Rather than supporting these countries by providing broad access, the EU appeared more concerned with defending its domestic industries in these areas that found it hard to compete by applying anti-dumping regulations. In such circumstances, the tension between the demands of a benevolent external development policy and aspects of internal EU economic policy are difficult to reconcile.

At the political level engagement remained tentative – a function of the informal nature of the process mitigating against attempts to raise potentially contentious political issues and set proactive agendas. Human rights, a key focus in EU foreign and development policy, first made its appearance on the Summit agenda at Seoul in 2000, having being vetoed at the previous two meetings – human rights questions were particularly sensitive for Indonesia (East Timor) and China (internal affairs). Also central to the human rights issue was the question of Myanmar and its possible inclusion in the Asia–Europe dialogue, with the EU adamantly opposed at the time to its formal participation in any form – including observer status. This issue saw a series of lower level ASEM meetings postponed during 1999. The EU subsequently refused to discuss Myanmar's membership at any ASEM meeting, and at ASEM-2 the UK declined entry visas to officials from Myanmar, thus precluding their participation. Following acceptance at ASEM-2 of the informality of the process however, and a continuing commitment to the ASEAN Way as an organizing principle (with its emphasis on sensitivity, non-confrontation and quiet diplomacy), the path was opened for Myanmar's entry. It had been decided, in other words, that disagreements on political matters would not be allowed to under-mine economic cooperation – the clear priority in Asia–Europe engagement. As a consequence, Myanmar acceded to ASEM at its fifth summit (convened in Hanoi in 2004) alongside the remaining ASEAN member states, Cambodia and Laos, and the new ten member states from the 2004 'big bang' enlargement of the EU. The inclusion of Myanmar was clear evidence of the EU's acceptance of the prioritization of the economic over the political. While holding out the possibility that further sanctions could be imposed in the absence of progress towards democracy, the Union had in practice abandoned its CFSP position on Myanmar, as well as the human rights, democracy and rule of law commitments that were intrinsic to its external relations and development policies.

As noted already, absent from the ASEM process during the first ten years was any substantive consideration of development. By ASEM-5 reference was being made to poverty reduction and promoting sustainable economic development, but this was firmly in the context of trade liberalization and a commitment to global governance institutions being seen as essential to achieving these goals. Thus the agreed Hanoi Declaration on Closer ASEM Economic Partnership only emphasized the facilitation of trade and investment through reducing barriers to trade, as well as sectoral cooperation on issues such as the protection of intellectual property rights, energy, transport, e-commerce and tourism.

The emergence of development?

The second ASEM decade has witnessed the apparent emergence of development onto the cooperative agenda. Alongside the mutual celebrations to be expected at the decennial meeting, the sixth ASEM summit (convened in Helsinki in 2006) gave for the first time detailed consideration to sustainable development, replacing the mere rhetorical commitments that had been made previously. An emphasis was placed on poverty reduction and the pursuit of the MDGs: with this in mind the need to increase resources for developing countries (from domestic sources as well as ODA) was highlighted, alongside the standard EU approach of providing technical cooperation and capacity building measures. Sustainable development was also incorporated into the Helsinki Declaration on the Future of ASEM which aimed to provide more substance to the process by defining focused areas for future action. These included strengthening multilateralism, globalization and competitiveness, health, science and technology, and intercultural dialogue, while still making it clear that the core focus remained on economic and financial cooperation. This agenda was not significantly different from the nature of the dialogue in ASEMs-1–6, and it remains to be seen whether the Declaration's agreement to set two-year work programmes of substantive cooperation at the summit level will produce meaningful results.

The meeting also continued the process of enlargement, extending invitations to attend the next meeting to Bulgaria and Romania (who were to accede to the EU on 1 January 2007), also, unexpectedly, to India (which had previously indicated a lack of interest in joining the dialogue) and to Mongolia and Pakistan, thus for the first time incorporating two South Asian states into the Europe–Asia dialogue and potentially changing the centre of gravity of the entire process.

Though the global financial crisis dominated much of the discussion at ASEM-7, convened in Beijing in 2008, the new focus on sustainable development continued, most prominently with the publication of the Beijing Declaration on Sustainable Development. While far from being a substantive document, the Declaration demonstrated the increasing profile of development-related issues in Asia–Europe relations, a function of the expansion of ASEM to incorporate members for whom ongoing poverty remains a particular challenge. Notably absent from the Declaration was any suggestion as to what ASEM might do to ensure their meeting the MDGs (on which the understanding of development was premised), other than supporting the activities of other fora such as the UN. This absence of concrete policies was a source of considerable criticism from civil society groups in the two regions. Although an ASEM Development Conference was subsequently convened in Manila in April 2009, it simply reiterated the key elements of the Beijing Declaration. While recognizing that 'the primary responsibility of each country to achieve its own development, complemented by an enabling international environment', the conference noted the importance of international cooperation in achieving MDG targets and consequently asserted the need to incorporate the principles of the Beijing Declaration into future ASEM discussions on relevant topics. Thus, the Conference followed the too familiar ASEM approach of continuing dialogue with little substantive result.

Future challenges

Clearly, ASEM has increased the profile of Asia within the EU's policy priorities. Whilst this was necessary, is it a sufficient reason for maintaining the ASEM framework as the principal mechanism for EU–Asian dialogue? To what extent has rhetoric masqueraded as progress? For some EU member states the initial commitment to ASEM was somewhat reluctant because of their already heavy summit obligations. The challenge for ASEM is to counter the growing general perception of 'forum fatigue' by graduating ASEM from its symbolic origins to a more substantive policy output level – without jeopardizing the informal, multi-dimensional and high-level advantages associated with the current dialogue (Yeo 2000). Others have been more critical of the elitism of the process, seeing the lack of effective public involvement as a fundamental problem (Holland and Chaban 2010). The management of the people-to-people dialogue at the 2008 Beijing meeting did little to appease these critics. The future legitimacy and viability of ASEM appears to depend on a greater role for civil society in the process – both in Europe and Asia (Köllner 2000: 11).

The generally non-contentious nature of the political dialogue also potentially threatens the future development of ASEM. Whilst a gentleman's agreement to avoid divisive political topics may have been the necessary price to pay in order to instigate the dialogue, ASEM continues to run the obvious risk of becoming vacuous if 'sensitive' issues remain taboo. Obviously, the problem of human rights and labour practices present major obstacles. In more general terms, the basic premise of ASEM – two regions coming together for dialogue – is arguably flawed. While the EU can justifiably be described as a region that speaks with a post-Lisbon 'single voice' (whether vocal or timorous) in a variety of forums, the 16 Asian states associated with ASEM do not function as a similarly cohesive group – or exist collectively outside the ASEM context. The heterogeneity within the ASEM membership can reduce the cohesion and effectiveness of the group. On the Asian side, the tensions between Japan and other members, the inclusion of China and latterly India, as well as the parallel expectations of ASEAN membership, cumulatively suggest limited scope for a common agenda among Asian ASEM states. With Australia, New Zealand and Russia becoming the latest new ASEM members at the October 2010 Brussels ASEM-8 summit (under a new 'third category' modality), it is hard to envisage how this enlargement will increase solidarity.

As already stated, ASEM represents a constructed reality. The Asian ASEM states have to date represented Asia for Europe. The gradual enlargement from 10 to 16 Asian states represented a redefinition of the Asian region for Europe. If the original grouping constituted an economic view of the region, incorporating great powers and 'Tiger' economies, this new version suggested a more nuanced view with an inevitable impact on the EU's Asia policy and on the ASEM process. Has the gradual incorporation of states that are clearly defined as 'developing countries' signified a move from a trade and business view of Asia to one at least partially coloured by the reality of underdevelopment? The incorporation of Cambodia, Laos, Myanmar, Mongolia, India and Pakistan, while also representing the inclusion of South alongside East Asia, makes it increasingly difficult to ignore the reality of underdevelopment. Indeed, the enlargement from ten Asian members in 1996 to 16 in 2008, despite more than a decade of economic growth (including the tripling of China's GDP), saw the GDP per capita of the Asian ASEM grouping fall nearly 13 per cent from US$3,830 to around US$3,350 (a drop from upper middle to lower middle income in the World Bank's definition).

While the reconstitution of Asia seems to have forced development onto the agenda, the increasing size and heterogeneity of ASEM – particularly with the accession of Australia, New Zealand and Russia – raises questions as to its capacity to make substantive progress on development or indeed any other issue. The clear risk is that this enlargement to the north and to the south will reinforce the rather shallow nature of discussions that is already characteristic of the ASEM process. The eighth ASEM, convened in Brussels in 2010, comprised 46 member states, plus the European Commission and the ASEAN Secretariat – and further enlargement on both the EU and Asian sides is almost certain. Consideration will therefore need to be given to the ongoing structure of the relationship, with more emphasis being placed on ministerial meetings and working groups, with development being an obvious candidate for expansion in this way.

In conclusion, how does ASEM compare with the EU's general pattern of relations with the developing world? First, it clearly further compounds the problem of defining what constitutes the developing world. ASEM includes advanced industrial and techno-logical societies such as Japan, South Korea and Singapore as well as underdeveloped countries such as Cambodia, Indonesia, Laos, Myanmar, Pakistan and Vietnam, but also includes the emerging global giants of India and China, as well as a re-emerging Russia. Once again, geography creates at least as many problems as it solves. Second, ASEM indicates to some degree that institutional-ized relations are not always necessary – or effective – in generating dialogue. Third, it also suggests that economic parity is essential if political conditionality is to be excluded: good governance and human rights have not played a universal role in shaping the EU's dialogue partners. Fourth, the history of EU relations with ASEAN and ASEM also underline the limited role that trade preferences can play in development. Despite receiving no preferential concessions, Asian trade with the EU has grown over the past decades whilst that with Europe's privileged partners has virtually collapsed. And fifth, the EU's motives for re-establishing a dialogue with Asia illustrate Europe's wider agenda to become an effective international actor and its activism in confronting American global unilateralism. With the enhanced potential for EU foreign affairs associated with the Lisbon Treaty's EEAS, in the second decade of the twenty-first century there may no longer be any *domaine reserves* that the EU feels obliged to respect.

The aid dimension

If EU–Asia trading relations have been comparatively modest, then Asia has been similarly treated in the deployment of European aid. To compound matters, prior to the 1990s aid did not necessarily go to those in the greatest need: political considerations have weighed heavily in the choice of recipient countries. For example, China only began to receive aid in 1985 and similar patterns can be found for the states of Indochina (Vietnam, Cambodia, Laos and Myanmar). Typically, the very poorest Asian countries were not the main aid recipients – these were primarily the ASEAN countries, such as Thailand and Indonesia. The only exception to this was the Indian subcontinent that received aid irrespective of implied conditionality. The scale of the aid problem distorts even the most generous of programmes when examined on a per capita basis. Nonetheless, the EU contribution remains small. For example, between 1976 and 1991 aid to Indochina totalled just ECU 123.6 million, or the equivalent of ECU 1.6 per capita. This has however increased significantly, with aid totalling €735 million between 2000 and 2009, or approximately €4.9 per capita. South Asia, the most favoured of the Asian regions, received only ECU 2.6 per capita (representing ECU 2,965 million) between 1976 and 1991. By 2000–09 this was still only €3.1 per capita (around €4,863 million).

With the exception of South Asia, EU aid has not been a major Asian development factor and for many states bilateral member state aid has remained more important. Of course, if taken cumulatively Europe's presence is enhanced and the Commission claims that the EU does practise a comprehensive global aid programme. Conversely, critics have described the presence of EU aid in the past as 'paper thin, not only in China and Indochina, but also in the Indian sub-continent' (Grilli 1993: 289). The aid that does exist has historically been almost totally agricultural and food aid. Following the launching of the EC's food aid programme, India and Bangladesh were the primary recipients: for example, nearly half of the cereals distributed between 1968 and 1974 went to Asia (compared with 4.5 per cent for Latin America). In contrast to the ASEM initiative that was designed to rejuvenate the lethargic EU–Asia relationship, no equivalent relaunch of aid to Asia was developed. The obligatory political conditionalities that now shape the EU's external relations in general can be seen as one of the disincentives to revising the EU's aid distribution.

During the first half of the 1990s EU aid to Asia increased by 82 per cent (compared with 68 per cent for Latin America). However, as a percentage of the EU's overall aid, the ALA share actually declined over this five-year period due to the shifting aid priority towards the CEECs (to 13.6 per cent of EU total aid). This was reversed in 1995 when EU aid commitments to both Asia and Latin America reached a record level of €1.2 billion. This represented 17 per cent of the EU's overall aid budget and was close to half the level of aid provided to the ACP states. As already noted in the previous chapter, Asia – not Latin America – was the greater recipient of EU aid. From 1976 to 1991 it consumed 67 per cent of the ALA aid budget. During the 1990s, while volumes of aid steadily increased, they were outpaced by those to Latin America and commitments to Asia dropped to 56 per cent of the ALA aid budget. However, this trend was reversed between 2000 and 2009 as Asia once again received roughly double the aid commitments compared with Latin America. Nevertheless, on a per capita basis Latin America received higher commitments (including regional allocations) of €8.3 between 2000 and 2009, compared with €2.6 for Asia. While development assistance to Asia has almost doubled since 2000 (Table 6.2), in 2009 it still constituted only 9.3 per cent of EU ODA, a significant drop from the mid-1990s level. As with Latin America, the sectoral distribution of aid has been dominated by food aid, humanitarian projects and NGOs. The longer-term sustainability of this aid remains an area where the EU contribution could undoubtedly be improved.

Notable within humanitarian assistance to Asia since 1997 has been a specific focus on 'uprooted people' and refugees. Council Regulation 443/97 on operations to aid uprooted people in Asian and Latin American developing countries (subsequently updated in 2001 and replaced by the DCI in 2006) created the legal base for this EU action to counter the effects of civil wars. This has generally taken two forms: in post-conflict situations where resettlement and rehabilitation initiatives act to consolidate peace processes; and, where conflict continues, the financing of operations designed to increase stability. While targeted at both Asia and Latin America, Asia has exhibited a greater degree of conflict and need for refugee assistance. During the latter part of the 1990s, assistance to Asia averaged around €38 million per year (€114 million in total commitments), largely focused on resettlement of displaced persons (Commission 2000f: 14), a trend which has continued. From 2001 to 2006 assistance remained high, averaging €45 million per year (€270 million in total), with funding for 2007–10 falling to €28 million per year (€112 million overall). The main beneficiaries in Asia have been Afghanistan, Bangladesh, Indonesia, Myanmar, Nepal, the Philippines, Sri Lanka and Thailand.

Far less prominent in Asia than in Latin America has been assistance for regional integration. As already noted in Chapter 5,

Table 6.2 *EU ODA commitments and disbursements to Asia (managed by EuropeAid and other DGs), 2000–09 (€ million)*

	2000		2002		2004		2006		2007		2008		2009	
	Com.	Dis.	Com.	Dis.	Com.	Dis.	Com.	Dis.	Com.	Dis.	Com.	Dis.	Com.	Dis.
East and South East Asia (bilateral)	168.4	201.2	296.6	232.7	394.7	209.5	351.2	283.7	269.4	303.4	356.2	351.8	291.8	259.0
South and Central Asia (bilateral)	381.0	213.8	521.4	401.9	421.8	456.6	694.9	614.8	611.7	547.5	637.8	718.3	746.1	729.4
Regional	11.6	6.7	67.1	2.7	46.5	42.4	86.0	53.7	109.7	83.3	127.0	118.0	55.6	63.5
Asia total	561.0	421.7	885.1	637.4	863.0	708.6	1,132.1	952.2	990.8	934.3	1,120.9	1,188.1	1,093.5	1,051.8
% dispersal		75.2		72.0		82.1		84.1		94.3		106.0		96.2
EU ODA total (€ billion)	7.1	4.0	6.5	5.9	7.5	6.9	9.8	8.1	9.9	8.5	12.0	9.2	11.8	9.9

Notes: East and South East Asia: Cambodia, China, Indonesia, Korea (DPR), Laos, Malaysia, Mongolia, Myanmar, Philippines, Thailand and Vietnam; South and Central Asia: Afghanistan, Bangladesh, Bhutan, India, Kazakhstan, Kyrgyz Republic, Maldives, Nepal, Pakistan, Sri Lanka, Tajikistan, Turkmenistan and Uzbekistan.
Source: EuropeAid Annual Report, various editions.

between 1976 and 1991, regional allocations accounted for only 3.7 per cent of all ODA to Asia, compared with 26 per cent for Latin America. This has changed somewhat since 2000, with regional allocations constituting 7.8 per cent of Asia's ODA total, compared with 25.7 per cent for Latin America. Aside from the ASEAN programmes already discussed, the promotion of regional integration has been a lower priority in the Asian region. Some tentative steps towards encouraging the South Asian Association for Regional Cooperation's (SAARC) FTA have been highlighted by the Commission, along with funding for dialogue on the benefits of regional integration to South Asia, but, given SAARC's slow progress under the weight of economic and political disagreements between Bangladesh, India and Pakistan, these have been accorded far lower priority than their ASEAN and Latin American equivalents.

Lastly, one specific, if untypical, 'aid' contribution was the EU's response to the Asian financial crisis. EU member states provided around 30 per cent of funding for the IMF, 27 per cent for the World Bank and 14 per cent of the Asian Development Bank. Cumulatively, Europe was the greatest provider of financial support to Asia providing some 18 per cent of the total value at €27 billion. In comparison with the USA, in 1998 the EU's development and humanitarian aid to Asia was twice that of America and the funding for three-quarters of the then existing debt-relief schemes came from Europe (Schmit 2000: 109).

What is clear from the above discussion is that the EU's aid to Asia has been largely reactive rather than proactive in its allocation. Absent is a clear, focused strategy for dealing with the developmental issues of the region. Rather, assistance has been focused on responses to crises, such as those related to food, conflict and economic collapse. This is an outcome of the low priority afforded to development in the EU's broader approach to Asia. The provision of assistance in some form is seen simply as a necessary component of a global strategy, a pillar reinforcing the EU's claim to be an effective global actor. The attainment of development goals comes a poor second.

Conclusion

While the EU–ACP relationship is defined by its developmental focus, what is clear from the above discussion is that EU–Asia relations essentially constitute an economic dialogue to which developmental rhetoric has been attached. While the states of South Asia attracted a certain level of development assistance, primarily in the form of food aid, those of East and South East Asia (around which the Asia policy essentially revolved) were viewed primarily as an economic threat. Subsequent ties with the Asian region centred on the development of trade and business relations, initially with the member states of ASEAN and from 1996 with the broader ASEM process. In both structures, development – increasingly defined as poverty eradication – has been seen as a function of trade and economic growth, sitting comfortably therefore with the EU's own interests. The lack of a clear strategy focused on inequality and under-development in Asia has meant that the few resources available are not targeted in a coherent fashion. The gradual expansion of ASEM – increasingly the preferred framework for engagement with the region – seems in recent years to have placed under-development on the interregional agenda. The extent to which these initial steps can be developed into a focused strategy assisting the poorest states will do much to determine the future prospects of the poorest Asian states. Indeed, given the emphasis on partnership within the ASEM, and the existence of significant, if inequitably distributed, wealth within Asia, the establishment of a developmental focus alongside the current economic, political and cultural pillars in the relationship, drawing on the financial and technical resources of both sides, would seem to offer the best opportunity for achieving sustainable results.

Chapter 7

Complementarity and Conditionality

Having reviewed the geographical and policy frameworks that shape EU development policy, in this chapter we address two broad conceptual issues: first, the introduction of the principle of complementarity guiding the internal organization of European policy; and second, the application of conditionality – both political and economic – in the EU's relations with the developing world. While the commentary is intentionally generalized, much of the empirical evidence is drawn from the Lomé Conventions. To that extent Lomé has provided a reflection of the EU's more general global approach: what was transposed in agreements with Asia or Latin America, for example, usually had their origins in the discussions previously held with the ACP. The application of Lomé – and latterly Cotonou – is also useful as they provide the most comprehensive EU perspective dealing now with 78 ACP states in total.

Political conditionality has become one of the most disputed policy areas between the EU and the developing countries. European demands for greater accountability by recipient countries has seen the introduction of a series of related principles applied and evaluated – good governance, democracy, human rights and the rule of law in particular. Economic conditionality has a longer history and is drawn from an international rather than specifically European agenda. The definition, application and evaluation of these concepts, however, remain contentious. In addition to these externally imposed EU criteria, the Union has also set itself a performance agenda to enhance the delivery of European development policy. The notion of complementarity (and the related ones of coordination, coherence and consistency) has come to dominate EU development policy, albeit with mixed success. We examine both the external imposition of political and economic conditionalities by the EU and its own internal requirements to mesh effectively EU-level and member state bilateral policies. In both these internal and external spheres the results have been mixed.

Complementarity

Writing in the early 1990s, Grilli, in his seminal work on European development policy, summarized Europe's disappointing experience towards constructing a common development approach in the following terms:

> Despite the progress achieved, Europeanization of development aid is still nowhere in sight ... Multilateralization of EC aid, the most direct route to Europeanization of external assistance ... failed to reach decisive results. Less direct forms of Europeanization of aid, from making assistance practices more homogeneous among EC members to the establishment of more common aid objectives among EC partners, have not advanced much either. After a promising start, this process seems to have slowed down to the point where progress is hardly discernible. (1993: 74)

With the notable exception of Lomé, Europe's presence as a development actor remained fragmented, ad hoc and fundamentally bilateral. If tentatively, the Commission had been calling for some form of coordination for more than two decades. By the end of the 1980s the Council did endorse this position at least with respect to the ACP states and SAPs. The endorsement, however, continued to reflect member state sensitivities. Existing bilateral autonomy in development aid was maintained and no precise remedy was advocated beyond 'an exchange of views and information ... to increase consistency and convergence between the approach of the Commission and the member states at all levels' (Council 1989: 118).

It was at the Maastricht Intergovernmental Conference that this deficiency was finally addressed at a treaty level by incorporating the principle of complementarity as a policy objective. Only since 1993 has this principle – in theory – become a key aspect of EU policy in general, as well as in the development sphere in particular, an attribute that has continued to find expression in the 2009 Lisbon Treaty. At one level the principle is simple enough: the Commission and the individual member states are required to work in tandem to avoid producing policies that either duplicate each other or, more seriously, promote contradictory objectives. However, the actual translation of principle into practice has typically been less easily achieved.

In part, the origin of the problem lies with the Commission. The decade in which Jacques Delors was Commission President was characterized by a rapidly expanding role for the Commission and an implicit federal and harmonization agenda. During the Maastricht debates the Commission clearly saw the principle of complementarity to its advantage and envisioned member state development policies eventually becoming aligned with a common EU policy. In a sense, this was in keeping with the Commission's preferred view on subsidiarity – that the centre was the natural level for policy implementation, not the member states. Such a perspective was, of course, bound to conflict with a number of member states and the Council's response was to reassert the importance and autonomy of bilateral development policy to some degree. As was the case with other innovative aspects of the Maastricht Treaty, pragmatism, as much as ideology, guided practice; it soon became apparent that the Commission's more ambitious agenda was politically unacceptable. Consequently, an emphasis on coordination was substituted to promote complementarity, though this compromise has only been partially successful. The Lisbon Treaty reflected a similar political compromise to balance any expanded EU-level competences with the growing resurgence of intergovernmentalism as symbolized by the enhanced role of the European Council and reorganization of the Commission's development portfolios (as discussed in Chapter 4).

Defining appropriate policy spheres for the EU that were distinct from those of the member states has been particularly fraught and complex. In particular, the process presented implicit threats to the Commission's legitimate original sphere of authority as well as having serious budgetary consequences. Critics maintain that the nature of European development assistance remains typically '27+1' with the Commission either filling in the gaps or simply duplicating the roles and initiatives operated by the member states. While acknowledging the challenge, the Commission sees the problem in a rather different light. As former Commissioner for Development, Louis Michel, commented in 2005, 'one of the EU's most central challenges in development cooperation remains to ensure a coherent and effective approach between 26 different actors, the 25 Member

States and the European Commission, with 26 development policies' (Commission 2005b). Others, too, have rejected a minimalist position and have argued for the EU's comparative advantage and defined specific roles that add value at the EU-level. These include, for example, the EU's greater economic and political neutrality; its ability to marshal greater amounts of financial assistance than any single bilateral member state programme; its greater choice of agencies for the implementing of aid; a greater geographic spread of aid; and the longer-term security and predictability offered by assistance through programmes such as Lomé and latterly Cotonou (Bossuyt et al. 1999: 6). A core issue for member states, however, is the financial implications of this choice. Should funding be primarily directed through bilateral programmes or through EU-level initiatives? In the context of shrinking aid and development budgets, particularly since 2008, in several member states there is little possibility of additional monies being allocated, just the decision of which mechanism to use to achieve policy goals. For example, of the three largest member state aid donors (France, Germany and the UK), who typically provide half of all EU ODA combined, only Germany increased its GNI percentage aid contribution between the years 2005 and 2008.

The logic of bureaucratic self-interest – and survival – is a powerful one. Consequently, while there has been some progress towards implementing this principle over the last two decades, competing political and bureaucratic factors have often conspired to moderate its effect. As one analysis concluded, 'complementarity still appears to be a political slogan rather than a practical reality' (ibid.: 1). For third country recipients, the added complexity and administrative costs associated with this multiplication of delivery agents can be considerable and results in a less than optimal use of EU and member state resources. The Lisbon Treaty is the latest attempt to address this shortcoming by seeking 'to enhance the efficiency and democratic legitimacy of the enlarged Union, as well as the coherence of its external action' (Commission 2007b: 4). It will be interesting to see how successful the EEAS is in achieving these goals – and the required level of bureaucratic support involved.

One historic example that can be used to illustrate the problems of achieving complementarity is in relation to poverty reduction – the EU's long-standing development objective and now an MDG key priority. In a study undertaken by the European Centre for Development Policy Management the application of complementarity during the first five years following the implementation of the Maastricht Treaty was assessed (1993–97). Four major weaknesses were identified that outweighed the gains made through increased consultation and an exchange of information and learning between the Commission and the Council. First, it was found that the control of policy remained a top-down excessively centralized approach. Second, the sequencing and linkages between different poverty reduction policies were found to be lacking. In particular, Council resolutions on implementing complementarity seemed to have little influence in modifying the member-state-level policy. Third, the EU actors remained largely divided in the level of commitment to the principle of complementarity and suspicious of the role it played in the wider political agenda between the Commission and the Council. Lastly, it was concluded that complementarity was largely a one-way street. The presumption was – on the part of the member states – that it was the Commission's role to ensure that EU policies became complementary to bilateral policies, not vice versa (Bossuyt et al. 1999: 12–13). From the perspective of 15 years further on, responsibility for assuring complementarity still resides with the Commission, and the member states remain stubbornly committed to their bilateral development programmes.

However, there is also evidence that the EU has recognized that a more effective and meaningful implementation of complementarity was needed and that improvements had to be made. Both the MDGs and the EU 'Consensus on Development' have gone some way to alleviating these concerns. The pressures for change have partly come from the awareness that sustainable development is enhanced by such collective action and the practical necessity to provide aid donors with value for money. More specifically, because both the EU and member states have considerably expanded their development priorities and interaction with civil society often their ability to administer and implement such a wide range of programmes individually is compromised. Indeed, as noted previously, one of the main thrusts of the investigation into Commission administrative malpractice in 1999 was that the Commission had increased its areas of activity without having the necessary human resources to do so effectively. Cooperation based on complementarity may provide a remedy to this shortcoming. The possibility for enhanced capacity and additional capability within the Commission is remote in the current political climate. Alternatively, recent reforms have seen the EU begin to replace its centralized bureaucratic approach to development in favour of decentralizing decision-making to local offices. Such a move is in keeping with an emphasis on 'local ownership' of development initiatives – it remains to be seen whether this trend will continue under the new Lisbon institutional structure that now encompasses development as an aspect of EU foreign affairs (see pp. 124–32).

Perhaps the most compelling rationale for emphasizing the importance of complementarity, however, is derived from the EU's own self-image and ambition. The words of the 1980 London Report that first called for Europe to become a significant international actor and to shape and not merely responded to international events has been at the heart of the EU's external relations ever since (and a driving motivation behind the reforms in Europe's international relations defined by the Lisbon Treaty). Undoubtedly, a more effective EU presence could be established in the international community if Commission and member state activity benefited from greater complementarity. Such arguments involve the nature of the integration debate itself. And of course, the prospect of an enhanced role for the EU is antagonistic to those states that advocate a strictly intergovernmental agenda for Europe's future. As noted in Chapter 1, such macro-theoretical ideas have a direct impact upon the shape and future of EU development policy and can under some circumstances play a greater role than issues that are specifically developmental in nature. Conversely, the Commission may also regard enhanced complementarity with suspicion if it is used to renationalize aspects of development policy, reduce EU budgetary allocations and constrain the EU's international role. Quite how committed the various European actors are to enhancing complementarity and their underlying motivations for doing so remain crucial questions for determining the future impact of an EU-level development policy.

As also noted in Chapter 1 and elsewhere in this book, EU policy-making in the 1990s established a number of additional general principles designed to support and promote complementarity: these were coordination, coherence and consistency. Coordination and coherence, like complementarity, were given legal recognition in the Maastricht Treaty, whereas the principle of consistency was subsequently incorporated in the Amsterdam Treaty of 1997. Collectively the introduction of these 'four Cs' was tantamount to recognition that previous policy frameworks had been inadequate: past experience had proved that the EU often faced profound difficulties in achieving effective policy collectively. Coordination provides a practical mechanism for enhancing complementarity. It focuses on coordinating the administrative actions of the member states, the Commission and recipient countries to maximize the effectiveness and execution of EU development policy. To bolster this trend, in the decade following Maastricht the Council issued a series of resolutions promoting this perspective covering development topics as diverse as gender, the environment conflict resolution, poverty, education and food aid (van Reisen 1999: 230); since 2000, the EU has produced its own 'Consensus on Development', of course, and forged a common commitment to the MDGs and achieving an EU-level 0.7 per cent ODA target. The most recent institutional restructuring that has seen the EEAS embrace aspects of development policy can also been seen as consistent with enhancing coordination, coherence and consistency.

The principle of coherence was introduced to ensure that all areas of EU policy were compatible with EU development objectives. This requirement was further enhanced by the addition of 'consistency' which involves linking all the EU's external activities (CFSP, CSDP, trade, environment and development) in a consistent and logical manner. Cumulatively, it is hoped that by operationalizing these principles effectively, the past experiences of contradictory policies being adopted either by different arms of the Commission or by member states can be avoided. Somewhat belatedly, policy-makers have come to appreciate that often decisions taken on matters to do with Europe's internal market, for example, can have unanticipated and unintended consequences for third countries outside the Union. An obvious example of this is the CAP: changes to price support mechanisms can influence agricultural exports which in turn may impact significantly on developing-country producers. The implications, however, are not just limited to agriculture but spread across a wide range of policies that are increasingly determined at the EU rather than national level. This interpretation is consistent with both the multilevel governance and path-dependency theoretical models discussed in Chapter 1. Of course, in practice the level of commitment to realizing complementarity, coordination and coherence depends ultimately on political will. It remains to be seen the extent to which the ambitious intentions agreed to in resolutions, agreements and treaties are matched in practice. Agreeing on the need for consistent and coherent policies is not the same as changing national behaviour to achieve that goal. And even where there is an intention to make such changes, bureaucratic processes can be slow to respond. Consequently, despite the legal authority of the Maastricht, Amsterdam and Lisbon Treaties and numerous Council resolutions, inconsistencies and even contradictions are likely to persist in EU development policy for the foreseeable future.

Conditionality: good governance, democracy, human rights and the rule of law

Conditionality can be dichotomized in a variety of ways: between political and economic aspects; internal and external supervision; or between positive and negative applications, for example. Conditionality can also be prescriptively explicit or general in its description, take legal or informal forms or be peculiarly 'European' and new in nature or derived from existing global standards and definitions. Political conditionality links rewards (such as a preferential trading agreement, aid or other forms of assistance) with both the expectation and the execution of policies in a third country that promote the goals of democracy, human rights, the rule of law and good governance. Economic conditionality is concerned with linking rewards to the adoption and promotion of specific macroeconomic policies (such as structural adjustment programmes, liberalization and free trade areas). Typically, both political and economic conditionality are externally monitored (by the EU) although in theory at least it is possible for the recipient states to perform this task through internal domestic mechanisms. Positive and negative forms of conditionality simply contrast promised benefits for future desired action with the threat of punitive sanctions where specific policy guidelines are violated (and such punishment is often automatically triggered). Explicit conditionality can prescribe in great detail the mechanism, form and outcome of a policy; alternatively, conditionality may just describe general outcomes and goals, leaving the methods and policies used to realize these to individual choice. Typically, it is argued that, to be effective, conditionality must take a legal treaty-based form to enable actions to be justiciable and visible: however, in the area of political conditionality informal expectations may in practice be equally effective. Finally, both political and economic conditionalities can either draw on approaches defined by international organizations that are universally recognized or create specific policies that apply to a particular context.

What has been the underlying rationale for conditionality? Obviously there is no single rationale promoting the EU's application of conditionality. A major influence has been the changing external political environment. The post-1989 democratization process within Eastern and Central Europe provided the catalyst and convinced the EP of the necessity for future EU international agreements to contain explicit guarantees to strengthen fledgling democracies. Significantly, the 1987 Single European Act had given the Parliament the power of veto in agreements with third countries, and even prior to the fall of the Berlin Wall Parliament had sought to introduce human rights clauses in a number of cases (Smith 1998: 260). Up until that point, Europe's external relations had generally been noted for their apolitical content (Grilli 1993: 102). Second, the original ambitions of the Maastricht Treaty were highly optimistic – if largely unfulfilled – about Europe's international role. It was envisaged that the CFSP would result in the EU becoming a significant international actor and, as such, Europe would be well placed to shape international affairs, a plaintive refrain that was still familiar at the launch of the Lisbon Treaty. Consequently, Maastricht provided an explicit role and responsibility for the EU to promote global democracy and development. Article J.1 specified these as central objectives of EU foreign policy as expressed through the CFSP process: Article 130u specifically linked these political conditions to EU development policy. Hence, the 1990s saw the revised Lomé as well as new agreements with Latin America and Asia all include political conditionality as an 'essential' element (and by 1995 these agreements also had suspension clauses in cases of democratic and human rights violations (Smith 1998: 264)). Third, it has become accepted wisdom by the EU that sustainable development can only result where there are secure and effective institutions that promote democracy and civil society. Experience had shown that economic conditionality was, by itself, inadequate. Thus, good governance, for example, has become an EU developmental prerequisite, not an optional extra. Fourth, many third countries have sought democratic conditionalities as a means for promoting and embedding domestic reforms. In part, the EU can serve as the umbrella under which domestic governments can protect human rights, the rule of law and democratic accountability more effectively than they can independently. Other states, of course, do not take such a sanguine view and regard conditionality as essentially inconsistent with sovereignty. Lastly, European public opinion has been influential in demanding an EU development role while requiring that EU resources are effectively managed and not used to support authoritarian regimes.

Good governance

The concept of 'good governance' only found a voice in the EU's development vocabulary in the 1990s. Its introduction – together with that of human rights, the rule of law and democracy – as a form of political conditionality, has progressively complemented the trade relations basis typical of earlier EU development policy. Thanks to a politically assertive EP, reference to this principle has now become mandatory in all formal agreements between the Union and third countries – developed or developing. As is often the case, while the formal Treaty expression of the concept can be clearly defined, operationalizing the idea has proved to be less easily achieved in practice. What, then, does the EU understand by 'good governance' and to what extent is this interpretation shared by the developing world?

First, and importantly, good governance is a broad and inclusive idea that can be expressed through a variety of measures. It includes all aspects of the management of public affairs – economic, political and administrative – and requires that such management be 'transparent, accountable, participatory and equitable' and 'encompasses every aspect of the state's dealings with civil society, its role in establishing a climate conducive to economic and social development and its responsibility for the division of resources' (International IDEA 1999: 34). Central to this is a belief that good governance implies the establishment of competent and effective institutions consistent with democratic principles. Evidence of corruption is inconsistent with the principle. Article 5 of Lomé IV linked the principle of good governance to the goal of sustainable development, although it did not make it an essential element of the Convention (unlike democracy, human rights and the rule of law, which were). The difficulty in measuring levels of 'good governance' no doubt precluded this: just how 'good' was good enough? Had the principle been an essential element it would have been subject to scrutiny and differentiation and used, where necessary, to justify sanctioning any state which failed to meet the EU-defined standard of good governance. It is this role of the EU as legislator, judge and jury of the principle that presents the greatest difficulty. A cynic might also point out that the

EU's own standard of good governance is imperfect given the findings of corruption that led to the resignation of the Commission in 1999, the repeated refusal of the EP to discharge the EU's annual accounts, or the furore over the imposition of media restrictions in Hungary in 2011. Any such events in a vulnerable developing country could well have seen 'good governance' abrogated.

Nonetheless, there are a number of features that can be identified as indicators of good governance (although inevitably these overlap to some degree with general democratic principles). First, there is equity in administration and resource allocation that is guided and protected through an impartial application of law. Second, good governance depends upon the state possessing the capacity to administer and manage the allocation of resources effectively. No matter how good the intention, the capacity to act remains crucial. Third, transparency in decision-making, accountability and scrutiny are fundamental. And lastly, development decision-making should be open and participatory with accessible mechanisms whereby all members of civil society can be involved and informed (ibid.: 35). The Cotonou Partnership Agreement went to considerable lengths to define the elements legally – although once again these were not given the force of an 'essential element'.

Democracy, human rights and the rule of law

In assessing human rights the EU relies on internationally accepted universal principles enshrined in the UN Charter, the Universal Declaration of Human Rights and elsewhere. Clearly, human rights are fundamental to good governance. However, the EU's self-appointed role as sole adjudicator with respect to developing countries is not without critics. In the Lomé Convention and the Cotonou Partnership Agreement, for example, the EU has an exclusive right to judge when human rights have been breached despite repeated calls by the ACP for the equivalent of an independent EU–ACP court to perform this function.

Respect for the law and the independence of the judicial system are again fundamental principles applied by the EU. Impartiality, equality before the law and the citizen's right to redress grievances form the 'essential' elements of all other EU–developing country relationships. In contrast to good governance, any breaches in these legal requirements are more readily recognizable. Assessing 'democracy', however, can be more problematic.

Democracy's security and promotion have become the new mantra for EU relations with the developing world. The new wisdom argues that only through democratic institutions and norms can economic development effectively be pursued. The obvious question is, of course, which form of democracy does this best? The nuances of democracy are almost boundless: to avoid becoming bemused by the labyrinth of this debate, the following basic elements are considered as the essential core around which a practical assessment of democratic behaviour can be measured. Democracy is a political system based on respect of the law, implying rights (including civil rights), where the rulers are accountable to the population who can through peaceful and accepted procedures change those leaders at periodic intervals. Democracy implies control of power through checks and balances. There is no one single constitutional framework that guarantees these conditions: legitimate democracies can, and do, take many forms. When defining and evaluating democratic procedures and good governance, Eurocentric myopia must be avoided. The challenge for the EU remains how best to judge democratic performance. At the simplest level the following aspects of civil rights are commonly considered as essential prerequisites to political rights: 'Freedom of communication and speech and writing, freedom of assembly and of petition, freedom to form associations and engage in peaceful protest, and freedom from arbitrary arrest and lawless punishment' (Engel, quoted in Hanf 1999: 4).

Obviously, there are some extreme situations where it is relatively easy to agree that there have been serious breaches in democratic behaviour. Coups, such as the ones that occurred in Fiji in 2000 and 2006, for example, are the most easily identifiable. However, determining an appropriate response within an acceptable time frame can prove harder to achieve. Outside of such crisis situations, regular elections offer the EU a basic and practical yardstick with which to measure 'democracy' and provide a mechanism through which conditionality can be successfully applied. Free and fair elections are clearly the leitmotif of democracies and increasingly election observation has become the recognized measure for assessing the quality of this democratic practice. However, election observation or monitoring – if it is to be of value – has to be regularized, comprehensive, employ rigorous criteria and focus on every aspect of the election cycle, from the drafting of the electoral law through to the final allocation of seats.

Prior to the creation of the CFSP, the EU had not been formally involved in election monitoring. Over the past two decades, however, the EU has become increasingly active in election observation. Indeed since the Union's first monitoring experiences (in Russia and South Africa in 1993–94) the EU has become an authoritative voice that is increasingly called upon to validate the 'free and fair' nature of elections in third countries. This change was in response to new Treaty obligations to support the development of democracy globally, the EU's own implicit agenda to become a major international actor, as well as a direct consequence of third countries demanding such a role from the EU in order to provide international credibility to their electoral processes (as was the case, for example, in the July 2011 Thai general election where EU observers were invited). The EU is well suited to this role. Its varied membership makes it less likely to impose a single model of democracy as its assessment criteria. Practices – as well as historical experiences – within the 27 vary considerably, but are equally valid expressions of democratic election. Of course, the conduct of elections and this kind of quantifiable assessment forms only one aspect of the wider question of good governance. Its empirical nature makes it an appealing and useful indicator but not a complete measure. In crisis situations, however, the role of election monitoring plays a vital role.

If demand can be equated with success, then the EU's recent election observation profile is impressive: typically between eight and ten missions have been undertaken annually, covering all continents with an average annual cost of around €13 million. During the 2006–08 period a total of 32 missions were undertaken. For example, in 2006 this covered elections in Africa (Zambia, Congo and Mauritania), the Middle East (Yemen, the West Bank and Gaza), Central and Latin America (Venezuela, Nicaragua, Bolivia and Mexico) and one each in Asia (Bangladesh), the Pacific (Fiji) and the Caribbean (Haiti), confirming the EU's global reach and role. As of 2011 there were seven ongoing election observation missions: three in ACP states (Guinea Bissau, Mozambique and Malawi in Africa), Bolivia, Ecuador, Lebanon and Afghanistan (EuropeAid 2011).

Another aspect of human rights that has a particular EU perspective – and one where the EU's normative shadow can clearly be seen – is capital punishment. Since 1998 the EU sought the abolition of capital punishment and today it is the leading actor and donor in the fight against the death penalty. The policy mechanisms involved fall under the European Instrument for Democracy and Human Rights, specifically the Guidelines on the Death Penalty, the objectives of which are 'to work towards universal abolition of the death penalty as a strongly held policy view agreed by all EU member states; if necessary with the immediate establishment of a moratorium on the use of the death penalty with a view to abolition' (Council of the EU 2008a). In addition to its own bilateral initiatives, the EU also acts multilaterally. Resolutions on the moratorium on the use of the death penalty were adopted by the UN in 2007 and 2008 and on 21 December 2010 the General Assembly approved a new resolution in favour of a universal moratorium (Bacon 2011). There are some signs for optimism with executions declining somewhat since 2007(Hood and Hoyle 2008): however, in 2009 there were still 5,679 recorded executions in the 58 states that retained capital punishment.

How influential has the EU's anti-death penalty policy been? While not a strict form of conditionality, a significant majority of ACP states have either abolished the death penalty or effectively have a moratorium in place. Over 30 ACP states no longer have capital punishment and a further similar number have not conducted an execution within the last ten years, although formally the death penalty remains in place. Just 10 of the 78 ACP countries (all bar one in Africa) are retentionist states: Botswana, Chad, the Democratic Republic of Congo, Equatorial Guinea, Nigeria, Somalia, Sudan, Uganda and Zimbabwe (and St Kitts and Nevis in the Caribbean). The situation in Asia suggests that this EU value has not so easily been absorbed. While five states have an effective moratorium in place (Brunei, Laos, Myanmar, South Korea and Sri Lanka), 11 (including two of the BRICS) continue to use the death penalty (Bangladesh, China, India, Indonesia, Malaysia, North Korea, Pakistan, Singapore, Taiwan, Thailand and Vietnam). With the exception of Suriname, where a moratorium has been operating for over a decade, all states in Latin America have abolished capital punishment. On balance, Europe's ability to change the global normative agenda related to this issue has been limited: it will remain part of the EU's foreign policy and Human Rights agenda, however, and Baroness Ashton has made removing the death penalty a 'personal priority' (Ashton 2010a).

Economic conditionality: liberalization, structural adjustment and debt

The hallmark of the last decade of EU economic policy towards the developing world is an unquestioning commitment to the philosophy of trade liberalization. Based originally on the Maastricht Treaty conviction (more recently reasserted in the Lisbon Treaty) that development is fundamentally dependent upon reintegrating the developing countries into the world economy, the EU has increasingly turned to free trade as its preferred option. Often, the arguments as much resemble religious belief as they do economic rationality. Essentially, whether the EU is acting within the WTO, bilaterally with any OECD state or with the developing worlds of Asia, Africa, Eastern Europe, Latin America or elsewhere, the philosophy is dominated by economic liberalization.

The prolonged and often acrimonious negotiations between the EU and South Africa during the late 1990s provided an early illustration of this new catechism. Prior to 1995 all of Europe's relations with the developing world involved some degree of preferential concessions on the part of the EU. The most established and formalized of these relationships was the Lomé Convention, which – as we have seen in Chapter 2 – gave the ACP countries non-reciprocal access to the EU market for a range of goods and products. In general, the Lomé approach had typified EU behaviour towards the rest of the developing world. After its transition to full democracy and the election of President Mandela in 1995, South Africa opened a dialogue with the EU with the expectation that membership of Lomé – or at least a similar arrangement – would be the basis of the new relationship. What actually transpired was that the EU effectively insisted that the economic relationship had to be based around a free trade area. Never before had the EU sought to make this the basis of its relations with any developing country. After some minor concessions, in 1999 an agreement was signed that committed both to establishing a free trade area, albeit over an asymmetrical time period extending over 12 years for South Africa. Free trade, however, is not an absolute notion from the EU's perspective. Specifically, the EU sought (successfully) to exclude a significant proportion of agricultural goods from the agreement. The internal politics relating to the CAP were of greater significance than the soundly argued economic development arguments of Pretoria. Thus trade liberalization is not an equal partnership. The

South Africa example was in many regards a test for the subsequent general application of this new economic philosophy by the EU. Consequently, it was unavoidable that FTAs became the focal point for the post-Lomé IV discussions of 1996–2000 and that EPAs came to characterize the new Cotonou Partnership Agreement.

In part, a free trade agenda has been a consistent theme throughout the EU's history: the novelty was its application to such widely disparate economies. FTAs were also seen as consistent with the EU's long-standing ideological support for regional integration. In a sense the agreement with South Africa was unique in that the FTA was bilateral. The EU's objective is rather to promote regional groupings – the Pacific Island states, East Africa, and so on – with which to formalize multilateral FTAs. Such an objective is internally driven, as the motivation behind the Union itself is the belief that regional integration is a better form of both political and economic organization. Consequently, the promotion of regional integration outside of the EU is something that is impossible for the Union to oppose.

Bolstering this ideological commitment is the more practical argument of trade. As the world's largest trader (representing around one-fifth of global trade), it is in the EU's direct self-interest to support the role of the WTO in regulating the global economy. As an open multilateral trading system based on rules, market access commitments, enforcement through a dispute settlement system and a future liberalization agenda, the WTO both mirrors and facilitates the EU's wider social and economic agenda. In such a context, the EU has significantly more to gain from general trade liberalization than it has to lose from opening up its markets to the developing world. Of course, the EU can also argue that it is in the long-term self-interest of the developing countries to embrace trade liberalization. It is a matter of personal preference to determine the extent to which the EU's insistence on FTAs can be construed as altruistic. There can be no doubt, however, that the confluence of American and European views has combined to dictate the fundamental purpose of the WTO. The creation of global rules demanding equal treatment (based on MFN) for like cases in trading relations have been effectively used by the EU to argue that aspects of the previous preferential arrangements with the developing world were no longer sustainable. Even were the EU to want to maintain non-reciprocal arrangements, WTO rules have reduced the areas where this can operate legally (WTO Article 24 prohibits such non-reciprocal regional trade agreements). The Lomé Convention was successful in obtaining a WTO waiver for non-compliance with the MFN principle for ACP states. This waiver continued initially under Cotonou's interim EPAs; however, the EBA represented an important concession to the principle of equality of treatment by the EU. The EU made a clear choice: to embrace FTAs as a standard basis for all trade rather than attempt to redraft the WTO rules to make allowances for the EU's particular North–South context. For some, it is suspiciously convenient for the EU to employ WTO rules as an excuse for introducing free trade arrangements when FTAs are clearly its preferred economic option for the developed and developing world.

The EU's approach to international economics has become largely consistent with the mainstream policies of the Bretton Woods institutions. Indeed, making EU policy consistent with IMF and World Bank policies has become an additional aspect of coordination. Since 1996 the Commission and the World Bank have adopted a series of measures towards a joint approach to SAPs (van Reisen 1999: 70). While Europe's autonomy remains clear, increasingly an implicit consensus between these institutions has emerged on macro-economic development issues. Despite being a major contributor (providing over half of all ODA for example) the EU has yet fully to counter the influence of the USA in these forums. One explanation why a more distinct EU perspective in these international organizations has failed to emerge is purely institutional. The role of the EU in the IMF, World Bank and the UN is diluted because membership is through member states bilaterally: the EU as such does not have a seat and consequently Europe is unable to project its own exclusive voice. Obviously, the recent attempts to ensure coherence and coordination between national and EU-level policy has gone some way in moderating this; however, in terms of influencing the agenda of the Bretton Woods institutions Europe continues to punch well-below its weight, and some minor institutional concessions made in 2010 have actually seen this EU influence diluted further. Of course, development policy is not unique in this regard and this pattern is generally reflected wherever policy areas are shared between the EU and the member states.

The incorporation of SAPs as a form of conditionality first emerged during the negotiations for Lomé IV. Funds were earmarked and only made available for distribution where specific macro-economic policies were undertaken by the recipient state. In fact the EU had become a reluctant convert to this economic ortho-doxy and the motivation for adopting this approach came from the wider international community. From the 1970s onwards the poor performance of developing countries – especially those in Africa – were increasingly explained in terms of the domestic constraints placed upon their economies. The combination of over-valued exchange rates, high tariffs and rates of taxation, together with government controlled producer prices, were regarded in part responsible for the uncompetitive nature of many developing economies. This logic, coupled with the collapse in world prices for many primary commodities, led to what was at the time an irre-sistible policy conclusion. Domestic structure of production incen-tives had to be changed and the chosen international agent for this process became SAPs.

The EU did not enthusiastically embrace SAPs, and their negative consequences saw their popularity wane considerable by the end of the 1990s. Nonetheless, they became formal aspects of conditional-ity for a decade under Lomé IV. The EU through its member states sought to influence the design of SAPs by the IMF to accommodate more directly EU priorities and thereby counter – to a degree – the predominance of Washington in setting the Bretton Woods agenda. The imposition of SAPs also symbolized the changed balance in the original concept of partnership that defined European–ACP rela-tions. Prior to Lomé IV Europe accepted the principle that develop-ing countries had the democratic and sovereign right to determine their own aid priorities. The accelerating decline of primary product economies during the preceding decades effectively undermined the acceptance of this principle and emasculated their bargaining power. As Grilli (1993: 38) notes, the EU was 'in effect trying to establish control over the policy environment governing the use of the aid resources as a condition of the disbursement of part of its economic assistance'.

One of the most catastrophic consequences of the post-1970 economic crises faced by the developing world was the accumula-tion of indebtedness. The combination of mismanagement, declin-ing revenues and the effective devaluation of local currencies due to the liberalization of exchange rates demanded by structural adjust-ment, saw most developing countries unable to service their borrowing requirements. Africa has been the worst affected. By 2000, Africa's cumulative debt stood at US$375 billion, and equated to three-quarters of the continent's GDP and four times the value of its annual exports (*The Economist* 2000: 50). Europe's approach to this issue was both tardy and reluctant. As discussed in Chapter 3, the initial response was that debt, per se, was not an EU-level problem. Developing countries were typically indebted to various international organizations or had financial obligations to individual member states. Looked at in this way, the EU accounted for less than 5 per cent of the developing countries' global indebtedness. Indeed, the general character of EU financial assistance to the ACP countries was in the form of grants, not loans. Consequently it was argued as early as 1988 that the EU was not the appropriate mechanism for orchestrating debt relief. Either the G7 or the so-called Paris Club was given the initial responsibility for handling the issue. Grilli has suggested that this was especially revealing. It indicated that any debt concessions would be made unilaterally and not subject to the normal ACP–EU process of negotiation: simply, the 'form and substance of the European debt initiative could not have been farther away from the model of Lomé' (1993: 39).

The pattern over past decades illustrates the scale of the financial challenge. For example, the assessment of the Jubilee 2000 international campaign at the start of the millennium concluded that debt for the very poorest group of countries (the Heavily Indebted Poor Countries – HIPC) had risen by an average of 7.4 per cent per annum each year between 1980 and 2000, while these HIPC economies recorded just a 1.1 per cent growth over the same period. In 1980 total HIPC debt stood at US$58 billion: by 1997 this had grown to US$199 billion. The plight of two countries (Madagascar and São Tomé and Príncipe) – both ACP members – was particularly severe. More than 60 per cent of their revenue went on debt servicing alone (Holland 2002: 129–30). In a response to this deteriorating situation, debt relief was reintroduced onto the EU agenda in the mid-1990s (van Reisen 1999: 122). However, the major initiatives by EU member states have predominantly been bilateral and outside the EU framework. In the most important contemporary example – the HIPC initiative – the EU's contribution and role was overshadowed by a number of member states acting bilaterally (principally the UK and Germany, with Italy and France in support – see pp. 202–3). As well as constituting the four most important EU member states, these four also shared responsibility through the then G7 group and membership of the boards of the IMF and World Bank. However, the importance of the link to the EU is clear. Thirty-five of the 40 HIPCs are members of the ACP group and the EU is the world's biggest aid donor. The impact on the HIPC will principally be determined by the EU acting both multilaterally and bilaterally through its member states.

The HIPC Initiative found its way on to the World Bank and IMF agendas and by 1998 the EU issued a formal decision announcing its participation in the scheme. Funds of €40 million were set aside with the monies coming from the interest accrued through the non-disbursement of the EDF, a condition that the ACP states did not regard as particularly generous (Council 1998). In contrast to this collective approach, 1999 saw both Germany and the UK lead new bilateral initiatives on debt, followed by Italy in 2000, leading to an observation by one lobby group that there seemed to be a novel competition underway for the title of world debt relief champion! The Blair Government went on record to committing the UK to the UN goal of halving the number of people living in absolute poverty by 2015 – a promise with little prospect of being honoured. The year 2000 was the British target for beginning a systematic programme of debt reduction for all 40 HIPCs with funding coming from the proposed sale of the IMF's gold reserves. The German government of Gerhard Schröder complemented this by suggesting that SAPs be cut from six to three years (but still play a central role in debt conditionality) and that in exceptional cases aid debt could be completely cancelled. These ideas shaped the eventual 1999 Cologne Initiative at which the G7 agreed to provide improved debt relief to a number of HIPCs. Under the new initiative some 33 countries (with a combined population of 430 million) became eligible for debt relief and estimates put the level of relief at US$70 billion, reducing the HIPC indebtedness by more than 50 per cent (*The Economist* 1999: 23). Estimates at that time suggested that around 15 per cent of the expenditure of HIPC countries was devoted to debt servicing, and, as a creditor, the EU was owed roughly €1,460 million (van Reisen 1999: 198, 122). The situation for Africa was even more extreme: up to 40 per cent of African public revenues went towards debt relief. In July 2000, the Commission allocated more than €1 billion to the HIPC Initiative Trust Fund, making the EU the single largest contributor (Commission 2000d).

Whatever the actual final figures, the point made by advocates of debt relief is that cancellation of the specific EU debt involves a comparatively modest amount and is one that can be accommodated within the EU's existing budget. Debt relief does not come without conditions, of course: recipient states need to demonstrate a commitment to sound economic management (which implies continuing to comply with the IMF's Enhanced Structural Adjustment Facility – ESAF – conditions). However, critics argue that the HIPC debt relief initiative was an inadequate gesture and that the EU and the member states should cancel all debt: the EU has been institutionally divided over this option. Further, lobby groups such as Jubilee 2000 proposed a list of 52 – not 40 – countries that should be included in any debt initiative (Holland 2002: 131). Even among those who accept that the HIPC initiative is the only practical option, there was criticism of its limited application. The conditionality attached to the HIPC debt initiative revolves around an assessment of debt sustainability. The IMF stresses macro-economic measures (such as the role of exports in servicing debt) in its decision on which countries qualify under the HIPC programme. Criteria based on human development issues and indexes are not considered. Consequently, the immediate effect of the HIPC initiative was slow: by the year 2000, just four countries had benefited from debt relief.

Momentum took off, however, soon after the turn of the millennium with the launch of the EU's Barcelona Commitments to pursue debt sustainability. Some overall progress in debt reduction became evident, even in Africa where the debt service level fell from 4.2 per cent of GNI in 2001 (12.5 per cent of exports) to 1.6 per cent by 2008 (3.6 per cent of exports), though these levels have again risen since the financial crisis of 2008, jumping to 1.9 per cent of GNI in 2009 (6.1 per cent of exports). Finally, however, the request from debtor developing countries for the abolition of all debt was eventually accepted by the international community. In 2005, the G8 (involving the UK, France, Germany and Italy, together with the Commission representing the EU) under a British G8 presidency initiative, agreed to honour the commitment given in 1996 to take substantive action on debt relief. All debt owed to the World Bank, IMF and the African Development Bank by 18 HIPCs was rescheduled for payment by the G8 nations, effectively cancelling debts worth €33 billion. The 18 nations that benefited (14 from Africa) were: Benin, Bolivia, Burkina Faso, Ethiopia, Ghana, Guyana, Honduras, Madagascar, Mali, Mauritania, Mozambique, Nicaragua, Niger, Rwanda, Senegal, Tanzania, Uganda and Zambia. To qualify for debt relief, countries had to 'tackle corruption, boost private-sector development' and eliminate 'impediments to private investment, both domestic and foreign' (G7 2000: §3), a process monitored by the IMF and World Bank. A further €12.4

billion in relief was foreshadowed (the possibility was raised dependent upon conditionality criteria), affecting 20 more HIPC countries (conditional on anti-corruption and good governance criteria). However, for many of these countries internal conflicts have seen only marginal progress towards satisfying these G8 prerequisite goals, with debt relief consequently delayed.

This initiative provoked two divergent responses. For the EU, it was a clear success as it represented the first such action in the G8's 30-year history (Holland 2008: 355). For others, including NGOs and many developing countries, the limited scope and comparatively small sums involved were a disappointment. The exclusion of Bangladesh and Indonesia from the initial initiative, and the failure to agree on relief for Africa's greatest debtor and largest economy, Nigeria, was seen as especially critical. Nigeria's debt alone – estimated at US$36 billion in 2005 – was close to the entire relief given to the initial 18 HIPCs: European consensus on addressing this in 2005 was blocked by objections from Austria, Denmark and the Netherlands. Some estimates put the total of developing countries in need of debt relief at 62, not just the HIPCs. There are many countries that are as equally poor and as highly indebted as the HIPCs, yet, due to inappropriate eligibility and debt sustainability criteria, they have been excluded from the HIPC classification (G24 Secretariat 2003: 3).

The IMF and the World Bank first developed the HIPC initiative in 1996 with the ambition to provide a permanent solution to the problem of repeated debt rescheduling for the poorest countries (IMF 2003). It took until 1999 before the idea was further elaborated and operationalized by establishing measurable political and economic conditionality criteria. In essence, the HIPC initiative provides debt relief to the most impoverished nations globally that agree to undertake prescribed economic reform. From an original list of 40 countries, 38, mostly African, were considered, in principle, to be eligible for relief under the initiative. To qualify, countries must be very poor; have a very heavy debt burden; maintain economic stability; and have a strategy for reducing poverty. Various reforms were identified that the HIPCs were also required to enact, such as action on debt sustainability and the implementation of capacity-building (Martin and Johnson 2001).

Procedurally, the HIPC initiative is divided into two periods: the first where countries progress towards the 'Decision Point'; and the second, when the 'Completion Point' is met. The Decision Point involves a three-year period during which countries work to establish a record of good economic policies and sustained poverty reduction as determined by the IMF/World Bank criteria. The World Bank/IMF then determine each country's debt level and for those countries whose debt is considered unsustainable (after full use of traditional debt relief mechanisms) a package of relief is identified. This is the Decision Point. The Completion Point is reached once key structural reforms and poverty reduction policies have actually been implemented. While full HIPC debt relief is only provided at the Completion Point, some interim relief may be provided before this (IMF 2003: note 1). Of course, as critics have noted, linking the delivery of relief in this staged way intrinsically adds to the conditionality of debt relief; and the daunting process, procedures and requirements have been described as 'mind-bogglingly complicated and lengthy' (Martin and Johnson 2001: 6), involving numerous agencies – the IMF, World Bank, Paris Club – as well as donors and the HIPC states. For example, not only does an HIPC need to provide reliable debt data and agreed upon exchange rates, this also has to be reconciled with the various external creditors prior to reaching the Decision Point, a process tantamount to a debt audit. The capacities required to undertake these 'multiple, complex and continuous tasks' (ibid.: 22) are – unsurprisingly – not that readily available in the HIPCs; consequently assistance in capacity-building is a fundamental HIPC need.

The HIPC framework covers external debt that is public and publicly guaranteed. The criterion for being 'poor' is to be a country that relies on highly concessional financing from the World Bank's concessional lending arm, the International Development Association. The Decision Point determines whether a state's debt is sustainable or not. If the external debt ratio for a country after traditional debt relief mechanisms is above 150 per cent for the present value of debt to exports, it qualifies for debt relief under the initiative (Paris Club 2005). Excluded from this measurement are several other types of debt that undoubtedly impact upon an HIPC's overall debt sustainability, such as private sector borrowings, short-term external debt and domestic government debt (Martin and Johnson 2001: 6). To further complicate the debt assessment, the value of the country's debt is typically a year out of date and potentially may miscalculate the level of relief required – a problem not made any easier by the international currency instability characteristic of the international environment since 2008.

Table 7.1 *HIPC progress, 2010*

	Decision Point	Completion Point	Creditor participation at completion (%)
Post-Completion Point countries			
Afghanistan	July 2007	January 2010	97.7
Benin	July 2000	February 2003	99.0
Bolivia	February 2000	June 2001	95.0
Burkina Faso	July 2000	March 2002	76.0
Burundi	August 2005	January 2009	96.0
Cameroon	October 2000	April 2006	94.0
Central African Republic	September 2007	June 2009	82.0
Congo, Democratic Republic	July 2003	June 2010	96.0
Congo, Republic	March 2006	January 2010	80.6
Ethiopia	November 2001	April 2004	92.0
Gambia	December 2000	November 2007	80.7
Ghana	February 2002	June 2004	89.6
Guinea Bissau	December 2000	November 2010	81.0
Guyana	November 2000	November 2003	81.0
Haiti	November 2006	June 2009	96.0
Honduras	July 2000	March 2005	92.0
Liberia	March 2008	June 2010	96.4
Madagascar	December 2000	October 2004	90.0
Malawi	December 2000	August 2006	97.0
Mali	September 2000	February 2003	93.5
Mauritania	February 2000	May 2002	76.0
Mozambique	April 2000	September 2001	88.0
Nicaragua	December 2000	January 2004	87.0

→

By early 2003, 26 countries had reached the Decision Point by meeting these conditionalities, with six achieving the Conclusion Point after satisfying all criteria. By 2005 a further 12 had fully satisfied these HIPC conditions and it was these 18 states that were selected for debt relief by the G8 in June 2005. By December 2010, 36 states had reached the Decision Point, of which 32 had gone on to reach the Completion Point, with a further four currently at the pre-Decision Point level – Eritrea, the Kyrgyz Republic, Somalia and

	Decision Point	*Completion Point*	*Creditor participation at completion (%)*
Niger	December 2000	December 2003	85.0
Rwanda	December 2000	March 2005	95.0
São Tomé and Príncipe	December 2000	February 2007	85.0
Senegal	June 2000	March 2004	81.4
Sierra Leone	February 2002	December 2006	81.0
Tanzania	April 2000	November 2001	90.0
Togo	November 2008	December 2010	80.0
Uganda	April 1997	April 2000	96.0
Zambia	December 2000	March 2005	97.0
Interim countries (between Decision and Completion Point)			
Chad	May 2001	Initially expected December 2002	–
Comoros	June 2010	Expected December 2012	–
Côte d'Ivoire	March 2009	Expected December 2011	–
Guinea	November 2000	Initially expected December 2002	–
Pre-Decision Point countries			
Eritrea	Yet to qualify	–	–
Kyrgyz Republic	Yet to qualify	–	–
Somalia	Yet to qualify	–	–
Sudan	Yet to qualify	–	–

Source: IMF Decision Point and Completion Point Documents (www.imf.org/external/np/hipc/index.asp?view=pre&sort=cty).

Sudan (see Table 7.1). The focus on HIPCs can have an unintended negative effect of disadvantaging those countries just above this poverty index. Consequently, there have been calls for better treatment of severely indebted low-income countries which are ineligible for the HIPC initiative, by providing additional debt reduction or budget support aid (HIPC 2005).

The example of debt relief serves to emphasize (all be it nega-tively) the constant challenge of complementarity for the EU. As shown above, in this key development policy area the EU is at the mercy of the member states and their respective domestic lobbies. It is almost an impossible task to expect the Commission to coordinate the British, German, French, Italian and Scandinavian proposals on HIPC policy, let alone make these complementary with the EU's own position. The EU seems unable to avoid the trap of formalizing policy goals that lead to high expectations before providing the Commission with the necessary scope and authority to execute such policies. While the complexities of policy-making at the EU level can provide a theoretical explanation for this, the dissonance does noth-ing to enhance the EU's image as an effective and single interna-tional actor. Bilateral action has proved to be resilient and remains a core aspect of the EU's multilateral development agenda.

Implementing conditionality

Despite the dominance of a bilateral approach towards debt reduc-tion, as the preceding sections have outlined the EU has collated a range of collective political and economic conditionalities to frame its relations with the developing world. These are commonly applied and represent the multilateral perspective based upon the consensus of the 27. But just how effective and consistently has political conditionality in particular been applied?

Isolating various elements within political conditionality – human rights, good governance, etc. – has presented the EU with an empirical challenge: simply, how does one measure violations? Are there degrees of compliance? Are all elements of equal importance or are some less significant? Wherever possible, the EU uses a carrot rather than stick approach. The emphasis is on recognizing, encour-aging and rewarding states to maintain or move towards acceptable standards of governance, preferring to withhold sanctions as very much the last resort. However, as one commentary noted, the EU does not provide any data to substantiate this claim, so conclusions can only be impressionistic (Smith 1998: 266). Given the financial constraints under which development policy operates it is probably almost impossible to 'reward' states for good behaviour as such resources are already committed elsewhere. Where a budget alloca-tion cannot be increased the only solution is to take funds from other existing areas, something that is itself politically difficult to achieve. An example of this dilemma occurred in mid-2000 when the EP sought to increase the aid provided to South Africa under the FTA. As an increase in the overall development budget was not acceptable, the Council proposed rechannelling funds previously committed to the emergency food aid budget to achieve this.

Cases of sanctions are easier to identify of course (although one should be aware of distinguishing between those sanctions agreed in principle and those actually enacted – the time lag between these two events can often be considerable). Table 7.2 provides data for the 1990s where violations of democratic or human rights resulted in the suspension of trading relations or aid. Four features are immediately apparent. First, with few exceptions, the offending countries were all members of the Lomé Convention. The explicit conditionalities introduced into Lomé in part explain this pattern. Second, around half the cases occurred prior to the Maastricht Treaty legally coming into force (on 1 November 1993), suggesting that the real change in approach pre-dated the CFSP debates and that, while a legal framework adds weight, the necessary prerequisite for action is a collective political will. Third, the offending states, as well as the notable omission from the list of other less peripheral states, are of relative unimportance to the EU economically. And fourth, there is an absence of cases in Asia.

The situation by 2009 was quite different. Table 7.3 provides information for sanctions that were only imposed because of violations in democratic practices, human rights, rule of law or good governance standards. The ACP now only represented half of those states targeted by EU sanctions, arguably an effect of conditionality, although the dominance of Africa amongst the ACP had not changed. Asia – Myanmar – appeared for the first time as a target of EU action. Looking at the specific cases amongst the ACP, often concerns over arms were a trigger for the imposition of EU sanctions based on democratic breaches. For example, in the Democratic Republic of Congo sanctions were linked to an arms embargo, covering inter alia: the recruitment of child soldiers; the targeting of children or women in situations of armed conflict; obstruction of humanitarian assistance; and the illicit trade of natural resources to support armed conflict. In Eritrea the EU sanctions concern the harbouring, financing, supporting, organizing, training or inciting of individuals or groups to perpetrate acts of violence or terrorist acts against other states or their citizens in the region. Similarly, in Somalia the EU sanctions are designed to restrict individuals from

Table 7.2   *EU sanctions based on violations of democracy, human rights, the rule of law or good governance, 1990–98*

		Reason for EU action		
	Year	Human rights	Rule of law	Democracy
ACP states				
Sudan	1990	√		√
Haiti	1991		√	√
Kenya	1991			√
Zaire	1992			√
Togo	1992			√
Malawi	1992			
Equatorial Guinea	1992	√	√	
Nigeria	1993	√		√
Gambia	1994		√	√
Comoros	1995		√	√
Niger	1996		√	√
Burundi	1996		√	√
Sierra Leone	1997		√	√
Other developing states				
Guatemala	1993		√	√
Transition economies				
Belarus	1997	√		√

Sources: Smith (1998: 267), *Bulletin of the EU* (1998–2000), *European Foreign Affairs Review* (1997–2000).

engaging in acts that threaten the peace, security or stability, or obstruct the delivery of humanitarian assistance. In Sierra Leone sanctions are limited to restrictions on leading members of the former military junta. And in Sudan, EU sanctions seek to place restrictions on the admission of individuals who impede the peace process, constitute a threat to stability in Darfur and the region, and commit violations of international humanitarian law or other atrocities.

Table 7.3   *EU sanctions based on violations of democracy, human rights, the rule of law or good governance, 2009*

	Reason for EU action		
	Human rights	*Rule of law*	*Democracy*
ACP states			
Côte d'Ivoire	√	√	
DR Congo	√	√	
Eritrea		√	
Haiti		√	√
Liberia	√	√	√
Sierra Leone		√	√
Somalia	√	√	
Sudan	√	√	
Middle East			
Lebanon		√	√
Syria	√	√	√
Europe			
Belarus		√	√
Bosnia and Herzegovina		√	
Croatia		√	
Yugoslavia (Serbia and Montenegro)		√	
Asia			
Myanmar	√	√	√

Source: Commission (2010h).

Agreements with developing countries as well as the imposition of sanctions – and their removal – require unanimity in the Council. Parliament's involvement does not extend to suspension clauses and it can be technically if not politically ignored. If action is to be undertaken through the CFSP then the additional mechanism of joint action or common position are required. Consequently, there is ample opportunity to employ procedural arguments and allow bilateral preferences to prevent the emergence of EU action. In addition to cases of sanctions, the EU is active in other, less punitive ways – such as issuing critical démarches or joint statements in the UN and elsewhere, as well as through formal political dialogues. Increasingly, the withdrawal of EU ambassadors from third countries has been used to indicate concern. Clearly, the negative exercise of sanctions based upon political conditionality is subject to all kinds of constraints, and EU action in the past has in no sense been uniformly applied. The 'importance' of the transgressing state is often influential, as is any former colonial link with a member state. With the exception of the arms embargo, China has escaped punitive action along with a number of other Asian countries where labour practices and human rights are widely known to be suspect.

The nature of the economic partnership is also a factor. It can be relatively simple to impose a trade embargo on a state with which there is very little economic interaction: where European jobs are at stake the political costs are considerably higher. Often past experiences of ineffectual sanctions (such as those applied to South Africa in 1985–86 or Yugoslavia since 1991) are sufficient to deter the EU from taking punitive measures. Many critics have concluded that in terms of the application of political conditionality the EU simply employs double standards. Even those who are more sympathetic to the institutional, procedural and political constraints within which the EU operates argue that a more systematic and coherent approach is possible (Smith 1998: 273). The dissonance between the EU's formal presentation of its foreign policy objectives of human rights and democracy and its performance to date has principally succeeded only in widening the publicly perceived 'capabilities–expectations gap' and compromised the EU's claim to be an important international actor. The record under the new authority of the High Representative for Foreign Affairs will be closely scrutinized to see whether the Lisbon Treaty can deliver on this promised ambition and expectation.

Conclusion

In conclusion, both the goals of complementarity and conditionality, if successfully executed, would enhance the EU's international character. However, as we have argued in this chapter, promoting EU-level policies that meld with those of the member states as well as with Europe's internal policy priorities is complex, challenging and probably impossible to realize perfectly. The link between development and democratic principles of good governance has become the accepted and inevitable face of North–South relations; the degree to which this conditionality is supervised and sanctioned remains variable, however. This variable application of conditionality historically has undoubtedly detracted from the EU's international credibility and influence, and remedying this perception should be a priority for the new EEAS. As is often the case with the EU, there is a tendency to exaggerate the expectations for new policy competences, whether this is for the CFSP, EMU or development and poverty reduction. Indeed, a cynic might accuse the EU of blatant and repetitive false advertising. Successive treaties have underlined the EU's policy on complementarity and introduced political and economic conditionalities – yet, there has been a worrying gap between the rhetoric and practice of what has been promised and expected: Lisbon must avoid this trap. Of course, this failing is not unique to the EU: what is unique, however, is that the EU cannot rely on a long history of international action to bolster its reputation. It is judged, and can only be judged, on how it deals with the present, and in the area of development policy its current performance is at best mixed, at worst, disorganized and incremental.

Chapter 8

The EU and the Global Governance Development Agenda

As remarked elsewhere in this text, the global and European development agenda of the 1990s focused unprecedented attention on the transition economies of Eastern and Central Europe. This understandable international response to the collapse of communism and the Soviet Union had the unintended consequence of further marginalizing the traditional developing world of the South. In an attempt to redress this imbalance, by the turn of the twenty-first century the international community began to develop a new perspective that sought to address these ongoing and increasingly global inequalities. The EU was a leading voice in setting this new agenda and worked collaboratively within the UN, the World Bank, the IMF, the G8 (and more recently the G20) and international campaigns such as 'Make Poverty History' over the last decade. In this chapter we examine the EU's role in this wider global governance development agenda, particular in relation to ODA commitments, untied aid, a renewed emphasis on Africa, and the UN's MDGs. By exploring the linkages between EU development policy and that of the international community a central question is raised: is the impact of development policy enhanced by such complementarity or reduced through duplication and competition?

Official Development Assistance

Before examining the EU's ODA contribution, the exact nature of development aid needs to be clarified – what is eligible for aid and what is not. ODA is defined by the DAC in the following terms. ODA involves:

donor flows that are for 'the promotion of the economic development and welfare of developing countries'. The directives that cover what can be reported as ODA exclude the supply or financing of military equipment or services and use of military personnel to control civil disobedience. (OECD-DAC 2005a)

More generally, the DAC's mandate (established in 1961) describes their function as 'making national resources available for assisting countries and areas in the process of economic development and for expanding and improving the flow of long-term funds and other development assistance to them' (OECD-DAC 1961). To qualify as ODA, funds have to be provided from official sources on concessional terms (meaning that loans can qualify), their main objective must be to promote the economic development and welfare of developing countries, and support of military aid and peacekeeping expenditures are excluded (Carey 2005). Consequently, the broad scope of the DAC's mandate can cover: financial aspects of development assistance; the environment; statistics; aid evaluation; gender equality; good governance and capacity building; conflict, peace and development; and harmonization of donor practices.

These definitions were supplemented in 2005 to include aspects of security as eligible for ODA budget support, a change reflecting the belief that to pursue sustainable development without a secure environment was a futile exercise (Holland 2008: 351). The changes and reforms agreed upon included to:

1. Improve civilian oversight and democratic control of security expenditure.
2. Facilitate a civil society security role to enhance compliance with democratic norms and principles of accountability, transparency and good governance.
3. Support legislation against the recruitment of child soldiers.
4. Develop civilian activities for peace-building, conflict prevention and conflict resolution.
5. Prevent the proliferation of small arms and light weapons.

(OECD-DAC 2005a)

Turning to bilateral aid levels since 2000, the cumulative importance of EU member state aid has been considerable. Although the USA has been consistently the largest single country donor during the first decade of the twenty-first century, figures since 2006 show that the EU and its member states now collectively contribute in excess of 60 per cent of all DAC ODA. Typically, the EU contributions have been dominated by four member states: in 2009, for example, France led with €8.9 billion, followed by Germany (€8.6 billion), the UK (€8.2 billion) and Spain (€4.7 billion), equivalent to over €30 billion or around US$43 billion in support. The distribution of aid, however, displayed a difference in geographical priorities, with aid from four EU states having a strong sub-Saharan African focus, this being the priority for the UK, France, the Netherlands and Sweden as of 2008, while Germany's focus was the Middle East and North Africa (closely followed by sub-Saharan Africa), and Spain concentrated aid on Latin America and the Caribbean (World Bank 2010a: 410–12). South Asia was also a British aid focus, and to a lesser extent that of the Dutch, reflecting their respective historical ties.

The EU's ODA record is less impressive, however, if viewed in a broader context: as of 2009 only four member states had met the agreed UN 1970 ODA target of 0.7 per cent GNI – Sweden, Luxembourg, Denmark and the Netherlands (see Figure 8.1). The most recent data shows that the EU27 average stood at 0.42 per cent by 2009, ahead of all other OECD economies with the exception of Norway (on 1.06 per cent), and the EU's figure compared rather favourably with the USA's GNI percentage contribution that has only reached 0.21 by 2009 (OECD-DAC 2011) – although the USA remains the highest volume contributor (US$28.8 billion in 2009 – more than twice the level of the next highest, France on US$12.6 billion). A further six member states had previously committed to meeting the 0.7 per cent figure by 2015 (Belgium, Finland, France, Ireland, Spain and the UK) and Sweden achieved its goal of reaching an ODA/GNI ratio of 1 per cent in 2006. However, all of the EU12 post-2004 member states fell significantly below even the USA's ODA/GNI ratio, as did one founding member (Italy) as well as Greece, even prior to the unfolding of its debt crisis (see Figure 8.1 and Table 8.1).

Table 8.1 reveals some striking patterns in ODA member state contributions over the 2006–09 period, both in terms of value and as a percentage of GNI. First, the 2004–07 enlargement marked a profound ODA dichotomy between old and new members states. In 2009, the EU15 provided €48,217 million in ODA, the equivalent to 0.44 per cent of their combined GNI: in comparison, the EU12

FIGURE 8.1   EU member state ODA as percentage of GNI, 2009

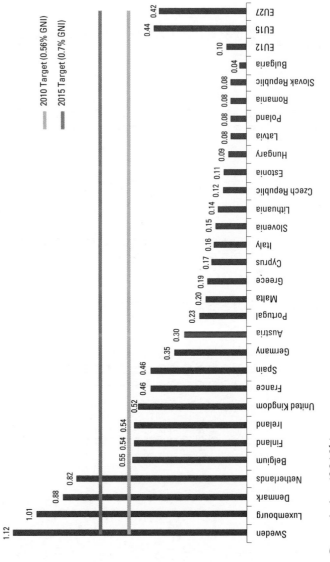

Source: Commission (2010b).

Table 8.1 EU member state ODA, 2006–09

	2006		2007		2008		2009	
	€m.	% GNI	€m.	% GNI	€m.	% GNI	€m.	% GNI
Austria	1,194	0.47	1,320	0.50	1,165	0.42	823	0.30
Belgium	1,576	0.49	1,425	0.43	1,651	0.47	1,868	0.55
Bulgaria	1	0.00	16	0.06	13	0.04	12	0.04
Cyprus	21	0.15	18	0.12	27	0.17	29	0.17
Czech	128	0.12	131	0.11	146	0.11	161	0.12
Denmark	1,782	0.80	1,872	0.81	1,941	0.82	2,017	0.88
Estonia	12	0.09	16	0.12	14	0.09	14	0.11
Finland	665	0.39	716	0.39	790	0.43	924	0.54
France	8,446	0.46	7,212	0.38	7,596	0.39	8,927	0.46
Germany	8,313	0.35	8,978	0.37	9,644	0.38	8,605	0.35
Greece	338	0.16	365	0.16	480	0.20	436	0.19
Hungary	119	0.14	75	0.08	72	0.07	83	0.09
Ireland	814	0.53	870	0.55	918	0.58	718	0.54
Italy	2,901	0.20	2,897	0.19	3,081	0.20	2,380	0.16
Latvia	10	0.06	12	0.06	14	0.06	15	0.08
Lithuania	18	0.08	30	0.11	41	0.13	35	0.14
Luxembourg	232	0.90	274	0.91	283	0.92	289	1.01
Malta	7	0.15	8	0.15	6	0.11	11	0.20
Netherlands	4,344	0.78	4,542	0.81	4,848	0.80	4,614	0.82
Poland	236	0.09	265	0.10	264	0.08	249	0.08
Portugal	316	0.21	343	0.22	425	0.27	364	0.23

Romania	3	0.00	80	0.07	94	0.07	99	0.08
Slovak	44	0.10	49	0.09	65	0.10	53	0.08
Slovenia	35	0.11	38	0.11	51	0.14	51	0.15
Spain	3,038	0.31	3,755	0.37	4,635	0.43	4,719	0.46
Sweden	3,151	0.99	3,170	0.93	3,286	0.98	3,267	1.12
UK	9,931	0.51	7,191	0.36	7,919	0.43	8,267	0.52
EU 27	47,673	0.41	45,668	0.37	49,468	0.40	49,029	0.42
EU 15	47,039	0.43	44,930	0.39	48,663	0.42	48,217	0.44
EU 12	634	0.09	739	0.09	805	0.09	812	0.10

Source: Commission (2010c: 44).

managed just €812 million between them, representing 0.10 per cent of their GNI. Totalling the respective figures raised the EU27 amount to just over €49 billion, while lowering the average GNI to 0.42 per cent. Within the EU15 a further division was apparent that distinguished between those member states who had met their ODA commitments by 2009 (led by Sweden at 1.12, Luxembourg at 1.01, Denmark at 0.88 and the Netherlands at 0.82 per cent of GNI) and the largest contributors in value (France and Germany) who continued to hover around the EU GNI average (0.46 and 0.35 per cent respectively). Also evident over the 2008 to 2009 period has been a significant increase in the ODA/GNI ratio of the UK (from 0.43 to 0.52) and France (from 0.39 to 0.46), alongside a decline for Germany (from 0.38 to 0.35, representing an ODA reduction of €1 billion – 10 per cent). There was less variation in contributions between the newer member states, although the contributions of the larger countries were especially disappointing (Hungary at 0.09, and Poland and Romania at 0.08 per cent of GNI each).

In terms of volumes of aid, over half of the EU27 ODA commitments for 2009 (of €49,029 million) came from the EU3, led by France and Germany who each provided 18 per cent, and the UK on 17 per cent. A further quarter was provided by the combined contributions for Spain, the Netherlands and Sweden. Strikingly, although consistent with its historical record, Italy only provided modest ODA support, representing just 5 per cent of the overall total, making it the least generous of the EU15 member states. However, even this figure outshone the combined effort of the EU12, which collectively accounted for a mere 2 per cent of the EU's ODA total (Commission 2010c: 15).

The full impact of the 2008 global financial crisis or the debt crisis faced by several EU member states in 2010–11 has yet to be accurately measured against ODA commitments. What was already clear by 2009, however, was that no additional EU aid would be forthcoming: what was less certain was whether prior promises would, or could, in fact be kept. The initial response (some six months after the crisis commenced) by the then Commissioner for Development, Louis Michel, was hardly encouraging, as he conceded that 'we have not come here to announce to you any huge new sums … Of course our ambitions are limited. But we are going to keep putting the pressure on' (*Deutsche Welle* 2009). The extent of the 'ambition' was for the more effective disbursement of existing EDF commitments, with a target of 72 per cent set by 2011. While the aid trajectory had been generally positive, the four-year period prior to the financial crisis had already seen bilateral fluctuations in GNI aid allocations. Overall, the EU27 percentage aid has been static across this period, with any real funding increases offset by the impact of enlargement on GNI calculations. The EU did, however, achieve its 0.39 per cent 2006 target that was agreed by the member states at the 2002 Monterrey International Conference on Financing for Development (OECD-DAC 2005b). However, only the most confirmed optimists consider it plausible that the EU can meet its 0.7 per cent ODA target by 2015 (unless the GNI of the EU member states declines so dramatically as a consequence of the global financial crisis that their percentage share rises without any actual additional funds being required!).

Putting rhetoric to one side, the EU has had only limited success in either increasing the levels or maximizing the impact of member state and EU development funding. As the Union's public diplomacy frequently proclaims, the EU together with the member states supplies more than half of all OECD aid, yet a lack of adequate coordination has reduced its potential and effectiveness. In November 2004, the Council invited the Commission to 'prepare specific and ambitious proposals' concerning development policy (Commission 2005b). The Commission's response of 12 April 2005, drafted by Louis Michel and commonly known as the 'MDG package', called for groups of countries to pool their aid efforts, with leadership roles going to those countries with the relevant specific expertise. It was hoped that this new approach would reduce duplication and streamline the typically multiple and differing demands made by individual donors that can often overwhelm the administrative capacity of recipient states. Effective implementation of this policy, of course, depends upon the cooperation of the member states, and the history of development aid is littered with examples of national political criteria and donor competition that have compromised the goal of poverty reduction. If the EU is to reach the 50 per cent reduction in global poverty set by the MDGs by 2015, the Commission's coordinating role will be crucial (Holland 2008: 353).

There were three elements within Michel's new approach designed to increase the volume and effectiveness of the development aid provided by the Commission and the member states (Commission 2005b, 2005g, 2005h). Its adoption, of course, was subject to Council and EP approval. Specifically, these were to:

- Increase EU member state ODA to 0.56 per cent of GNI by 2010 (worth €66 billion) and to 0.7 per cent (€92 billion) by 2015.
- Achieve greater coherence between Community policies, better coordination between member states and the EU, and more ownership of aid by the recipient countries.
- Prioritize Africa.

(Commission 2005e)

The funding target was always ambitious, and in the revised context of the global financial crisis is proving impossible to achieve. To have met the 0.56 per cent figure by 2010 would have required an increase of over €15 billion on the 2008 level of ODA: while European development funding remains outside the Community budget, given the fiscal constraints imposed upon the 2007–13 EU budget, such an unprecedented increase in member state funding was always unlikely to be realized. Missing the target – yet again – was therefore no surprise. Given the economic disparity between the EU15 and the EU12, the new member states were given lower ODA targets (of 0.17 per cent by 2010 and 0.33 per cent by 2015: Commission 2005g: 6) – goals that seem equally unobtainable, however.

The designation of Africa as the EU's development priority was similarly radical, broke with past practice and sat uncomfortably with the existing ACP focus of the Cotonou Agreement. These contradictions notwithstanding, EU policy, in cooperation with the global community, now seeks to: empower African governance through support for the African Union; support African regional integration and foster South–South trade; promote social cohesion and sustainable peace. Of most significance was the EU decision finally to address the debt burden, something that had not been considered an EU responsibility previously (see p. 61). Finally, the Commission called for the untying of aid – something first advocated under the 2002 Barcelona Commitments (see Box 8.1) – and member state compliance in tender procedures for bilateral aid (Commission 2005b).

Despite claims of innovation by the Commission, the 'coherence' aspects of the MDGs package simply repeated the shortcomings previously identified during the policy review that lead to the Cotonou Agreement. The only new practical initiative was the agreement to draft a coherence report after the September 2005 UN summit and the next international assessment of the MDGs. This signalled an important change in approach; however, the EU's

---

Box 8.1   The Barcelona Commitments

- Increase EU ODA to 0.39 per cent of GNI by 2006 and examine the means and time frame for each member state to reach the UN 0.7 per cent ODA goal. The member states commit individually to reach a baseline target of at least 0.33 per cent GNI to ensure that the EU achieves the collective 0.39 per cent goal.
- Improve aid effectiveness through closer policy coordination and harmonization of procedures, and to take concrete steps to this effect before 2004.
- Take measures with regard to untying of aid to Least Developed Countries.
- Increase Trade-Related Assistance.
- Support the identification of relevant Global Public Goods.
- Explore innovative sources of financing.
- Support the reforms of the International Financial Systems and strengthen the voice of developing countries in international economic decision-making.
- Pursue efforts to restore debt sustainability in the context of the enhanced HIPC initiative.

---

attempts to promote policy coherence were no longer to be confined to the coordination of the EU and member state levels, but now extended to incorporate the wider framework of global efforts to achieve the 2015 MDGs (Holland 2008: 353).

Aid is certainly an essential element in global development but obviously not a sufficient condition. By way of illustration, in 2003 only in one region (sub-Saharan Africa) did official aid have a significant impact on GNI levels, accounting for 6.0 per cent of GNI and 15.9 per cent of imports. The next highest grouping was South Asia, with ODA at 0.8 per cent of GNI and 4.2 per cent of imports (World Bank 2005: 350–2). Trade and investment remain the more important components from an EU policy perspective and the key to Cotonou's ambition to see the 'gradual integration into the global economy' of developing countries through the creation of EPAs.

While increasing ODA to reach the 0.7 per cent GNI target

remains an EU commitment, a new emphasis on the quality of 'real aid' has emerged that attempts to measure the percentage of aid that actually improves people's lives, a calculation somewhat different to the standard statistical ODA arithmetic. One, albeit disputed, 2005 estimate suggested that just two-fifths of aid could be considered 'real', the remainder being absorbed by overpricing, inefficient cooperation or used to fund programmes not strictly aid associated (Holland 2008: 356). In fairness to the ODA figures, they should be viewed as neutral regarding the quality of aid – they do not attempt to measure the benefits of ODA to developing countries, but simply try to quantify the donor costs of the aid programme. Nonetheless, there is now a broad international consensus on the need to maximize the human impact of aid and to minimize its dilution through diversion, excessive bureaucratic regulations or misapplication (Carbone 2007). The former World Bank President, James Wolfensohn, has criticized the amount of ODA accounted for by relief of export credit debt, expensive expatriate-provided technical cooperation, tied aid and excessive transactions costs, such as multiple uncoordinated missions and studies. Similar sentiments were also echoed by the Director of the UN's Millennium Project who questioned whether EU consultants or developing countries benefited the most from EU policy (Sachs 2005). Tied aid is especially inefficient: in 2002 the DAC estimated the extra costs of goods and services tied to donor country sourcing at between US$5 and 7 billion (Carey 2005).

The 2005 DAC Paris Declaration, involving 17 EU member states, the Commission and 30 ACP countries, was an important initiative in addressing the issue of aid quality as an aspect of the MDGs. It acknowledged that coordination on the side of the donors as well as enhanced capacity to absorb aid was needed in order to improve implementation effectiveness. It provided for detailed joint commitments, including mutual accountability mechanisms, and stipulated a five-year implementation and evaluation plan to facilitate measurable thresholds (OECD 2006). The overall purpose of the Declaration was to initiate and enable a systematic discussion of aid effectiveness issues between donors and specific country partners, something that had previously proved difficult to establish. While the initiative increased multilateral complementarity, it also compounded the complexity of development policy.

Another new area where the international community sought consensus was in relation to tied aid. Typically, aid from individual

DAC countries had required that preference be given to companies, consultants and products from the donor country, rather than allow recipient countries to choose in the competitive framework of an open procurement market. With around half of all ODA tied, distortion, cost escalations and less aid value for money were the commonly perceived negative consequences. In order to accelerate development in the poorest regions, in 2001 the OECD agreed to begin to 'untie their ODA to the Least Developed Countries to the greatest extent possible', while committing themselves to 'sustain adequate flows of ODA in terms of quality, volume and direction', so as to ensure that aid to the LDCs would not decline as a consequence of this policy change (OECD-DAC 2001: Article 2). The expectation was that untying aid would increase competition, help develop the local private sector and signal to the LDCs that donor countries were genuinely committed to providing effective aid to support development, even at the expense of their own direct economic self-interest. This seemingly simple and ethical idea has proved complex and slow to implement in practice (Holland 2008: 357).

Somewhat inauspiciously, the governing OECD guidelines noted that 'untying is a complex process' and thus 'different approaches are required for different categories of ODA, and actions by Members to implement the Recommendation will vary in coverage and timing'. However, it was agreed that by 1 January 2002 the DAC members would untie their individual ODA to the LDCs in the following areas:

* Balance of payments and structural adjustment support.
* Debt forgiveness.
* Sector and multisector programme assistance.
* Investment project aid.
* Import and commodity support.
* Commercial services contracts.
* Procurement related activities of Non-Governmental Organisations.

(OECD-DAC 2001: 3)

Certain technical cooperation and most significantly, as well as contentiously, food aid were excluded from the scope of the policy. Consequently in those areas where aid remains tied distortions will continue to proliferate: for example, it has been estimated that the continued tying of aid for food relief generally increases the cost of food stuffs by almost 30 per cent, compared with commercial transaction estimates (OECD-DAC 2005c: 10).

In the 2009 DAC Untied Aid Report (Clay et al. 2009: 10), five EU member states reported a minimum of 90 per cent of aid as untied. Greece reported the lowest ratio among DAC members at just 13 per cent. What was of greater importance, however, was the historical change in attitude and perception. Within a comparatively short timescale untied procurement had become the norm and effective transparency meant tenders were accessible to all OECD competitors. For example, in 2003, almost 75 per cent of all reported tender contracts were awarded to companies located outside the donor territory and almost 40 per cent went to developing countries (ibid.: 9), though this calculation was made from only a limited number of donor responses. By 2007, as the contract reporting mechanisms became more firmly established, the figures were somewhat different – 38.5 per cent of contracts reported were awarded outside the donor territory, with 31 per cent going to the developing world. Importantly, in practice, all of the aid to those categories was untied (Carbone 2007). The success of this LDC initiative has seen calls for the policy of untying of aid to be extended to a further 21 low income developing countries. The European Commission responded to this OECD initiative by agreeing to continue to examine the further untying of EU aid (while appreciating this was a member state competence primarily). In keeping with a long tradition of self-congratulation as the world's leading development donor, at the 2005 UN Summit President Barroso stated that the EU had 'shown its determination to turn worthy aspirations into action' in relation to untying aid (Commission 2005c). It will be interesting to see whether this humanitarian perspective survives the inevitable reconsideration of aid procurement in the wake of the global financial crisis.

A final concern facing aid – whether tied or untied – that should be noted has been the attempt by some member states to blur the distinction between anti-poverty resources and allocations for security and foreign policy expenditure. This post-9/11 tendency to view almost all policy from a security perspective clearly has potentially serious and far-reaching implications for the traditional understanding of development aid: as one critic noted, 'development assistance which prioritizes the achievement of human development goals is at risk. A rapid increase in aid has been channelled to meet new security imperatives' (Woods 2005: 407).

Prioritizing Africa

Timing can often be crucial in facilitating policy innovation. Despite the ACP grouping, Africa had become increasingly marginalized in the EU's global priorities since the early 1990s. In the second half of 2005 this neglect was finally reversed and sub-Saharan Africa re-emerged as an EU policy priority. This rediscovery was largely thanks to an EU member state (the UK) holding the EU and G8 presidencies simultaneously, giving Britain an unprecedented opportunity to influence the global development agenda. Africa appeared as a key theme in the British EU presidency goals and was also the focus of G8 discussions which complemented the UN's September 2005 review of the MDGs. Africa took precedence over other developing regions because – as is discussed later in this chapter – it was the continent that was the least likely to meet any of the eight MDGs by 2015, with 2050 the more realistic if still optimistic date (Holland 2008: 348). Africa's domestic plight has been extensively recorded: 40 per cent of all Africans live on less than €1 a day; three out of every four persons who die from AIDS are African; 18 of the world's 20 poorest per capita income countries are in Africa; African life expectancy has been falling over the last 30 years; and Africa's share of world trade continues to decline (G8 2005a; Commission 2005h). For historical, political and economic reasons, Europe is uniquely placed to assist as the EU is Africa's most important donor of development aid and largest trading partner. Collectively, the EU and the member states provide close to two-thirds of all development aid to Africa and around half of all EU aid goes to sub-Saharan Africa (Commission 2005h). Interestingly, Eurobarometer findings suggest that EU public opinion also regards Africa as an area where the EU could have the greatest impact on development.

The July 2005 Gleneagles meeting was the first time the G8 had reviewed commitments made under its 2002 Africa Action Plan. The outcome was an agreement to double annual aid to all developing countries to €41.9 billion (over the 2004–10 period) with 80 per cent of this figure coming from the EU and its member states – with a half of this total designated for Africa. This funding was to be entirely new and not an accounting transfer between budget lines and was in addition to the €46 billion previously agreed in debt cancellation for the 18 HIPCs (see pp. 202–8). The G8 called for coherent, coordinated and mutually reinforcing actions with the ambition to 'accelerate the self-sustaining growth of Africa and end aid dependency in the long term' (G8 2005a: §6). The Gleneagles communiqué argued, if ambitiously, that such an increase in financial aid for Africa could, if implemented fully, have a dramatic impact, including the delivery of universal free basic healthcare and primary education, universal access to HIV/AIDS treatment, promoting employment prospects and raising millions out of abject poverty (G8 2005b).

In a related initiative focused on the African Union, the G8 made the link between development and security by outlining a range of initiatives aimed at improving the conflict prevention and resolution capacity of the continent. The most notable innovation saw the G8 offer to train and potentially equip 75,000 African troops by 2010 to facilitate the policing of security both within the African continent and worldwide. Programmes in support of good governance and transparency were also promoted that involved the African Union and its NEPAD (New Partnership for Africa's Development) programme. Continuing this African theme, in 2005 the Paris Club of donors agreed to a partial relief programme for Nigeria's €15.1 billion debt. At the EU level, an additional €1 billion specifically for trade development was committed so that emerging African exports could take advantage of EU market access opportunities in practice and not just in theory (Holland 2008: 349).

The Commission's long-awaited Africa Strategy was launched in October 2005 (see Box 8.2) and greeted with cautious optimism by some (Kingah 2006). The objective of the new Strategy was to provide a coordinated framework for action applicable to the EU and the member states designed to focus additional resources on the key issues for achieving the MDGs for Africa. The Strategy aimed to provide more and better development aid, to increase the speed of implementation, to improve aid effectiveness and to prioritize and increase aid for Africa. Peace and security, good and effective governance, trade, interconnectivity, social cohesion and environmental sustainability were seen as necessary, if not sufficient, elements for sustainable development (Commission 2005c). In order to assist Africa in reaching the MDGs, the EU agreed to provide at least an additional annual €10 billion by 2010 (Michel 2005), and specific mechanisms for promoting joint programming, alignment of procedures and increasing budgetary aid were outlined. Two examples are the ambitious Governance Initiative and the Partnership for Infrastructure. Under the Governance Initiative, the EU will provide

Box 8.2   EU Strategy for Africa 2005

The main themes of the EU Strategy for Africa:

- The Strategy focuses on: peace, security and good governance; economic growth, trade and infrastructure; and MDGs of health and education, sanitation and environment.
- The Strategy supports sustainable development through a Governance Initiative and a Partnership for Infrastructure.

Implementing 'more, better and faster'

The Strategy is based on the June 2005 European Council commitment to Africa to do 'more, better and faster' through:

- *Finance*: by 2010 at least 50 per cent of the additional annual development aid budget will go to Africa. EU Aid to Africa will increase from €17 billion in 2003 to around €25 billion in 2010.
- *Budgetary support* will increasingly be used to implement development projects faster and strengthen African ownership.
- *Coordination* of EU donors will be strengthened through concrete initiatives, including the formulation of an Action Plan in 2006 to enable progress on issues such as Joint Programming.
- *Coherence* with policy areas such as trade, agriculture, fisheries and migration will be strenghtened

Source: Commission (2005f).

support for reforms triggered by the African Peer Review Mechanism, a unique tool for good democratic governance by and for Africans. In the context of the Partnership for Infrastructure, the EU will continue to promote its belief in regionalism by supporting programmes that facilitate interconnectivity at a continental level, thereby promoting regional trade, integration, stability and development. This builds on the €50 million already allocated to support the institutional and operational development of the region's embryonic integration body, the African Union. The Strategy identified three ways of building closer and more effective links with the African Union: through political dialogue, existing agreements and by the creation of a pan-African programme (Commission 2005h). The Strategy, if indeed new, relied heavily on a familiar element: success was dependent upon the ability of the EU and member states to coordinate effectively policies and to engage in complementary actions. As the then Commissioner for Development and Humanitarian Aid stressed, 'one of the EU's most central challenges in Development cooperation remains to ensure a coherent and effective approach between 26 different actors, the 25 member states and the European Commission, with 26 Development policies' (Commission 2005c); an observation that was sadly repetitive to anyone familiar with the previous three decades of EU development policy (Holland 2008: 350).

The subsequent 2007 EU–Africa Lisbon Summit under the Portuguese presidency (the first such high level meeting since 2000) sought to build on this initiative by forging a new 'strategic partnership' in a wide-ranging agreement covering topics of peace and security; governance and human rights; commerce and regional integration; energy; climate change; migration and employment; and science, information technology and space. A €10 billion annual increase in EU support to Africa was pledged, and a commitment to hold a further summit in 2010 given – and subsequently honoured (Commission 2007a). But the Agreement met with strong criticism and the inclusion of Zimbabwe's President Mugabe at the meeting demonstrated the significance of a parallel development and reflected the growing concern over the emergence of China as an actor in Africa. Confronted by China's expanding trade and development role in the continent (which came without any apparent conditionality) the EU became increasingly concerned that its good governance conditionality would see its influence diminish. The Agreement was signed under inauspicious circumstances and difficulties in the relationship were further compounded when around half of the sub-Saharan ACP countries failed to meet the 31 December 2007 deadline for signing EPAs (see pp. 82–5), something that many commentators had long foreseen (Hadfield 2007).

The Union's concern with China has continued. Most notably, its focus on resource extraction from the African continent and the use of non-conditional aid transfers as a mechanism for guaranteeing access and supply has been a key facet in debates on China's emerging role on the global stage. The Commission's most recent communication should be viewed in the context of this increased competition for resources. Asserting that 'development policies can play a crucial role in creating win–win situations where both developed and developing countries benefit from the sustainable supply of raw materials', the draft communication advocates a greater role for EU development policy and lending practices in securing raw material from the continent (Willis 2011b). Whether the exigencies of resource supply will outweigh the Union's governance agenda is yet to be seen.

MDGs: from consensus to momentum

As we have illustrated in this chapter, through a series of incremental changes the EU modified its development policy from 2000 onwards; however, the most substantial and concerted change came with the EU's embrace of the MDGs, a rare example of effective multilateralism in practice. The 1996 DAC *Shaping the 21st Century* report (OECD-DAC 1996) set the underlying principles that came to be widely endorsed by the international community (Michel 2005). The report led to the formulation of the UN's Millennium Declaration and what were to become the MDGs which, in September 2003, were finally adopted as the eight MDGs which now bind the UN's members to development targets by 2015. Seven of these goals encompass all the traditional aspects of development, from poverty reduction to education, gender inequality, health (such as mortality, HIV/AIDS) and environmental sustainability. The eighth goal is more complex and subjective, invoking a 'global partnership for development' to address the underlying economic structures for development (see Box 8.3).

A distinctive feature – from an EU perspective – of the MDGs is the complementarity with EU development priorities: indeed, in 2005 Commissioner Louis Michel went as far as to suggest that 'the MDGs endorse to a large extent the European suggestions and positions. We can be satisfied: it is always better to have the glass half full rather than have an empty one' (Michel 2005). However, as this section illustrates, policy coordination and multilateralism counts for little without adequate financial commitments. And as for satisfaction – the question is for whom?

Box 8.3   UN Millennium Development Goals

Goal 1 Eradicate extreme poverty and hunger:
- Reduce numbers living on less than a dollar a day;
- Increase employment;
- Reduce hunger.

Goal 2 Achieve universal primary education

Goal 3 Promote gender equality and empower women:
- Remove gender disparities in education.

Goal 4 Reduce child mortality

Goal 5 Improve maternal health:
- Reduce mortality;
- Increase access to reproductive healthcare.

Goal 6 Combat HIV/AIDS, malaria and other diseases

Goal 7 Ensure environmental sustainability:
- Integrate principles of sustainability;
- Protect biodiversity;
- Increase access to potable water and sanitation;
- Improve lives of slum dwellers.

Goal 8 Develop a Global Partnership for Development:
- Develop open and rule-based trading and financial system;
- Address needs of LDCs, landlocked countries and Small Island Developing States;
- Deal with the debt problem;
- Increase affordability of essential pharmaceuticals;
- Increase access to technology.

For more details, see: www.undp.org/mdg/basics.shtml.

MDG goal 1 – concerning hunger and poverty – was a modified version of the long-standing EU commitment to addressing global poverty. The changed wording, from an EU perspective, is of note: in earlier and more optimistic times the EU's policy had called for poverty eradication, subsequently reformulated as poverty reduction, while under the MDGs this was redefined in terms of 'extreme poverty and hunger'. While it is important to note that data on poverty measures are estimates only, and as a consequence are often imprecise and variable in reliability from country to country, World Bank regional data addressing the 2001 MDG baseline of halving the number of people who live in extreme poverty (originally less than US$1 a day, now less than US$1.25) by 2015 offers a clear overall picture. Four regions (Europe and Central Asia, Middle East and North Africa, South Asia, and sub-Saharan Africa) saw an increase in the numbers of people living in poverty over the 1990–2005 period, though it is important to note that in only one of these – Europe and Central Asia – did this reflect an overall increase in the percentage of the population living in poverty. Nevertheless, the poverty figures are still extremely high – in sub-Saharan Africa, 50.9 per cent of the population was living on less than US$1.25 per day in 2005, with 72.9 per cent on less than US$2 per day. The figure for those on US$2 per day was even higher for South Asia, with India in particular registering a staggering 75.6 per cent. By contrast, China has undergone a remarkable decrease in poverty over the same period, from 60.2 per cent in 1990 to 16.8 per cent by 2005. Only two regions registered an overall decrease in the ratio of those living in extreme poverty during the time frame – East Asia and the Pacific, and Latin America and the Caribbean.

At the launch of the MDGs, the proportion of the world's people who were hungry had declined from one-fifth to one-sixth since 1985; but this still represented 852 million people. While most were in Asia (India 221 million and China 142 million), sub-Saharan Africa with 204 million hungry was the only region of the world where hunger was continuing to increase, even though in 14 sub-Saharan African countries hunger had been reduced by at least 25 per cent during a decade (G8 2005b). According to UN predictions, if these trends continue, this region will fail to meet the hunger MDG (UN 2005d: 11).

Universal primary education and gender equality (MDGs 2 and 3) were also principally a sub-Saharan African concern where less than two-thirds of children were enrolled in primary school. Four out of five children in the developing world – and just half of children in sub-Saharan Africa – had completed a primary school education, a statistic virtually unchanged over a decade and compounded by continued gender differences which have seen the primary gender equality goal by 2005 unrealized (UN 2005i: 36). For secondary education, the figures were even less encouraging. For example, in South Asia the female secondary enrolment rate stood at 47.1 per cent and in sub-Saharan Africa at only 29.7 per cent (UN 2005h: 5). Given this pattern, the MDG 2015 educational deadline seems unlikely to be met.

One area where gender inequality showed significant improvement was in female representation in parliament. However, of the 49 countries in the world where female parliamentary representation stood at under 10 per cent, 11 were in sub-Saharan Africa and 12 in the Asia–Pacific region, figures that had only marginally improved since 1990 (IPU 2010).

The theme of gender equality – in relation to child and maternal mortality rates – was expressed through MDGs 4 and 5. Although mortality rates for children aged under 5 have fallen, estimates still suggested that 10.8 million children a year – 30,000 a day – continued to die from preventable or treatable causes in the new millennium, with 41 per cent of these deaths in sub-Saharan Africa and 34 per cent in South Asia (G8 2005b). Just six countries (India, Nigeria, China, Pakistan, the Democratic Republic of Congo and Ethiopia) accounted for half of all childhood deaths and 90 per cent of deaths occurred in just 42 countries (UN 2005j: 53). Contemporary analyses have concluded that none of 47 countries in sub-Saharan Africa was 'on track' to reduce child mortality by the MDG target of two-thirds by 2015. Based on 2005 data, there remained a substantial difference in child mortality rates between rich and poor: the ratio of deaths to 1,000 live births was 7 for industrialized countries, 88 for developing countries and 120 for the world's poorest countries (ibid.: 62).

Maternal mortality constituted MDG 5: the 2015 target was to reduce the death of women in pregnancy and childbirth by three-quarters. In the UN's 2005 assessment, the maternal mortality MDG was the one towards which countries had made the least progress (ibid.: 77). Overall levels of maternal mortality remained largely unchanged since 1990 with current estimates of deaths put at about 530,000 a year. In the great majority of countries where historically most maternal deaths have occurred, there has been little change: in other countries, where levels of HIV/AIDS and malaria are high and growing, the number of maternal deaths and the maternal mortality ratio have even increased (ibid.: 5). The geographical spread of maternal mortality followed a familiar pattern, with sub-Saharan Africa having by far the highest mortality ratio of any developing area, accounting for 47 per cent of all deaths in 2000. African women have a 1 in 20 chance of dying in childbirth (ibid.: 79).

MDG 6 is arguably the most ambitious of the MDGs and concerns the diseases most prevalent in the developing world – HIV/AIDS, malaria and TB – with the goal of reversing their rise and pervasiveness by 2015. Evidence to date suggests that this goal is likely to be unobtainable. Unlike MDGs 1–5 the benchmark against which to measure HIV/AIDS success is somewhat opaque and lacks precise measurement. Because the scale of the problem is so enormous, simply halting the further spread of HIV/AIDS can hardly be seen as a success. Once again, the geographical distribution pattern is skewed. In total numbers, 2005 estimates indicated that 39 million people carried the virus worldwide, 25 million of whom were from Africa, with an annual death rate of 3 million, which exceeds that for malaria and TB, making it the planet's most deadly communicable disease (UN 2005c: 1). In sub-Saharan Africa, 7 out of 100 adults were living with HIV and 57 per cent of HIV cases were among women (G8, 2005b). In Southern Africa more than a quarter of the adult population was HIV-positive and, importantly, the rate of infection for young women (15–24 years) was three times that for young men (UN 2005b: 54). AIDS remains the leading cause of death worldwide for the 15–49 generation. One consequence has been the prolific increase in orphans, with some 15 million already orphaned by the disease by 2004. Around 80 per cent of these orphans (12.3 million) were again to be found in sub-Saharan Africa (ibid.: 111): by 2010 this figure was estimated to have risen to 18.4 million out of a global AIDS orphan population of 40 million. Funding towards this MDG has increased significantly over a decade: in 1996 it was around US$300 million but by 2004 the total support from all sources was calculated at US$6 billion globally. Yet this figure was considered to be less than a third of the annual amount needed (US$19.9 billion) in order to achieve the MDG and bring the disease under control (ibid.: 132); yet again, the bulk of funding was needed for sub-Saharan Africa.

Although it generally attracts less public and media attention than AIDS, malaria is endemic in many of the world's poorest countries, infecting an estimated 350–500 million people a year, leading to between 1.1 and 2.7 million deaths annually. A series of eradication programmes in the 1950s–60s saw malaria disappear from the former Soviet Union, southern Europe, the United States, all but one of the Caribbean islands, and Taiwan (UN 2005c: 13). The comparatively recent global re-emergence of the disease dates from the 1990s as a result of drug resistance and failing health systems in the poorest countries of the developing world. Consequently, the disease is especially virulent in tropical Africa where 90 per cent of the global malaria deaths each year occur (ibid.: 15). Malaria is estimated to have slowed economic growth in African countries by 1.3 per cent a year (ibid.: 20). The original malaria MDG – like that for HIV/AIDS – lacked a realistic basis for quantification, although a revised 2015 target of 75 per cent reduction in deaths based on 2005 baseline data was subsequently proposed (ibid.: 88–9). The policy strategy has been largely informed by the multilateral consensus built around the 'Roll Back Malaria' WHO initiative of 1998, the impact of which was badly undermined by a lack of funding (ibid.: 24). This impediment was partly removed with the creation of a G8-sponsored 'Global Fund to Fight AIDS, Tuberculosis and Malaria' which initially provided US$3 billion over a two-year period for all three diseases (with $921 million for Malaria programmes in 80 countries, $1.8 billion for HIV/AIDS in 119 countries and $500 million for TB in 80 countries)(ibid.: 26). While positive, significantly greater support is needed if the MDGs are to be achieved.

Tuberculosis in many ways mirrors malaria and AIDS. Around 95 per cent of TB deaths are in the developing world, killing a total of 1.7 million people a year, with numbers growing by about 1 per cent annually; in 2002, for example, nearly 9 million new cases were notified (UN 2005g: 24). TB is the prime cause of death for those with HIV/AIDS. Estimates suggest some 11 million people have both HIV/AIDS and TB: sub-Saharan Africa again has been the region with the greatest increase (7 per cent between 1997 and 2002). The revised MDG together with the new 'Global Plan to Stop TB II' calls for the global prevalence of TB and death rates to be halved between 1990 and 2015 (ibid.: 73). Effective treatment is available: inadequate funding and ineffective delivery prevent this from reaching about half of those infected (G8 2005b). The MDG strategy is to maximize participation in the DOTS initiative ('Directly Observed Treatment, Short-Course', the internationally recommended control strategy for tuberculosis) that has been operational in 180 countries since 1995. However, the excluded countries tend to be the poorest, African and where TB incidence is extreme. Fully 80 per cent of TB cases are found in just 22 countries (UN 2005g: 25) and 13 of the 15 countries with the highest estimated incidence rates per capita are in Africa. Nonetheless, the necessary medical and operational knowledge exists to achieve the 2015 targets provided that adequate political and financial investment is made – 2005 estimates put the gap between what was spent and what was needed at around US$1 billion per year (ibid.: 74).

MDG 7 (environmental sustainability) and MDG 8 (a global partnership for development) widen the context of global development issues and serve as prerequisites for the success of the other goals. The environmental sustainability focus intersects directly with the other goals through its emphasis on sanitation, water access, sound ecological practices, reduced pollution, infrastructure, conservation, soil degradation and deforestation, climate change, and biodiversity. Despite some 1.3 billion people living on marginal lands and one-fifth of humanity lacking access to safe water, historically the need for environmental sustainability has been marginalized in development and poverty reduction strategies (UN 2005e: 62). The links between the environment and poverty, food security and health are now better established, as is how the environment and ecosystems shape global economic well-being: consequently, the environmental MDGs emphasize mainstreaming sustainability across all development strategies. Where feasible quantifiable measures have been set (reducing by 50 per cent the number of people without sustainable access to safe drinking water, using 1990 as the baseline) as well as more qualitative targets such as achieving 'significant improvement' in the lives of at least 100 million slum dwellers by 2020 (MDG 7 targets 3 and 4 – see Box 8.3).

In 2002 the WHO estimated that at least 1.1 billion people lacked access to safe water and 2.6 billion lacked access to basic sanitation (predominantly in Asia and sub-Saharan Africa), deprivations that resulted in 3,900 child deaths each day due to dirty water or poor hygiene (UN 2005e: 3–4). To meet these MDGs, the global funding necessary between 2001 and 2015 is estimated to be around 'US$68 billion for water and US$33 billion for sanitation, for a total of US$101 billion'. That amounts to $6.7 billion per year – less than half what Europe and the USA spend annually on pet food ($17 billion) (ibid.: 102). As for sustainability, water underpins and is relevant to achieving all of the MDGs, but most analysts agree that to meet just the MDGs concerned with access to clean water and sanitation will require a profound change in water management and international priorities and resources.

The challenge of making 'significant improvement' to the lives of 100 million of the world's 924 million slum dwellers and promoting alternatives to future slum formations (MDG 7 target 4) is equally daunting, even if the measures were recognized by the UN as less quantifiable. Urban slums are widespread in the developing world (representing 43 per cent of these regions' populations in 2005) and at extreme levels in the LDCs (rising to 78 per cent) (UN 2005a: 1). Asia has the highest slum totals: China and India together account for more than half of the world total. Long-term projections envisage substantial increased urbanization, almost all within the developing world: by 2015 the urban population is expected to overtake those in rural areas in the developing world. The UN has estimated that to achieve the MDG target US$18 billion per year for 16 years is needed (2005–20), a total of US$294 billion, equivalent to US$440 for each individual slum dweller (ibid.: 9).

MDG 8 is both the most detailed (listing six specific targets) and yet the most generalized in its operational development goals – creating a global development partnership based on an 'open, rule-based, predictable, non-discriminatory trading and financial system' (MDG 8 target 1 – see Box 8.3), phrasing that is familiar to those who have followed the EU's development paradigm shift under Cotonou. Thus the goal seeks to address inequalities in the current international trading system and suggests how to correct this imbalance so as to provide developing countries with the possibility for greater economic growth and, therefore, greater capacity to reduce poverty. The broad ambition is consistent with the EU's trade liberalization approach with the ACP and Latin American and Asian developing countries as discussed in earlier chapters. However, the selective preferences that are the hallmark of the EU approach are a target of this MDG; in particular:

> The poorest countries have frequently received limited benefits from preference schemes, in part because preferences do nothing to address their multiple supply-side constraints. Benefits are also often gained at the expense of other developing countries, and they are smaller than would be the case with either direct transfers or multilateral liberalization. (UN 2005f: 217)

While the MDGs do not promote trade as the panacea for development, the contextual importance of trade regimes is paramount: were developed countries to open significantly their markets to developing countries (who would also became more open), poverty could be reduced faster, especially in the poorest ones. While there may be a broad consensus on these principles, the implementation of reciprocal liberalization has remained problematic, especially in the restricted markets for global agriculture, textiles and services, and FTAs in general having proved less than satisfactory to date. More positively, although initially no specific deadlines were set for any aspect of MDG 8, as discussed earlier progress has been made towards the targets of debt relief and meeting ODA commitments, at least by the EU, even if a UN Summit proposal to ensure this was rejected in 2007(Michel 2005). In other areas, despite provisional target dates, at best trends rather than actual changes are all that is discernible, suggesting that comprehensive trade liberalization in favour of development looks set to remain a work in progress.

Conclusion

In summary, the growing complementarity of EU development policy with the UN's MDGs is a positive sign. Europe's overlapping memberships within the G8, G20, Paris Club and the OECD presents it with a strategic advantage to lead and fundamentally influence the international development agenda. For optimists, the increased cooperation since 2000 and the joint perspective of the MDGs shared by the EU and the UN suggests a brighter development future. Yet on balance, while improved global statistics for some of the MDGs were becoming apparent by 2005, an overall MDGs assessment looked more pessimistic (Commission 2010g: 36–48), particularly given the little substantive improvement for the continent most seriously affected – Africa. There had been some progress – for example declining levels of maternal death during childbirth and lower mortality rates in children under five in sub-Saharan Africa (to a figure of 17.2 per cent in 2003); but this decrease was minimal in comparison with the equivalent European figure of 0.21 per cent. Hunger continued to decline, albeit slowly, and there was measurable progress in achieving universal primary education, although again the picture for sub-Saharan Africa was the most critical with less than two-thirds of children enrolled in school. Gender equality advanced through empowerment initiatives and at least a commitment to sustainable development practices had become widely articulated. More critically, while global poverty rates were in decline (particularly in Asia), the reverse was the case for sub-Saharan Africa. Finally, no effective reduction in HIV/AIDS, TB and malaria has been realized, with these diseases still remaining the leading causes of death in sub-Saharan Africa.

Despite this growing challenge and diminishing time frame, the Commission has remained optimistic, diplomatically at least, as reflected in the comments made by President Barroso at the September 2010 UN High Level Summit on Millennium Development Goals:

> The European Commission is and will remain fully committed to ensure progress towards the Millennium Development Goals. I firmly believe that they are achievable with strong political commitment from all partners and the right policies and resources. With only five years away of our target date, we now need to move up a gear. Some progress has been made to which the EU and the Commission contributed largely. But more remains to be done. Donors must live up to their promises and developing countries must take their future in their own hands ... By working together we can and we will reach the goals by 2015. (Commission 2010f)

The initiatives made in debt relief, ODA and trade reform notwithstanding, outside of the Commission this optimism is not widely shared, with few brave enough to conclude that the MDGs are either on schedule or likely to meet the 2015 deadline. The EU's leadership role in development has never been more necessary.

Chapter 9

Conclusion: Themes and Future Directions

In this concluding chapter the conceptual link between EU development policy and the process of European integration raised in
Chapter 1 is revisited. While atheoretical examinations of EU politics can still be found, increasingly the importance of integration
theory has come to be recognized as the essential starting point for
discussions of any EU activity. To understand the motivations and
rationale behind European policies – as well as the chosen policy
mechanisms – requires a theoretical framework. Often, explanations are not to be found in the more immediate issues related to a
specific policy sector, but in the wider debates concerning the kind
of integration process envisaged. Understandably, most examinations of Europe's relations with the developing world have located
themselves theoretically within the discourse of development studies
and a brief survey of these approaches was given in Chapter 1.
However, the perspective of this book has been upon the European
process of establishing policies that are developmental in nature;
consequently the issues pertaining to the wider integration debates
are of central relevance. Simply, which of the competing approaches
to integration can best explain EU development policy? We have
suggested a range of concepts rather than a single theoretical framework as the more appropriate approach. As has been shown, there
are clear intergovernmental policy competences involved (ODA,
debt relief, EDF), a new institutionalism is evident (EBA), neo-functional spillover has occurred (EPAs, the security and development
nexus), multilevel governance has shaped decision-making (the
Cotonou reforms) and there is the clear expression of constructivist
values and norms (MDGs, the death penalty) – all of which combine
to shape the nature of EU development policy. Such policy diversity
demands conceptual complementarity and not a single theoretical
lens.

241

The preceding chapters have provided an overview of the complex mosaic of frameworks that define the EU's relations with the developing world. The emphasis of the book reflects that of the EU itself: both historically and contemporarily the most intense dialogue has been with the ACP countries, with Asian and Latin American relations given considerably less attention. However, the debate surrounding Cotonou and the changing development paradigm promoted by the EU has come to colour all sectors of European development policy. In that respect, policy towards the ACP has shaped and determined the nature of the EU's developing-world relations globally. Even the latest initiative – the MDGs – has been largely driven by African needs.

What, then, might the next decade of EU development policy look like? Are we likely to see 'more' Europe, 'less' Europe, or perhaps a more effective Europe? In late 2010 the Commission began the latest development review process with the release of a Green Paper – EU Development Policy in Support of Inclusive Growth and Sustainable Development: Increasing the Impact of EU Development Policy – following a broad-based consultative tradition that first began in the mid-1990s as part of the Lomé reform process (Commission 2010d). A renewed debate on EU development policy was certainly timely given the recent geopolitical and institutional changes, the approaching EU financial framework for 2014–20, as well as the ongoing ramifications for global development of the financial and economic crisis. Indeed, as the Green paper acknowledged, a decade of progress towards the MDGs had been 'mixed' but the achievement of the MDGs by 2015 remains Europe's 'first and overriding priority' (Commission 2010d: 3–4). The gravity of the challenge was bluntly summarized by the Green Paper in the following terms:

> The review of progress on the MDGs therefore makes it clear that the world needs to do more in support of countries' efforts towards the MDGs, not just in terms of ODA levels, but at least as importantly, in terms of how aid is granted and used. In particular, aid alone will never succeed in pulling millions of people out of poverty ... development assistance can only be effective by addressing the underlying causes of insufficient progress towards the MDGs. Aid ... must tackle the roots of poverty rather than its symptoms, and primarily be a catalyst of developing countries' capacity to generate inclusive growth ... in support of poverty

reduction strategies. It is thus increasingly obvious that MDGs will not be achieved without more and more inclusive growth. (Commission 2010d: 4)

The focus of the Green Paper was on how to leverage new opportunities to reach the MDGs, in particular to reduce poverty. Four objectives to be pursued collaboratively by the EU and the member states were outlined. These were how to (i) ensure the greatest impact of EU development policy; (ii) facilitate more inclusive growth in developing countries as a means of reducing poverty; (iii) promote sustainable development to drive progress; and (iv) achieve durable results in agriculture and food security. Based on the Green Paper consultations, in mid-2011 a provisional 'roadmap' to modernize EU development policy was published by DG-DEVCO. The changed international context since the 2005 'European Consensus on Development' was instrumental in informing the new policy direction, including 'developing more appropriate and differentiated EU policy responses towards low income and middle income countries and emerging powers' (Commission 2011: 2). The implications appear profound; the EU's traditional global approach to development looks set to be replaced by one based on strategic targeting. Development assistance for the BRICS and other G20 countries is likely to be reduced or even ended, with EU resources becoming concentrated on 'Neighbourhood' states, North and sub-Saharan Africa and the LDCs. Further, a renewed emphasis on the role of political conditionality underpinning the realization of the MDGs has surfaced in the wake of the 2011 Arab Spring, with a promise by the EU to implement its 'policy on governance more strictly and consistently' (Willis 2011d). The fate of these new policy directions is of course subject to EU institutional approval, something that had yet to be conferred prior to the publication of this book. However, if adopted and implemented, a significant redesign of EU development ambitions will have occurred.

To conclude, a number of broad themes can be identified from this survey of EU relations with the developing world. First, development policy still remains an undervalued and under-researched aspect of EU activity. In the academic literature it has gained only spasmodic attention, although a new generation of scholars has begun to work more intensely in the area since the launch of the MDGs: and, as discussed in Chapter 1, in contrast to the analysis of most other EU policy sectors, it is rarely addressed from the conceptual premise of integration theory. In part, this discontinuity is explained by the ambiguous nature and origin of development policy. The national funding base of the EDF is symbolic of this uncomfortable blend of national and supranational competences. While a distinct EU role exists, it is often conditional on national bilateral support and its function in the wider integration process obscured.

A second and perhaps a dominant theme is that EU development policy is subject to the shadow of complementarity. Ensuring that the different elements of EU-level development policy are consistent and do not produce unintended consequences or conflicts of interest is a substantial organizational task. The creation of the EEAS may provide the needed capacity to realize this bureaucratic goal, given the significant development competences that have been brought under the High Representative's auspices. However, as was shown in the analysis of the EBA and the implementation of Cotonou, ensuring consistency across different development policy spheres remains problematic. In isolation, the EPAs under Cotonou, the provisions for ACP non-reciprocity as well as the extension of this to all LDCs under the EBA can all be regarded as rational and appropriate policy responses. But cumulatively, these individual EU initiatives contain inherent conflicts and contradictions. This tendency is further exacerbated when one then tries to align EU-level policies with the 27 bilateral policies of the member states, even if development policy is often a terra incognita for the post-2004 members. Consequently, it should not be surprising to find examples where EU policy fails the complementarity test: what is more surprising is the frequency with which complementarity is achieved.

A third theme and one that appears to be currently in the ascendant is that development policy forms an important aspect of the EU's international role and should be understood within the broader intention to establish a single foreign policy international 'presence' as witnessed by the ESS's security–development nexus. Indeed, the continuing constraints of the essentially civilian nature of EU action – despite the eight 'military' CSDP missions so far conducted – make development policy initiatives an attractive mechanism for extending 'presence'. The EEAS now has the institutional authority to match security with development, and this relationship over the coming years will be a litmus test for the efficacy of the Lisbon Treaty reforms.

A fourth and familiar theme, as well as a danger, is the failure to match expectations with capabilities once again. As argued elsewhere in this book, it seems counter-productive for the EU to establish development policy goals – such as poverty eradication – that are effectively unachievable. Indeed, as the mid-point review of the MDGs have suggested, all eight MDGs are possibly unobtainable within the 2015 time frame adopted. Less grandiose, but more attainable objectives may be needed to enhance the reality of the EU's role in a global context.

A further current theme also with strong historical resonance is that of 'partnership' and who sets the development agenda. At best, the rhetoric of partnership had been imperfectly applied throughout the Lomé and Cotonou periods with this becoming increasingly characteristic more recently, despite the consultation processes embedded in the 2010 Green Paper described above. The new financial context, a growing acceptance of the impending failure to meet the MDG goals and the never-ending search for coherence under Lisbon have driven the EU to adapt its development strategy without abandoning its belief in both free trade and regional integration as the solution to global poverty. If not imposed unilaterally, clearly the voice of the ACP and other development actors have not shaped this new partnership debate: the EU's own priorities have dominated.

Lastly, the theme of how best to structure the EU's relations with the developing world is once again of prime importance. The role assigned to the ACP as the EU's principal interlocutor is rapidly fading and the predictions of ACP group fragmentation under Cotonou's EPAs appear prescient. Quite what new architecture will be designed remains uncertain, although the proposals contained in the 2010 Green Paper provide some insights: a reduced geographical concentration, the transition of the BRICS and similar emerging economies out of a development relationship, balanced against continued support for the LDCs within the overarching framework of the MDGs.

In the Introduction we considered the theme of whether development policy was a core EU function or might constitute an area for 'enhanced cooperation' under the Lisbon Treaty. The analysis here, especially in light of the theoretical discussion given above, argues very strongly that development policy still constitutes a core EU activity. Popular support for the integration process requires more than the advantages provided by monetary union or a common market. A wide and comprehensive range of policies is needed in order to generate public awareness and belief in the added value of integration. Without external policies such as relations with the developing world, the 'idea' of Europe is diminished. The challenge has always been for the EU to harness its various external policy sectors to this end – to enhance the integration process – and this responsibility now rests with the Lisbon Treaty to reinvigorate a new EU. From an integration perspective it would be mistaken for the EU to surrender development policy to the national level. The 'Consensus on Development', Cotonou, the EBA and the MDGs have all been ambitious attempts to redesign the EU's role. However, the greatest challenge still lies ahead – defining development policy as an exclusive EU competence and making that policy a future success. Intergovernmental theory suggests that the member states will not accept the demise of bilateralism quite that easily, however.

Finally, a valuable text should raise as many questions as it provides factual answers. To fulfil this task, we finish by raising some questions to encourage further debate. What can development policy tell us about the EU? First, where should development policy be located in the EU's policy spectrum? The mainstreaming of development policy as EU foreign affairs has been flagged by Lisbon: development policy is part of the EU's global role and ambitions, and the EU will undoubtedly be judged on the extent to which it can successfully deliver on its commitments. Second, the last decade has witnessed an increased development policy consensus between the EU and that of the wider international community through the adoption of the MDGs. While laudable in many respects, this merging of agendas also raises the question of whether it is necessary to have separate EU, UN or other multilateral perspectives. Would development be more effective if delivered through an empowered and exclusive UN mechanism? Third, are there clear international roles that the EU performs best, despite the persistence of bilateralism across all of Europe's external relations with the exception of trade? At a minimum, political conditionality seems best operationalized at the EU level and presents the EU with a distinct and appropriate function. Fourth, how successful has the EU been in spreading regional integration through its development policy? While not as robust and embedded as perhaps wished, regional integration has become very much a global phenomenon and one undisputedly advocated and led by Brussels. But is it the necessary foundation for economic development as advocated by the EU? Fifth, what is the link between public opinion and development policy? What is often a pervasive gap for the EU between consent and legitimacy remains a potential challenge for an EU facing economic and financial constraints: how might public opinion influence future development policy in the context of ongoing financial constraints? Sixth, and most provocatively, has the EU correctly defined the nature of development and adopted the appropriate policies? Is the solution really to be found in free trade and EPAs? And lastly, to what extent will the future of EU development policy be determined by Europe itself – its values, interests and aspirations – rather than be driven as a response to the policies adopted by other new players: simply, is the future for development Chinese?

Bibliography

ACPSec (2010) '*ACP Press Statement: ACP–EU Sign Second Revised Cotonou Agreement in Ouagadougou, Burkina Faso.*' www.acpsec.org/en/com/91/pr_cotonou_revised2_e.htm.> (accessed 22 June 2011).

Africa Renewal (2008) 'Trade Talks Reach Impasse at Europe–Africa Summit.' *Africa Renewal*, 21(4): 23.

Allen, D. and Smith, M. (1999) 'External Policy Developments.' *Journal of Common Market Studies*, 37 (Annual Review): 87–108.

Allen, D. and Smith, M. (2008) 'Relations with the Rest of the World.' *Journal of Common Market Studies*, 46 (Annual Review): 165–182.

Arts, K. and Dickson, A.K. (2004) 'EU Development Cooperation: From Model to Symbol?' In K. Arts and A.K. Dickson (eds), *EU Development Cooperation: From Model to Symbol.* Manchester: Manchester University Press: 1–16.

Ashton, C. (2010a) '*Speech to the European Parliament on Human Rights.*' SPEECH/10/317, 16 June. http://europa.eu/rapid/pressReleasesAction.do?reference=SPEECH/10/317.

Ashton, C. (2010b) '*Speech to the European Parliament's Foreign Affairs Committee.*' SPEECH/10/120, 23 March. http://europa.eu/rapid/pressReleasesAction.do?reference=SPEECH/10/120.

Avery, G. and Missiroli, A. (eds) (2007) '*The EU Foreign Service: How to Build a More Effective Common Policy.*' EPC Working Paper No. 28. Brussels: European Policy Centre.

Bacon, P. (2011) 'Human Rights, Transformative Power and EU–Japan Relations.' In K. Fukuda (ed.), *European Integration after the Treaty of Lisbon.* Tokyo: Waseda University Press.

Bessa-Rodrigues, P. (1999) 'European Union-MERCOSUL: In Search of a "New" Relationship?' *European Foreign Affairs Review*, 4(1): 81–98.

Bossuyt, J., Carlsson, J., Laporte, G. and Oden, B. (1999) *Improving the Complementarity of European Union Development Cooperation: From the Bottom Up.* ECDPM Discussion Paper 4. Maastricht: ECDPM.

Bretherton, C. and Vogler, J. (2006) *The European Union as a Global Actor.* Abingdon: Routledge.

Brown, W. (2004) 'From Uniqueness to Uniformity? An Assessment of EU Development Aid Policies.' In K. Arts and A.K. Dickson (eds), *EU Development Cooperation: From Model to Symbol.* Manchester: Manchester University Press: 17–41.

Bulletin of the EU (1997) 'Parliament Resolution on European Union Humanitarian Aid and the Role of ECHO and on the Commission Communication to the Council and the European Parliament on Linking Relief, Rehabilitation and Development.' *Bulletin of the European Union*, 1/2: 1.3.59. http://europa.eu/archives/bulletin/en/9701/p103059.htm.

Bulletin of the EU (1998–2000) http://europa.eu/archives/bulletin/en/welcome.htm.

Bulmer, S. (1983) 'Domestic Politics and EC Policy-Making.' *Journal of Common Market Studies*, 21(4): 349–63.

Bulmer, S. (1994) 'The Governance of the European Union: A New Institutionalist Approach.' *Journal of Public Policy*, 13(4): 351–80.

Carbone, M. (2007) *The European Union and International Development: The Politics of Foreign Aid*. Abingdon: Routledge.

Carbone, M. (2009) 'Mission Impossible: The European Union and Policy Coherence for Development.' In M. Carbone (ed.), *Policy Coherence and EU Development Policy*. Abingdon: Routledge: 1–20.

Carey, R. (2005) 'Real or Phantom Aid?' *DAC News*, June–August. www.oecd.org/document/29/0,2340,en_2649_33721_34990749_1_1_1_1,00.html.

Checkel, J.T. (2003) '"Going Native" in Europe? Theorizing Social Interaction in European Institutions.' *Comparative Political Studies*, 36(1–2): 209–31.

Christiansen, T., Jorgensen, K.E. and Wiener, A. (1999) 'The Social Construction of Europe.' *Journal of European Public Policy*, 6(4): 528–44.

Clay, E.J., Geddes, M. and Natali, L. (2009) 'Untying Aid: Is it Working? An Evaluation of the Implementation of the Paris Declaration and of the 2001 DAC Recommendation of Untying ODA to the LDCs.' www.oecd.org/dataoecd/51/35/44375975.pdf.

Coates, B. and Braxton, N. (2006) *Slamming the Door on Development: Analysis of the EU's Response to the Pacific's EPA Negotiating Proposals*. Oxford: Oxfam International.

Commission of the European Communities (1969) *The External Trade of the European Community 1958–1967*. Current Notes on the European Community No. 5. London: European Commission.

Commission of the European Communities (1971) 'Commission Memorandum on a Community Policy for Development Co-operation.' SEC (71) 2700. *EC Bulletin*, Supplement 5/71. Brussels: European Communities. http://aei.pitt.edu/4411/01/002200_1.pdf.

Commission of the European Communities (1972) *Memorandum from the Commission on a Community Policy on Development Co-operation: Programme for Initial Actions*. SEC (72) 320. http://aei.pitt.edu/4364/01/001551_1.pdf.

Commission of the European Communities (1973) 'Memorandum of the Commission to the Council on the Future Relations Between the Community, the Present AASM States, and the Countries in Africa, the Caribbean, the Indian and Pacific Oceans Referred to in Protocol 22 to the Act of Accession.' COM (73) 500 final. *Bulletin of the European Communities*, Supplement 1/73. http://aei.pitt.edu/4279/01/002298_1.pdf.

Commission of the European Communities (1974) *Food Crisis and the Community's Responsibilities Towards Developing Countries*. COM (74) 300 final. http://aei.pitt.edu/4392/01/001604_1.pdf.

Commission of the European Communities (1986) *Ten Years of Lomé: A Record of EEC–ACP Partnership 1976–1985*. Europe Information: Development DE 55. http://aei.pitt.edu/7565/01/31735055261311_1.pdf.

Commission of the European Communities (1990) *Thirteenth Annual Report from the Commission to the Council and the European Parliament on the Implementation of Financial and Technical Co-operation to Developing Countries of Asia and Latin America as of 31 December 1989*. COM (90) 204 final. http://aei.pitt.edu/4257/01/001920_1.pdf.

Commission of the European Communities (1992) *Humanitarian Aid from the European Community: Emergency Aid, Food Aid, Refugee Aid*. Europe Information: Development DE 70. http://aei.pitt.edu/9618/01/31735055261303_1.pdf.

Commission of the European Communities (1994a) *Fifteenth Annual Report from the Commission to the Council and the European Parliament on the Implementation of Financial and Technical Assistance to Asian and Latin American Developing Countries at 31 December 1991*. COM (94) 541 final. <http://eur-lex.europa.eu/LexUriServ/LexUriServ.do?uri=COM:1994:0541:FIN:EN:PDF.

Commission of the European Communities (1994b) *Towards a New Asia Strategy*. COM (1994) 314 final.

Commission of the European Communities (1995) *The European Union and Latin America: The Present Situation and Prospects for Closer Partnership, 1996–2000*. COM (95) 495 final. http://eur-lex.europa.eu/LexUriServ/LexUriServ.do?uri=COM:1995:0495:FIN:EN:PDF.

Commission of the European Communities (1996) *Creating a New Dynamic in EU–ASEAN Relations*. COM (96) 314 final. http://eur-lex.europa.eu/LexUriServ/LexUriServ.do?uri=COM:1996:0314:FIN:EN:PDF.

Commission of the European Communities (1997) *Guidelines for the Negotiation of New Cooperation Agreements with the African, Caribbean and Pacific (ACP) Countries*. COM (97) 537 final. http://

eur-lex.europa.eu/LexUriServ/LexUriServ.do?uri= COM:1997:0537: FIN:EN:PDF.

Commission of the European Communities (1999) *Evaluation of EU Development Aid to ALA States: Phase III – Synthesis Report*. http://ec.europa.eu/europeaid/how/evaluation/evaluation_reports/reports/ala/951401_en.pdf.

Commission of the European Communities (2000a) 'EU Deploys 160 Strong Election Observation Team in Zimbabwe'. Press Release IP/00/553, 30 May. http://europa.eu/rapid/pressReleasesAction.do?reference=IP/00/553.

Commission of the European Communities (2000b) *Commission Proposes 'Everything but Arms' (EBA) Initiative: Duty-free, Quota-free Access for all Products from all Least Developed Countries into the EU*. Press Release IP/00/1034, 20 September. http://europa.eu/rapid/pressReleasesAction.do?reference=IP/00/1034.

Commission of the European Communities (2000c) *Commission Sets Out Political Guidelines for the Future of EC Development Policy*. Press Release IP/00/410, 26 April. http://europa.eu/rapid/pressReleasesAction.do?reference=IP/00/410.

Commission of the European Communities (2000d) *Debt Relief: Commission Warns against Dilution of the Enhanced HIPC Initiative*. Press Release IP/00/779, 13 July. http://europa.eu/rapid/pressReleasesAction.do?reference=IP/00/779.

Commission of the European Communities (2000e) *Reform of the Management of External Assistance*. http://www.acp-programming.eu/wcm/dmdocuments/com_com_16_may_2000.pdf.

Commission of the European Communities (2000f) *Report from the Commission on the Implementation of Council Regulation (EC) 443/97 of 3 March 1997 on Operations to Aid Uprooted People in Asian and Latin American Developing Countries*. COM (2000) 367 final. http://eur-lex.europa.eu/LexUriServ/LexUriServ.do?uri=COM:2000:0367:FIN:EN:PDF.

Commission of the European Communities (2000g) *The European Community's Development Policy*. COM (2000) 212 final. http://eur-lex.europa.eu/LexUriServ/LexUriServ.do?uri=COM:2000:0212:FIN:EN:PDF.

Commission of the European Communities (2002a) *Latin America Regional Strategy Document 2002–2006*. http://www.eeas.europa.eu/la/rsp/02_06_en.pdf.

Commission of the European Communities (2002b) *The European Development Fund in a Few Words*. DE 112. http://www.pedz.uni-mannheim.de/daten/edz-l/gdd/02/fed_en.pdf.

Commission of the European Communities (2005a) *Accelerating Progress Towards Attaining the Millennium Development Goals: Financing for*

Development and Aid Effectiveness. COM (2005) 133 final. http://eur-lex.europa.eu/LexUriServ/LexUriServ.do?uri=CELEX:52005DC0133:EN:HTML.

Commission of the European Communities (2005b) *European Commission Adopts 'European Union Strategy for Africa'.* Press Release IP/05/1260, 12 October. http://europa.eu/rapid/pressReleases Action.do?reference=IP/05/1260.

Commission of the European Communities (2005c) *Financing for Development: Facing up to the Challenge of our Generation.* Speech by José Barroso to the UN Summit Special Plenary on FfD, New York. SPEECH/05/509, 14 September. http://europa.eu/rapid/pressReleases Action.do?reference=SPEECH/05/509.

Commission of the European Communities (2005d) *Proposal for a Joint Declaration by the Council, the European Parliament and the Commission on the European Union Development Policy: 'The European Consensus'.* COM (2005) 311 final. http://eur-lex.europa.eu/LexUriServ/LexUriServ.do?uri=COM:2005:0311:FIN:EN:PDF.

Commission of the European Communities (2005e) *Questions and Answers: The Commission's 'MDG Package' (Millennium Development Goals).* MEMO/05/124, 12 April. http://europa.eu/ rapid/pressReleases Action.do?reference=MEMO/05/124.

Commission of the European Communities (2005f) *Questions and Answers: The 'European Union Strategy for Africa'.* MEMO/05/370, 12 October. http://europa.eu/rapid/pressReleasesAction.do?reference=MEMO/05/370.

Commission of the European Communities (2005g) *Speeding up Progress Towards the Millennium Development Goals: The European Union's Contribution.* COM (2005) 132 final. http://eur-lex.europa.eu/LexUriServ/LexUriServ.do?uri=COM:2005:0132:FIN:EN:PDF.

Commission of the European Communities (2005h) *The European Commission Approves Proposals to Increase the Volume and Effectiveness of Development Aid.* Press Release IP/05/423, 12 April. http://europa.eu/rapid/pressReleasesAction.do?reference=IP/05/423.

Commission of the European Communities (2006) *EU Donor Atlas 2006: Volume I.* Brussels: European Commission. http://ec.europa.eu/development/body/publications/docs/eu_donor_atlas_2006.pdf.

Commission of the European Communities (2007a) *EU and Africa Aim for Deep Transformation of their Relationship at 2nd EU–Africa Summit in Lisbon.* Press Release IP/07/1864, 6 December. http://europa.eu/rapid/pressReleasesAction.do?reference=IP/07/1864.

Commission of the European Communities (2007b) *Reforming Europe for the 21st Century.* COM (2007) 412 final. http://register.consilium.europa.eu/pdf/en/07/st11/st11625.en07.pdf.

Commission of the European Communities (2008) *Green Paper: Future*

Relations between the EU and the Overseas Countries and Territories. SEC (2008) 383 final. http://ec.europa.eu/development/icenter/repository/1_EN_ACT_part1_v8.pdf.

Commission of the European Communities (2010a) *Commission Further Reshuffles its Senior Managers after the First Package Decided by this College in June.* Press Release IP/10/1398, 27 October. http://europa.eu/rapid/pressReleasesAction.do?reference=IP/10/1398.

Commission of the European Communities (2010b) *EU Donor Profiles.* http://ec.europa.eu/development/icenter/repository/eu_donors_profiles_2010.pdf.

Commission of the European Communities (2010c) *Financing for Development – Annual Progress Report 2010: Getting Back on Track to Reach the EU 2015 Target on ODA Spending?* SEC (2010) 420 final. http://ec.europa.eu/development/icenter/repository/SEC_2010_0420_COM_2010_0159_EN.PDF.

Commission of the European Communities (2010d) Green Paper: EU Development Policy in Support of Inclusive Growth and Sustainable Development – Increasing the Impact of EU Development Policy. COM (2010) 629 final. http://ec.europa.eu/development/icenter/repository/GREEN_PAPER_COM_2010_629_POLITIQUE_DEVELOPPEMENT_EN.pdf.

Commission of the European Communities (2010e) *Overview of EPA: State of Play.* http://trade.ec.europa.eu/doclib/docs/2009/september/tradoc_144912.pdf.

Commission of the European Communities (2010f) *President Barroso at the UN High Level Summit on Millennium Development Goals to Push for a Global Commitment and Shared Responsibility in the Fight Against Poverty.* Press Release IP/10/1137, 16 September. http://europa.eu/rapid/pressReleasesAction.do?reference=IP/10/1137.

Commission of the European Communities (2010g) *Progress Made on the Millennium Development Goals and Key Challenges for the Road Ahead.* SEC (2010) 418 final. http://eur-lex.europa.eu/LexUriServ/LexUriServ.do?uri=SEC:2010:0418:FIN:EN:PDF.

Commission of the European Communities (2010h) *Restrictive Measures (Sanctions) in Force: Measures Adopted in the Framework of the Common Foreign and Security Policy.* http://ec.europa.eu/external_relations/cfsp/sanctions/docs/measures_en.pdf.

Commission of the European Communities (2011) *Roadmap: Initiative to Modernize EU Development Policy.* http://ec.europa.eu/governance/impact/planned_ia/docs/2011_dev_003_modernising_development_en.pdf.

Cosgrove-Twitchett, C. (1978) *Europe and Africa: From Association to Partnership.* Farnborough: Saxon House.

Cotonou (2005) *Agreement Amending the Partnership Agreement Between* the Members of the African, Caribbean and Pacific Group of States, of the One Part, and the European Community and its Member States, of the Other Part, Signed in Cotonou on 23 June 2000. http://ec.europa.eu/world/agreements/downloadFile.do?fullText=yes&treatyTransId=2901.

Cotonou (2010) *Second Revision of the Cotonou Agreement – Agreed Consolidated Text, 11 March 2010.* http://ec.europa.eu/development/icenter/repository/second_revision_cotonou_agreement_20100311.pdf.

Council and Commission of the European Communities (2000) *The European Community's Development Policy: Statement by the Council and the Commission.* http://ec.europa.eu/development/icenter/repository/EU_com_Dev_policy_en.pdf.

Council of the EC (1981) *Council Regulation on Financial and Technical Aid to Non-Associated Developing Countries.* Regulation (EEC) No. 442/81.

Council of the EC (1989) 'Resolution of 16 May 1989 on Coordination in Support of Structural Adjustment in ACP States.' *Bulletin of the European Communities*, 5.

Council of the EU (1996) 'Council Regulation (EC) No. 1257/96 of 20 June 1996 Concerning Humanitarian Aid.' *Official Journal of the European Union*, L163: 1–8.

Council of the EU (1998) 'Council Decision of 6 July 1998 Concerning Exceptional Assistance for the Heavily Indebted ACP Countries.' *Official Journal of the European Union*, L198: 40–1.

Council of the EU (2006) 'Decision of the ACP–EC Council of Ministers of 2 June 2006 Specifying the Multiannual Financial Framework for the Period 2008 to 2013 and Modifying the Revised ACP–EC Partnership Agreement.' 2006/608/EC. http://eur-lex.europa.eu/LexUriServ/LexUriServ.do?uri=OJ:L:2006:247:0022:0025:EN:PDF.

Council of the EU (2007) *Conclusions of the Council and the Representatives of the Governments of the Member States Meeting Within the Council on Security and Development.* Doc. 15097/07. Brussels: European Union.

Council of the EU (2008a) *EU Guidelines on the Death Penalty: Revised and Updated Version.* www.consilium.europa.eu/uedocs/cmsUpload/10015.en08.pdf.

Council of the EU (2008b) 'The European Consensus on Humanitarian Aid.' *Official Journal of the European Union*, C25: 1–12.

Council of the EU (2010) 'Council Decision Establishing the Organisation and Functioning of the European External Action Service.' *Official Journal of the European Union*, L201: 30–40.

Courier, The (1988) 'The Adjustment Process in Africa: A European Council Resolution.' 111: 73.

Court of Auditors (1997) 'Special Report No 2/97 Concerning

Humanitarian aid from the European Union between 1992 and 1995 together with the Commission's Replies.' *Official Journal of the European Union*, C143: 1–65.

Court of Auditors (1999) 'Special Report No 4/99 Concerning Financial Aid to Overseas Countries and Territories under the Sixth and Seventh EDF Accompanied by the Replies of the Commission.' *Official Journal of the European Union*, C276: 1–24.

Court of Auditors (2006) 'Special Report No 3/2006 Concerning the European Commission Humanitarian Aid Response to the Tsunami together with the Commission's Replies.' *Official Journal of the European Union*, C170: 1–21.

Cox, A. and Koning, A. (1997) *Understanding European Community Aid: Aid Policies, Management and Distribution Explained.* London: ODI.

Cram, L., Dinan, D. and Nugent, N. (eds) (1999) *Developments in the European Union.* London: Macmillan.

Dauster, J. (1998) 'MERCOSUR and the European Union: Prospects for an Inter-Regional Association.' *European Foreign Affairs Review*, 3(4): 447–9.

Dent, C. (1997) 'The ASEM: Managing the New Framework of the EU's Economic Relations with East Asia.' *Pacific Affairs*, 70(4): 495–516.

Desesquelles, G. (2000) 'The Non-governmental Actors.' *The Courier*, 181: 6–9.

Deutsche Welle (2009) 'EU Advances Aid for Developing Nations.' 8 April. www.dw-world.de/dw/article/0,,4163761,00.html.

DEVCO (2011) *Final Organisation Chart of DG DEVCO (1/6/2011).* http://ec.europa.eu/europeaid/who/documents/organigramme-devco_en.pdf.

Development Council of the European Union (2000) '2263rd *Council Meeting – Development – Brussels, 18 May.*' PRES/00/156. http://europa.eu/rapid/pressReleasesAction.do?reference=PRES/00/156.

Doidge, M. (2008) 'Regional Organisations as Actors in International Relations: Interregionalism and Asymmetric Relationships.' In J. Rüland, G. Schubert, G. Schucher and C. Storz (eds), *Asian–European Relations: Building Blocks for Global Governance.* London: Routledge: 32–54.

Doidge, M. (2011) *The European Union and Interregionalism: Patterns of Engagement.* Farnham: Ashgate.

Duddy, J.-M. (2010) 'Namibia asks EU to "Step Back".' *The Namibian*, 17 September. www.namibian.com.na/news/full-story/archive/2010/september/article/namibia-asks-eu-to-step-back.

ECDPM, ICEI and ODI (European Centre for Development Policy Management, Instituto Complutense de Estudios Internacionales, Overseas Development Institute) (2005) 'Assessment of the EC Development Policy.' DPS Study Report. http://ec.europa.eu/development/ body/tmp_docs/ecdpm_report.pdf.

ECHO (2008) *Fact Sheet A1: Types of Financing Decisions and Related Procedures.* Brussels: European Union.

ECHO (2010a) *Annual Report 2009.* SEC (2010) 0138 final. Brussels: European Union.

ECHO (2010b) '*ECHO Offices.*' http://ec.europa.eu/echo/files/about/what/field_offices.pdf.

ECHO (2010c) *Technical Note: Methodology for the Identification of Priority Countries for the European Commission Humanitarian Aid 'GNA and FCA'.* ECHO C2/EN D (2010). Brussels: European Union.

Economist, The (1999) 'How to Make Aid Work.' 26 June. www.economist.com/node/215635?%20story_id=215635.

Economist, The (2000) 'The Poor Who are Always with Us.' 1 July. www.economist.com/node/3002.

EEAS (2011) '*Organisation Chart of the EEAS.*' www.eeas.europa.eu/background/docs/organisation_en.pdf.

Elgström, O. (2000) 'Lomé and Post-Lomé: Asymmetric Negotiations and the Impact of Norms.' *European Foreign Affairs Review,* 5(2): 175–95.

EuropeAid (2001) *Report on the Implementation of the European Commission's External Assistance.* D (2001) 32947. Brussels: European Community. http://ec.europa.eu/europeaid/multimedia/ publications/documents/annual-reports/europaid_annual_report_2000_en.pdf.

EuropeAid (2005) *Annex to the Annual Report 2005 on the European Community's Development Policy and the Implementation of External Assistance in 2004.* SEC (2005) 892. Brussels: European Commission. http://ec.europa.eu/europeaid/multimedia/publications/documents/annual-reports/europeaid_annual_report_2005_full_version_en.pdf.

EuropeAid (2009) *Annual Report 2009 on the European Community's Development and External Assistance Policies and their Implementation in 2008.* COM (2009) 296. Brussels: European Commission. http://ec.europa.eu/europeaid/multimedia/publications/documents/annual-reports/europeaid_annual_report_2009_en.pdf.

EuropeAid (2010) *Annual Report 2010 on the European Union's Development and External Assistance Policies and their Implementation in 2009.* COM (2009) 296. Brussels: European Commission. http://ec.europa.eu/europeaid/multimedia/publications/documents/annual-reports/europeaid_annual_report_2010_en.pdf.

EuropeAid (2011) '*Election Observation Missions.*' http://ec.europa.eu/europeaid/what/human-rights/election_observation_missions/index_en.htm.

European Council (1981) 'Council Regulation (EEC) No. 442/81 of 17 February 1981 on Financial and Technical Aid to Non-Associated Developing Countries.' *Official Journal of the European Communities,* L48/9.

European Foreign Affairs Review (1997–2000) 'Common Actions and

Positions Adopted by the Council of the European Union in the Framework of the Common Foreign and Security Policy', *European Foreign Affairs Review*, 2–5.

European Parliament (1997) *Report on the Commission's Green Paper on Relations between the European Union and the African, Caribbean and Pacific (ACP) Countries on the Eve of the 21st Century – Challenges and Options for a New Partnership (COM(96)0570 – C40639/96)*. PE 223.237/fin. Brussels: European Parliament.

European Parliament (2000) 'European Parliament Resolution on the Communication from the Commission to the Council and the European Parliament: Assessment and Future of Community Humanitarian Activities (Article 20 of Regulation (EC) No 1257/96) (COM(1999) 468 C5-0044/2000 2000/2016(COS)).' *Official Journal of the European Communities*, C135: 72–5.

European Parliament, Commission and Council (2006) 'The European Consensus on Development.' *Official Journal of the European Union*, C46: 1–19. http://ec.europa.eu/development/icenter/repository/european_consensus_2005_en.pdf.

Fangchuan, H. and Niemann, U. (eds) (2000) *Asia and Europe – Towards a Better Mutual Understanding*, Second ASEF Summer School, 22 August–5 September 1999, Beijing: Peking University.

Focke Report (1980) *From Lomé I to Lomé II; Texts of the Report of the Resolution Adopted on 26 September 1980 by the ACP–EEC Consultative Assembly*. Luxembourg: European Parliament.

Frisch, Dieter and Boidin, Jean-Claude (1988) 'Adjustment, Development and Equity.' *The Courier*, 111: 67–72.

G7 (2000) '*G7 Finance Ministers Conclusions on Development*.' Endorsed 8 September 2000. www.canadainternational.gc.ca/g8/ministerials-minis-terielles/2005/development-conclusions-developpement_080900. aspx.

G8 (2005a) '*G8 Communiqué on Africa*.' G8 Summit, Gleneagles, 6–8 July. www.canadainternational.gc.ca/g8/summit-sommet/2005/africa-afrique_05.aspx.

G8 (2005b) '*Factsheet: Africa's Progress Towards Meeting the MDGs*.' www.fco.gov.uk/Files/kfile/G8%20Press%20Factsheet%20-20MDGs%20 (FINAL),0.doc.

G24 Secretariat (2003) '*G-24 Secretariat Briefing Paper on the Heavily Indebted Poor Country (HIPC) Initiative*.' www.g24.org/hipc.pdf.

Gavas, M. (2010) '*A U-Turn on the European External Action Service? Where is Development?*' European Development Cooperation Strengthening Programme Blog, 27 October. http://international-development.eu/2010/10/13/a-u-turn-on-the-european-external-action-service-where-is-development.

Giddens, A. (1984) *The Constitution of Society: An Outline of the Theory of Structuration*. Cambridge: Polity.

Giscard d'Estaing, V. (2007) '*Le Blog de Valéry Giscard d'Estaing: Pour le Démocratie en Europe.*' 5 July. http://vge-europe.eu/index.php?post/2007/07/05/Quelques-reponses-4.

Glaser, T. (1990) 'EEC–ACP Cooperation: the Historical Perspective.' *The Courier*, 120: 24–28.

Grilli, E. (1993) The European Community and the Developing Countries. Cambridge: Cambridge University Press.

Grisanti, L. (2000) 'Europe and Latin America: The Challenge of Strategic Partnership.' *European Foreign Affairs Review*, 5(1): 1–7.

Hadfield, A. (2007) 'Janus Advances? An Analysis of EC Development Policy and the 2005 Amended Cotonou Partnership Agreement.' *European Foreign Affairs Review*, 12(1): 39–66.

Hanf, T. (ed.) (1999) *Watching Democracy at Work: Writing State of Democracy Assessments and Organizing Election Observations. A Practical Guide.* Freiburg im Breisgau: Arnold Bergstraesser Institut.

Harding, G. (2000) 'Nielson Unveils Blueprint for Development Policy Overhaul.' *European Voice*, 6, 23 March. www.europeanvoice.com/article/imported/nielson-unveils-blueprint-for-development-policy-overhaul/40374.aspx.

Hewitt, A. and Whiteman, K. (2004) 'The Commission and Development Policy: Bureaucratic Politics in EU Aid – From the Lomé Leap Forward to the Difficulties of Adapting to the Twenty-first Century.' In K. Arts and A.K. Dickson (eds), *EU Development Cooperation: From Model to Symbol.* Manchester: Manchester University Press: 133–48.

HIPC (2005) '*Debt Relief and Financing the MDGs.*' Communiqué of the 11th Meeting of HIPC Finance Ministers, Maputo, 16 March. www.dri.org.uk/pdfs/MM11_Maputo05Communique_eng.pdf.

HIPC CBP (2005) 'HIPC Initiative and PRSP Progress: January 2005.' *Strategies for Financing Development: The Newsletter of the HIPC CBP and the FPC CBP*, 22 (First Quarter): 8–9. www.hipc-cbp.org/files/en/open/Newsletters/Debt22_UK.pdf.

Holland, M. (1994) '*Plus ça Change...? The European Union Joint Action and South Africa.*' CEPS Paper No. 57. Brussels: Centre for European Policy Studies.

Holland, M. (2000) 'Resisting Reform or Risking Revival? Renegotiating the Lomé Convention.' In M. Green-Cowles and M. Smith (eds), *The State of the European Union Volume 5: Risks, Reform, Resistance, and Revival.* Oxford: Oxford University Press: 390–410.

Holland, M. (2002) *The European Union and the Third World.* Basingstoke: Palgrave.

Holland, M. (2004) 'When is Foreign Policy not Foreign Policy? Cotonou, CFSP and External Relations with the Developing World.' In M. Holland (ed.), *Common Foreign and Security Policy: the First Ten Years.* London: Continuum: 111–26.

Holland, M. (2008) 'The EU and the Global Development Agenda.' *Journal of European Integration*, 30(3): 343–62.

Holland, M. and Chaban, N. (2010) (eds) 'Reflections from Asia and Europe: How do we Perceive One Another?' *Asia–Europe Journal*, 8(2), Special Issue.

Hood, R. and Hoyle, C. (2008) *The Death Penalty: A Worldwide Perspective*. Oxford: Oxford University Press.

Human Resources and Security (2010) '*Key Figures Card: Staff Members.*' http://ec.europa.eu/civil_service/docs/key_figures_2010_externe_en.pdf.

ICG (International Crisis Group) (2001) *The European Humanitarian Aid Office (ECHO): Crisis Response in the Grey Lane*. Thematic Issues Briefing No. 1. Brussels: International Crisis Group.

IDD (International Development Department) and Associates (2006) *Evaluation of General Budget Support: Synthesis Report*. Birmingham: University of Birmingham.

IMF (2003) G-24 *Secretariat Briefing Paper on the Heavily Indebted Poor Country (HIPC) Initiative*. www.g24.org/ResearchPaps/hipc.pdf.

International Monetary Fund. Available at: http://www.g24.org/hipc.pdf.

International IDEA (1999) *Dialogue for Democratic Development: Policy Options for a Renewed ACP–EU Partnership*. Stockholm: International IDEA.

IPU (Inter-Parliamentary Union) (2010) '*Women in National Parliaments.*' www.ipu.org/wmn-e/classif.htm.

Jones, R.A. (2001) *The Politics and Economics of the European Union: An Introduction Text*. Cheltenham: Edward Elgar.

Karl, K. (2000) 'From Georgetown to Cotonou: The ACP Group Faces up to New Challenges.' *The Courier*, Special Supplement: 20–3.

Kelsey, J. (2007) 'Going Nowhere in a Hurry? The Pacific's EPA Negotiations with the European Union.' *Victoria University of Wellington Law Review*, 38: 81–103.

Keohane, R. and Hoffmann, S. (1990) 'Conclusions: Community Politics and Institutional Change.' In W. Wallace (ed.), *The Dynamics of European Integration*. London: Pinter/RIIA: 276–300.

Keukeleire, S. and MacNaughtan, J. (2008) *The Foreign Policy of the European Union*. Basingstoke: Palgrave Macmillan.

Kingah, S.S. (2006) 'The European Union's New Africa Strategy: Grounds for Cautious Optimism.' *European Foreign Affairs Review*, 11(4): 527–53.

Köllner, P. (2000) 'Whither ASEM? Lessons from APEC and the Future of Transregional Cooperation between Asia and Europe.' Paper presented at conference '*Asia-Europe in a Global Economy: Economics, Economic Systems and Economic Cooperation*', Seoul, Korea, 1–2 September.

La Prensa Gráfica (2007) 'Mercosur y Europa reiniciandiálogo TLC'

[MERCOSUR and Europe reinitiate dialogue on FTA], 29 May. www.bilaterals.org/spip.php?article8457.

Leo, S. (2009) 'Acordo entre Mercosul e UE viraprioridade' [Agreement between MERCOSUR and EU becomes a priority]. *Valor Econômico*, 31 July.

Lister, M. (1997a) *'Europe's Lomé Policy in Perspective.'* European Development Policy Study Group Discussion Paper No. 2. www.edpsg.org/cgi/go.pl?www.edpsg.org/Documents/Dp2.doc.

Lister, M. (1997b) *The European Union and the South: Relations with Developing Countries*. London: Routledge.

Manservisi, F. and Falkenberg, K. (2006) *'Letter of 20 October 2006 to Kaliopate Tavola, Lead Spokesperson of the Pacific ACP Regional Negotiating Team.'* TRADE/KFF D(2006) 12520. www.bilaterals.org/IMG/pdf/EC_Falkenberg_Manservisi_to_Tavola_Oct-06.pdf.

Marks, G., Hooghe, L. and Blank, K. (1996) 'European Integration from the 1980s: State-Centric v. Multi-level Governance.' *Journal of Common Market Studies*, 34(3): 341–78.

Martin, M. and Johnson, A. (2001) *Implementing the Enhanced HIPC Initiative: Key Issues for HIPC Governments*. London: Debt Relief International. www.dri.org.uk/pdfs/EngPub2_HipcII.pdf.

McMahon, J. (1998) 'ASEAN and the Asia-Europe Meeting: Strengthening the European Union's Relations with South-East Asia?' *European Foreign Affairs Review*, 3(2): 233–51.

Michel, L. (2005) *'Are the Developed Countries Hitting the Millennium Development Goals?'* Speech to the Friends of European and Friedrich-Ebert-Stiftung, Brussels. SPEECH/05/534, 22 September. http://europa.eu/rapid/pressReleasesAction.do?reference=SPEECH/05/534.

Michel, L. (2008) *Economic Partnership Agreements: Drivers of Development*. Brussels: European Commission.

Moeller, J.O. (2007) 'ASEAN's Relations with the European Union: Obstacles and Opportunities.' *Contemporary Southeast Asia*, 29(3): 465–82.

Monnet, J. (1978) *Memoirs*. New York: Doubleday and Co.

Moravcsik, A. (1991) 'Negotiating the Single European Act: National Interests and Conventional Statecraft in the European Community.' *International Organisation*, 45(1): 19–56.

Moravcsik, A. (1993) 'Preferences and Power in the European Community: A Liberal Intergovernmentalist Approach.' *Journal of Common Market Studies*, 31(4): 473–524.

Moravcsik, A. (1995) 'Liberal Intergovernmentalism and Integration: a Rejoinder.' *Journal of Common Market Studies*, 33(4): 611–28.

Moravcsik, A. and Nicolaïdis, K. (1999) 'Explaining the Treaty of Amsterdam: Interests, Influence and Institutions.' *Journal of Common Market Studies*, 37(1): 59–85.

OECD (2006) *The Paris Declaration's 12 Indicators of Progress.* Paris: OECD. www.oecd.org/dataoecd/57/60/36080258.pdf.

OECD-DAC (1961) *The Development Assistance Committee's Mandate.* Paris: OECD. www.oecd.org/document/62/0,2340,en_2649_33721_1918654_1_1_1_1,00.html.

OECD-DAC (1996) *Shaping the 21st Century: The Contribution of Development Co-operation.* Paris: OECD. www.oecd.org/dataoecd/23/35/2508761.pdf.

OECD-DAC (2001) 'DAC *Recommendation on Untying Official Development Assistance to the Least Developed Countries.*' DCD/DAC (2001)12/final. www.oecd.org/dataoecd/14/56/1885476.pdf.

OECD-DAC (2005a) *Conflict Prevention and Peace Building: What Counts as ODA.* Paris: OECD. www.oecd.org/dataoecd/32/32/34535173.pdf.

OECD-DAC (2005b) *Official Development Assistance Increases Further – but 2006 Targets Still a Challenge.* Paris: OECD. www.oecd.org/document/3/0,2340,en_2649_201185_34700611_1_1_1_1,00.html.

OECD-DAC (2005c) *Implementing the 2001 DAC Recommendation on Untying ODA to the Least Developed Countries: 2005 Progress Report.* Paris: OECD. www.oecd.org/dataoecd/15/22/35029066.pdf.

OECD-DAC (2007) *European Community: Development Assistance Committee (DAC) Peer Review.* Paris: OECD. www.oecd.org/dataoecd/57/6/38965119.pdf.

OECD-DAC (2010) *Development Co-operation Report 2010.* Paris: OECD.

OECD-DAC (2011) '*Statistical Annex of the 2011 Development Co-operation Report: Tables 1 to 14.*' www.oecd.org/dataoecd/52/9/41808765.xls.

O *Estado de S. Paolo* (2007) 'Negociações entre Mercosul e UE recomeçamem 2008' [Negotiations between MERCOSUR and the EU to recommence in 2008], 18 December. www.estadao.com.br/economia/not_eco97681,0.htm.

Official Journal (2001) 'Written Question E-3137/00 by Francisca Sauquillo Pérez del Arco (PSE) to the Commission.' *Official Journal,* C151 E/088: 78–9.

O'Neill, R. and Vincent, R.J. (1990) *The West and the Third World.* New York: St Martin's Press.

Paris Club (2005) '*HIPC Initiative and Enhanced HIPC Initiative.*' www.clubdeparis.org/en/presentation/presentation.php?BATCH=B04WP04.

Patten, C. and Nielson, P. (2000) '*Chris Patten European Commissioner Responsible for External Relations, and Poul Nielson European Commissioner Responsible for Development and Humanitarian Aid on Zimbabwe Elections European Parliament Strasbourg, 4 July 2000.*'

SPEECH/00/255.   http://europa.eu/rapid/pressReleasesAction.do? reference=SPEECH/00/255.

Peterson, J. (1995) 'Decision-Making in the European Union: Towards a Framework for Analysis.' *Journal of European Public Policy*, 2(1): 69–93.

Peterson, J. and Blomberg, E. (1999) *Decision-Making in the European Union*. London: Macmillan.

Petit, B. (2000) 'The Cotonou Agreement is the Only One of its Kind in the World.' *The Courier*, Special Supplement: 18–19.

Phillips, L. (2010) 'Frustrated with EU "Pressure Tactics", Africa Ready to Walk Away from Trade Talks.' *EU Observer*, 26 November. http://euobserver.com/19/31366.

Phillips, L. (2011) 'EU Wins New Powers at UN, Transforming Global Body.' *EU Observer*, 3 May. http://euobserver.com/9/32262.

Pierson, R. (1996) 'The Path to European Integration: A Historical Institutionalist Perspective.' *Comparative Political Studies*, 29(2): 123–63.

Rampa, F. (2007) *Implementation of Article 37(4) of the Cotonou Agreement: Provision of Technical Support to Assist the Pacific ACP Region in the Review of EPA Negotiations*. Draft Interim Report Submitted to the Pacific Islands Forum Secretariat. Maastricht: ECDPM.

Ravenhill, J. (1985) *Collective Clientelism: The Lomé Conventions and North–South Relations*. New York: Columbia University Press.

Reisen, M. van (1999) *EU 'Global Player': The North–South Policy of the European Union*. Utrecht: Eurostep International Books.

Richardson, J.J. (1996) *Policy-Making in the European Union*. London: Routledge.

Rostow, W.W. (1960) *The Stages of Economic Growth: A Non-Communist Manifesto*. Cambridge: Cambridge University Press.

Ruggie, J.G. (1998) 'What Makes the World Hang Together? Neo-utilitarianism and the Social Constructivist Challenge.' *International Organization*, 52(4): 855–85.

Rüland, Jürgen (2001a) *ASEAN and the European Union: A Bumpy Interregional Relationship*. Bonn: Rheinische Friedrich-Wilhelms-Universität.

Rüland, J. (2001b) 'ASEM – Transregional Forum at the Crossroads'. In W. Stokhof and P. van der Velde (eds), *Asian–European Perspective: Developing the ASEM Process*. Richmond: Curzon Press: 60–76.

Sachs, J. (2005) 'The Time for Action.' *DAC News*, September–October.www.oecd.org/document/37/0,2340,en_2649_33721_353209 97_1_1_1_1,00.html.

Santos, I. (2009) 'Memo to the Commissioner for Development.' In A. Sapir (ed.), *Europe's Economic Priorities 2010–2015: Memos to the New Commission*. Brussels: Bruegel: 95–9.

Sartori, G. (1976) *Parties and Party Systems*. Cambridge: Cambridge University Press.

Schmit, L. (2000) 'The ASEM Process: New Rules for Engagement in a Global Environment.' In H. Fangchuan and U. Niemann (eds), *Asia and Europe – Towards a Better Mutual Understanding*, Second ASEF Summer School, 22 August–5 September 1999. Beijing: Peking University: 105–20.

Smith, H. (1995) *European Foreign Policy and Central America*. New York: St. Martin's Press.

Smith, K. (1998) 'The Use of Political Conditionality in the EU's Relations with Third Countries: How Effective?' *European Foreign Affairs Review*, 3(2): 253–74.

Stevens, C. (2006) 'The EU, Africa and Economic Partnership Agreements: Unintended Consequences of Policy Leverage.' *Journal of Modern African Studies*, 44(3): 441–58.

Sun S. (2002) 'Asia–Europe Summit Targets Terrorism.' *China Daily*, 24 September.

Teló, M. (2007) 'Between Trade Regionalization and Various Paths towards Deeper Cooperation.' In M. Teló (ed.), *European Union and New Regionalism: Regional Actors and Global Governance in a Post-Hegemonic Era*. Farnham: Ashgate: 127–52.

UN (2005a) *A Home in the City*. London: Earthscan. www.unmillennium project.org/reports/tf_slum.htm.

UN (2005b) *Combating AIDS in the Developing World*. London: Earthscan. www.unmillenniumproject.org/reports/tf_hivaids.htm.

UN (2005c) *Coming to Grips with Malaria in the New Millennium*. London: Earthscan. www.unmillenniumproject.org/reports/tf_malaria. htm.

UN (2005d) *Halving Hunger: It Can be Done*. London: Earthscan. www.unmillenniumproject.org/reports/tf_hunger.htm.

UN (2005e) *Health, Dignity and Development: What Will it Take?*. London: Earthscan. www.unmillenniumproject.org/reports/tf_ watersanitation.htm.

UN (2005f) *Investing in Development: A Practical Plan to Achieve the Millennium Development Goals*. London: Earthscan. www.unmillennium project.org/reports/fullreport.htm.

UN (2005g) *Investing in Strategies to Reverse the Global Incidence of TB*. London: Earthscan. www.unmillenniumproject.org/reports/tf_tb.htm.

UN (2005h) *Taking Action: Achieving Gender Equality and Empowering Women*. London: Earthscan. www.unmillenniumproject.org/reports/tf_ gender.htm.

UN (2005i) *Toward Universal Primary Education: Investment, Incentives, and Institutions*. London: Earthscan. www.unmillenniumproject.org/ reports/tf_education.htm.

UN (2005j) *Who's Got the Power? Transforming Health Systems for Women and Children.* London: Earthscan. www.unmillenniumproject. org/reports/tf_health.htm.

UNDP (2007) *Human Development Report 2007/2008: Fighting Climate Change – Human Solidarity in a Divided World.* Basingstoke: Palgrave Macmillan.

UNDP (2009) *Human Development Report 2009: Overcoming Barriers – Human Mobility and Development.* Basingstoke: Palgrave Macmillan.

UNDP (2010) *Human Development Report 2010: The Real Wealth of Nations – Pathways to Human Development.* Basingstoke: Palgrave Macmillan.

Vasconcelos, Á. (2007) 'European Union and MERCOSUR.' In M. Teló (ed.), *European Union and New Regionalism: Regional Actors and Global Governance in a Post-Hegemonic Era.* Farnham: Ashgate: 165–84.

Vernier, G. (1996) 'The Lomé IV Mid-term Review: Main Innovations.' *The Courier*, 155: 8–13.

Wendt, A. (1992) 'Anarchy is What States Make of It: The Social Construction of Power Politics.' *International Organization*, 46(2): 391–425.

Willis, A. (2011a) 'Brussels Wants to Halve Recipients of EU Trade Benefits.' *EU Observer*, 11 May. http://euobserver.com/9/32306.

Willis, A. (2011b) 'Commission Targets Africa in EU Drive for Raw Materials.' *EU Observer*, 2 February. http://euobserver.com/9/31735.

Willis, A. (2011c) 'EU Aid Policy to Target Fewer States and Good Governance.' *EU Observer*, 31 May. http://euobserver.com/851/32429.

Willis, A. (2011d) 'Outcry at EU Plan to Mix Aid and Foreign Policy.' *EU Observer*, 10 February. http://euobserver.com/9/31786.

Woods, N. (2005). 'The Shifting Politics of Foreign Aid.' *International Affairs*, 81(2), 393–409.

World Bank (1990) *World Development Report 1990: Poverty.* Oxford: Oxford University Press.

World Bank (2005) *World Development Indicators 2005.* Washington, DC: World Bank.

World Bank (2010a) *World Development Indicators 2010.* Washington, DC: World Bank.

World Bank (2010b) *World Development Report 2010: Development and Climate Change.* Washington, DC: World Bank.

World Bank (2011) 'How We Classify Countries.' http://data.worldbank. org/about/country-classifications.

WTO (2001) *European Communities – The ACP–EC Partnership Agreement.* WT/MIN(01)/15, 14 November. www.wto.org/english/ thewto_e/minist_e/min01_e/mindecl_acp_ec_agre_e.htm.

Yeo, L.H. (2000) 'ASEM: Looking Back, Looking Forward.' *Contemporary Southeast Asia*, 22(1): 113–44.

Index